♦ ♦ ♦

"THERE'S A WIRE JUST COME IN, MARSHAL EARP."

"For me?"

"No sir," Wilbur said, "it's a wire advising Sheriff Behan that there is a warrant out for your arrest, sir . . . for murder."

"Has Behan seen that wire yet?" Wyatt asked, looking around.

"No, sir."

"I would appreciate it if Behan didn't see it for a half hour," Wyatt said.

"You bet," said the little man.

"Thank you, Wilbur."

Wilbur looked at him, and then said in a kind of awe, "You gonna kill 'em all, ain't ya . . . "

Wyatt did not answer but rode on.

♦ ♦ ♦ ♦ ♦ ♦ ♦ ♦ ♦ ♦ ♦ ♦ ♦ ♦

Shortly thereafter, a mounted troop of cavalry rode through Tombstone ready for war. China Mary watched impassively as a young cavalry trooper pulled out a wanted poster and hammered it into place over a wanted poster that said:

Wanted Dead or Alive for Murder— Curly Bill Brocious.

Over that poster, the trooper hammered the new one into place:

Wanted Dead or Alive for Murder— Wyatt Earp.

Wyatt Earp

A Novel by Dan Gordon

Based on the Screenplay by Dan Gordon and Lawrence Kasdan

WARNER BOOKS

A Time Warner Company

WARNER BOOKS EDITION

Cover design by Diane Luger
Cover art photography by Ben Glass

Warner Books, Inc.
1271 Avenue of the Americas
New York, NY 10020

 A Time Warner Company

Printed in the United States of America

First Printing: July, 1994

10 9 8 7 6 5 4 3 2 1

This book is dedicated to the memories of
A.L., Goddess and David Gordon.

And it is for Jo Ann, who walked beside me where others
would not have followed, who stood beside me when others
would have run.

ACKNOWLEDGMENTS

There are an awful lot of people to acknowledge on a first published novel so I would ask the reader to bear with me for a few lines. First and always, to Zaki, Yoni and Adam, who never tired of hearing the story or its characters, nor of ribbing its author. To Jerry Zeitman, the best friend I've ever had, who fights my fights as if they were his own. To Lenore Marcus who provided constant encouragement and an acid test literary sense and joined in the ongoing mind-reading games that were part and parcel of this project. To Anne Douglas Milburn for her editorial skills and advice and constant enthusiasm for this story. To Pierce O'Donnell and his able aides de camp, Robert Barnes and Julien Adams, without whom this version of the text would never have seen the light of day. To John Schulman and Zazi Pope for their sense of fairness and their resolve to bring matters to a happy conclusion. Finally, but in no sense in order of importance, I am indebted to the numbers of historians who have spent their lives researching the saga of the Earp family. To name only a few would be to slight the many others whose collective works have added to the wealth of information that is published today. There is one, however, with whom I have had the pleasure of speaking on more than one occasion and to whom every writer of fact or fiction about the Earps owes at the very least a tip of the hat, respect and gratitude, Glenn Boyer.

Wyatt Earp

PART ONE

Dodge City

CHAPTER ONE

His pa looked like a killer, but not the drugstore-tabloid-variety assassin who would slit your throat with a straight razor just to test the edge. He looked like a righteous Old Testament type of god who spoke in lightning bolts and would drop you where you stood for not heeding the Word. Like all the Earp men, Judge Nicholas P. Earp stood well over six feet, was ramrod straight, long and rangy-limbed with sinews that stood out and rippled like cords down his arms and a white patriarch's beard that flowed down to his chest. Nicholas Earp had the same pale-blue eyes that set all the Earps apart, marking them as men to be reckoned with and feared. To his fifteen-year-old son Wyatt it was not so much that his father looked like the Sunday school pictures of God, but to Wyatt Nicholas Earp *was* God, and he was fleeing from him now.

Wyatt was leaving their Missouri farm, running away to enlist on the Union side in the great War Between the States just as his brothers had before him. He was running slower now, down way past the unpainted wooden farmhouse, through the cornfield on this bright and golden morning in 1863 with the wind rippling through the stalks like a water current, sweeping Wyatt along ahead of it. Then he heard a sound rumble up behind him faster than the wind, louder than his footfalls or heartbeat pounding. It was the sound of a horse's hooves cantering back behind him. He ducked low behind a row of still-green corn before he allowed himself to turn and look.

He could see his father through the cornstalks, could see the horse snort steamy breath, and up above the big mare's head, the thick chest, the big arms, and his pa's eyes boring straight down into his. He had tried to run and Nicholas Earp had come after him. There was nothing to do but stand and wait for lightning.

"Where you headed, Wyatt?" the voice of his father demanded, snapping Wyatt to attention.

"Nowheres," said the boy, feeling his pitiful fifteen years of age. His father's gaze drilled through the top of his skull into his brain so that he thankfully remembered to say, "sir," before the big leather linked belt might come slithering out from the loops in his father's pants and snake out to smack him one just for forgetting.

"Where you headed, Wyatt?" his father asked again, blocking out the sun from where his horse stood pawing at the red earth.

The shame spilt over Wyatt, hot on his skin, flushing red to the bone. "To town, sir."

And then he did what he heard about in school, and it felt just like the words in the book: he screwed his courage up, and that's just what it felt like, twisting a screw into a hard plank to stand up to the Judge. He ran his hand through his blond hair that hung down past his ears, swept it back in what he hoped was a manly gesture, squared his shoulders, and looked his father straight in the eye. "I'm going to enlist, Pa."

"Are you?" said the big man on the horse.

There was no sound in the cornfield but the wind through the stalks and the horse snorting nervously, hooves pawing on the red earth. All were drowned out by the sound of Wyatt's heart beating loud in his ears as he screwed his courage up even tighter and said, "Yes, sir."

"You figure soldiers don't need food?"

His father paused for an answer, but he knew from experience it was not the kind of question he'd better answer without thinking. He knew his pa was winding up for a sermon. The sun flared back behind his father's head as he moved ever so slightly, so Wyatt had to squint, looking up at his pa.

"You figure soldiers don't need bread?" Nicholas demanded, and the sun shot like rays out behind him. There was no sound except for the wind.

"You figure all life is about is flags and trumpets, brass buttons and pretty charges?" The wind picked up a bit as if to say, Amen to that as well.

The old man leaned down over the horse's head, so he heard the leather creak in the saddle like the door to a house full of ghosts, and he watched his father's Adam's apple bob above his shirt button and the veins stand out in his forehead as the eyes still bore down into his own. "You figure you owe your country before your family?"

And there it was laid out on the table, the line carved deep before him. Stand on this side or that.

To his father the Earps were a religion and there was only one prayer.

"Family comes first," he said. "Countries break apart. This family doesn't. You're not turning your back on this family, are you, Wyatt?"

"No, sir." In a whisper choked with shame, choked with anger at not being allowed to be a man, choked at being forced to be a boy tending corn while his brothers wore brass buttons, sang of glory, and marched to war.

"I didn't hear you, boy," said the thunder that rode the horse. Nicholas Earp had been a justice of the peace and a territorial circuit judge, but he didn't just hand down fines or sentences. You couldn't just obey his laws. You had to embrace them.

"No, sir," he said, and snapped the "sir" like a flag that snapped the wind.

"Virgil and James will be coming home soon," his father said to the horizon, as if saying it would make it so. "Till then, you know what your job is, don't you?"

"Eighty acres of corn," the boy said, sullen.

The trial was over, the verdict in. Judge Earp looked down at his son. "Come home now, Wyatt. You're due a whippin'."

CHAPTER TWO

Virgil and James would be coming home soon, his father had said. And within two weeks it was true. Of the two brothers who had come back from the war, James was the one who had changed: shot up and gangrenous, hard-eyed and drunk. The wounds got healed, the ones you could see, the wounds you could see in every place but his eyes.

Judge Earp did not approve of the drinking. He had said as much in the beginning, but Virgil had leaned over to his father, put his hand on his father's hand, and said, "He's got a lot of pain, Pa." There was a force in Virgil's words, there was a sadness in the way he said it that let Wyatt know the pain was not only in what had happened to him but in what he had seen.

Late at night Wyatt had heard James cry, cry out in pain and terror. He had rushed in to James's room to see him sitting bolt upright, eyes bugged out like he had seen a ghost. When he had said so to his older brother, James just said, "Seen a thousand of them . . . ten thousand." It was then that Virgil appeared behind Wyatt in the doorway, gently moving his younger brother aside, walking into James's room, opening the bottle of whiskey he carried, and passing it to James as he pulled the gauze back on the wounds to change them. For Wyatt thereafter, the smell of whiskey and infection mixed forever in his mind. As Wyatt walked back toward his room, he turned and saw his father standing by the fireplace looking at the embers, flinching with the sounds of James's sobs as Virgil changed the dressings.

They would move, the Judge decided. This house, this family had become troubled, and so as if the troubles could be locked inside a building they would turn the key and flee them all. So Nicholas called the family together around the big oak table in the parlor. With Wyatt holding the baby, Adelia, on his knees with his eighteen-year-old sister Martha, and Virginia, his mother, motioning for James and Virgil to keep quiet, their pa laid out the family's plans.

"West," he said, "where it's better. West, in the land of promise, west, past whatever fiery tests of desert heat and naked savage may await us, there are fields of clover, milk and honey, land and gold, and happiness. It's a new chance for us."

And Wyatt knew that the chance he was talking about was not just for money or land, it was a chance to get away from war ghosts' cries on drunken nights and infectious smells on soiled sheets stained with bloody wounds that cracked and dried in the morning.

The Judge stood above them at the table spread before them. "Remember this, all of you. Nothing counts as much as blood. The rest are strangers."

"You already told them that, Nicholas," said Virginia.

"A hundred times," from James, belching into his buttons.

"Can't hear it enough," said Nicholas, drilling holes with the look at James, his drunken, broken son.

"Thousand times," said James, expanding on the theme.

There was silence and then the younger boy, Morgan, piped: "I heard you, Pa. Blood counts the most." And a few of them laughed enough to make Wyatt think it was a joke.

"Tell the baby, Pa. She ain't heard," said Wyatt, smiling till he saw the Judge.

And that night asleep in bed, the quilt up to his neck, there in the darkness he felt the old man's bony finger dig into his arm and shake him up awake, his eyes shining in the darkness. "It's not a joke."

And in the morning they were gone, eating dust and watching ruts of wagons gone before them through the desert, across the land on the Oregon Trail to promised peace and fabled riches, where the great land ended by the water . . . California.

But it held no salve to heal the wounds of war that scarred their family, and much to his surprise, Wyatt missed it. Missed the warmth and sense of safety, missed the family of his boyhood, when Pa was God and his brothers and he, too, were the disciples.

Seven years later, when Wyatt was twenty-two, he walked by a creek with a girl named Urilla. California had not worked out for him. It had not worked out for any of the Earps. The hardships of pioneer life were clearly not what James had had in mind.

"I seen enough hard times," James had told his father. They quarreled, and James said it was now his intention to find a little softness and ease in life. A soft woman of easy virtue, to be specific, if he could find one. Nicholas called him a degenerate, to which James had simply shrugged his shoulders and smiled his drunken smile and said, "No arguments there, Pa. No arguments there."

Virgil had not stuck around much longer. There was a restlessness about him since the war, and he allowed as if he might just have to go through a bit of shoe leather until he had gotten it walked off.

As for Wyatt, he had left Missouri much a boy and by the time he reached California with the wagon train was a young man, over six feet tall himself and bearing the brunt now of his father's anger and frustration at no longer being able to hold his family together. Wyatt struck out on his own, driving freight wagons from San Berdoo, past highwaymen and renegades bent upon thievery and murder.

It had all gotten old very quickly, so that at twenty-two, he asked himself now if maybe this was the reason he'd come back to Missouri, to re-create a family in his family's image.

But when he looked at this girl, try as he might, he didn't think of his family. Her name was Urilla Sutherland, and she was so pretty you could carve her face in a piece of ivory and young girls would wear it around their necks on velvet ribbons.

She smelled of soap, and his throat tickled every time he got in smelling distance and his face flushed red but not from shame, just from blood pumped faster like when he was scared. He was scared now, scared to ask her, scared not to ask her, scared of what she'd say or what she wouldn't say, wishing he could up and run yet wanting to be nowhere else but here, beside the girl with yellow hair, who made his throat tickle and blood pound. He figured he would just about bust if he didn't ask her quick, and then she spoke.

"What are you going to do with yourself, Wyatt?"

What did she mean by that? What was he supposed to do with himself? What would she want him to do with himself?

"Well . . . uh . . . well . . ." he said, and his tongue felt like a size-ten foot in a size-six boot.

"Well?" she said, and smiled that smile and brushed her yellow hair back from her eyes that looked now up and into his.

"Well, I kind of figured to read for the law." He stared down at his boot and then snuck a peek at her eyes to see if that was what she wanted.

"Is that what you want . . . to be a lawyer?"

"Well," Wyatt said, or thought he said; his lips had moved at least, but no sound had come out. So he "ahemmed" a little and took another run at it. "It kind of runs in the family."

"What does?" said Urilla, smiling at his discomfort.

"Well . . . lawyering. Pa's a judge and Granddad was a lawyer too, before him, and besides, I like it quite a bit myself." He was on a roll now, like a gambler who feels the cards starting to turn his way. A lawyer suited her just fine. "It's interesting, and I believe a man can make a handsome living at it." He had stated his case and laid his worth at her feet. Then she frowned, and he wished the earth could open just a crack and swallow him whole.

"I don't know," Urilla said, with a little frown that made his heart feel as if it had been whacked with a twelve-pound sledge. "I believe I'd like to live on a ranch," she said, and she looked off far as if she could see it just past the rise above them. "Some nice little spread with a sweet little house that I can turn into a castle for my husband, with a big feather bed where we'd stay snuggled up all warm on the coldest night."

As she lifted her eyes up to his, he gulped like a bullfrog and said, "Ranching is good . . . I like ranches."

After that Wyatt could pay her court, and he saw her every day for six months. Then Mrs. Sutherland asked Urilla when she expected Wyatt to propose.

"Mama," said Urilla, "Wyatt's proposed every day since he came back to town."

"Oh," said Mrs. Sutherland, and she smiled. This daughter of hers was no fool.

Beneath a tree upon a hill, all the Earps stood together once again. James was there and Virgil, Morgan was there and little Warren, his sister Martha, and Adelia, less a baby than before, was in Virginia's arms as Wyatt stood beside Urilla and her family and Judge Earp spoke out his blessing.

"Do you, Urilla, take . . ." And here the old man turned and looked at Wyatt, at the boy who was now a man and had finally come to understand the lessons of his father. He noisily cleared his throat like there was dust, but there was no dust on this fine clear day. "Do you, Urilla, take my son Wyatt to be your lawful wedded husband, to have and to hold, forsaking all others, to love, honor, and cherish in sickness and in health for richer or for poorer, till death do you part?"

"I do," said Urilla. She stood beside Wyatt and thought how pretty the words were but had no notion of what they truly meant.

When his father turned to Wyatt and asked the same question, Wyatt said, "I do." As if there were any doubts. As if there was anyone there on the hill who could possibly look at Wyatt and not know he would love, honor, and cherish Urilla Sutherland, forsaking all others, in any condition God threw their way, till death came to part them in old age, surrounded by children and grandchildren on the ranch he would build for the girl with the face so pretty you could carve it in ivory and wear it on a velvet ribbon.

"Then by the power vested in me by the state of Missouri, I now pronounce you man and wife."

* * *

"All together now," said the photographer. Wyatt and Urilla stood in the middle, with Nicholas, Virginia, James, Virgil, Morgan, and Warren on one side, and Urilla's parents and three brothers on the other. The photographer was just about to touch the flash powder and didn't even see James pull the flask out of his coat pocket to fortify himself with a snort, but he did hear the Judge when the Judge roared, "James!" like thunder cracking. Virg and Wyatt smiled and shook their heads, and James shrugged like a naughty boy. He put the bottle in his hip pocket and pulled a face for the camera, grinning with his eyes crossed above his nose.

The powder in the trough exploded with a blinding flash. "Perhaps," said the photographer with as much diplomacy as he could muster, "perhaps we could try one more, with all the eyes looking this way."

So Wyatt looked at the camera and tried not to smile and his brothers looked at Wyatt and tried not to laugh and the photographer said, "All right . . . one . . . two . . ." It would all have worked just fine except that Wyatt saw James look at Virgil with that same wall-eyed look that made Wyatt burst out laughing like a braying mule.

"I'm . . . I'm sorry. I just . . . I'm sorry."

"Pull yourself together," said the Judge. And the photographer, trying to avoid a family conflict, said, "One . . . two . . ." And then it was Virgil doing the donkey bray.

Then James looked at him stern and pulled himself up as straight as he could and said, "Virgil, try and pull yourself together. This is a very, uh . . . very somber . . . very sober occasion."

"I'm sorry," Virgil said. And James belched cheerfully. "S'okay . . . you want a drink?"

"No!" bellowed the Judge. "He doesn't want a drink!" The Judge yelled so loud, the photographer jumped a mile and touched his puck into his powder bag and damn near blew his leg off.

The wedding reception went downhill from there. James got in a fight with Urilla's brother and had to be pulled off, and Urilla didn't talk to Wyatt for a week thereafter.

But the anger passed and they found a piece of land that Urilla said she loved. She and Wyatt walked the acreage hand in hand, talking plans and seeing visions of their children frolicking as their lives all prospered. Wyatt built on to the little ranch house and Urilla made curtains and tablecloths, and by the time the new bedstead arrived from the store in St. Louis, the doctor confirmed that Urilla was pregnant. She would have the baby in the fall. By the time that summer had ended and the wheat was high and gold-colored and the air was just starting to chill, Urilla called out to Wyatt from the doorway of the house he had built for her. Wyatt thought she'd called him to supper, which was fine with him because he'd been working hard all day digging postholes for the new line of fence he was putting in.

But then he saw her lean against the doorjamb, saw the pain that flashed across her.

"It's the . . . Is it the . . . It's time . . . for the . . ."

"Baby!" Urilla shrieked with pain.

"Baby . . . Okay, sweetheart, go inside and I'll get the doc . . . I'll . . . You okay?"

Urilla nodded her head up and down and even managed to smile, and Wyatt was about to hug her and tell her how much he loved her when it hit her again and she said, "Hurry."

He hit the top rail of the corral with one foot and went up and over, sailing bareback onto his horse, no saddle, no bit, no reins, his fist grabbing mane, kicking flanks, jumping high, long, up over the fence, out of the corral and racing down to town.

Doc Ryerson was a man in his sixties and not given to taking orders from nervous husbands who hadn't had the good sense to saddle their horse before they came to get him. Babies had been born under his guidance for well over forty years, and he didn't need any help in doing it now.

Back at the house, Wyatt hovered in front of the closed bedroom door like a pup who's got to pee, till the doc came out and glared at him.

"How's she doin', Doc? She okay? What can I get for you? What do you need, Doc?"

Doc Ryerson just looked at him and said, dry as drought in Kansas, "I need to go to the outhouse, Wyatt, you think you can let me pass?"

The doc moved one way to pass, and Wyatt, trying to get out of his way, moved the same way and blocked it.

"Sorry," Wyatt said, and moved the other way, only to find the doc doing the same and blocking the way once again.

"Stand!" bellowed the doc, pointing his finger to one spot on the floor. "Stay!"

"Yes, sir," Wyatt said.

Doc Ryerson sighed. "Go out, son. Don't look at me like that. Go out! Go get some cigars. Go get drunk. Go do anything, just go out and stay out until I can get this baby born, hmm?"

Wyatt poked his head into the bedroom. Urilla was there in bed, tired but beautiful.

"How you doing?" Wyatt said, barely above a whisper, as he crossed toward her and took her hand.

"Okay, sweetheart."

"The doc told me to go out for a while."

Urilla squeezed his hand as if she knew how clumsy he'd been out in the front room. "That's probably a good idea." And then to soothe his wounded pride, "You haven't had any supper, have you?"

"Well . . ." Wyatt said, and thought that a meal might not be too bad after all. He hadn't eaten since breakfast, and before the baby business he'd been out digging postholes, and a fella can work up quite an appetite doing that.

"You go into town and get some supper."

"Oh my gosh," Wyatt said. "I haven't told your mother. Your mother's gonna skin me, Urilla."

But Urilla just smiled. "Then you go into town and tell my mother. But make sure she gives you some supper before she comes out here."

Wyatt leaned down toward her, and he could smell that soap smell on her and realized for the first time how much he truly did love her.

As if she could read his thoughts, she said, "I love you, Wyatt. . . . We're going to have everything we want now, aren't we."

And Wyatt raised her fingers to his lips and said, "I already do."

He had his own family now.

CHAPTER THREE

"My baby's having a baby . . . I can't believe it."

"There you go, Mother Sutherland," Wyatt said as he put his shoulder in a friendly sort of way to his mother-in-law's enormous rump, like you'd heft a flour sack. He pushed, she pulled, and the great weight sagged the buggy springs for just an instant and then the bounce back aided in accomplishing the desired effect. Mother Sutherland defied gravity and settled herself onto the seat of the old spring wagon just as dainty as you please. For a fat woman, she moved well.

Then Wyatt grabbed the reins before he was even halfway up into the buggy, slipped the brake, and gi'ed up the horses, throwing Mother Sutherland back against the board so that she had to grab her bonnet. He smacked the reins down hard, and the horses lurched the wagon and were off just like in the ranchers' races on the Fourth of July.

"I'll allow as how I'd like to live to see this grandchild, Wyatt," Mother Sutherland said, her hand clamped down on her bonnet like a potato masher.

But Wyatt didn't hear her; he was already thinking about Nick. For Nick is what it would be. No question about that. Nicholas on the paper that they'd file up at the courthouse, but Nick to him, little Nick whom he'd pull up in the saddle and ride around the ranch, little Nick he'd take out fishing by the creek where he had proposed.

And the boy would hear the story so many times about how scared he was, tongue-tied, bug-eyed, scared the day he asked the boy's ma to marry him, that little Nick would say, Oh, Pa, I've heard that a hundred times . . . a thousand times. Then Wyatt thought of James and knew if only James could find a girl like the girl who had now borne him a son, he'd be all right. And he wished for James and thought kindly of his father, for whom he'd name this son.

It was dark by the time they got back to the ranch, but he could see the warm light bouncing on the horizon up ahead. He could see the lighted window and fire upon the hearth, and instead of going faster, he reined the horses so he could memorize every moment to save for years thereafter, how it looked and how it felt the night his own son was born.

"Can't these horses go any faster, Wyatt? I'd like to see this grandchild before I die of old age."

Wyatt said nothing to his mother-in-law, just smiled and filed that sentence for the stories in years to come. Your grandma said, I'd like to see this grandchild before I die of old age. He memorized how she looked with her hand clamped down upon the now-crushed bonnet that sat there like a fallen encampment upon her head.

He pulled the buggy up before the house, stepped down on the brake, and hopped therefrom onto the ground. He was about to race into the house when he heard Mother Sutherland "ahem."

He turned back to her side of the spring wagon and let her lean upon his shoulder with one hand as she transferred her weight back down to earth and the wagon springs groaned. Then the springs seemed to sigh as the wagon returned to its normal height. Wyatt even remembered to open the door for his mother-in-law first.

Then he saw the doc. He sat in the chair by the fire with his head in his hands and the blood on his shirt and still on his hands, and it looked to Wyatt as though the old man's head must have weighed a ton, so slowly did he raise it. And then he saw the look upon the old man's face, and heard his voice so far away: "I couldn't save them . . . either of them."

"NO!" You could hear Wyatt's cry echo down the canyon, hear it bounce back off the mountains to be joined by yet another "NO!" that pierced the house's walls and made the horses whinny and strain against their harness, set the dogs a-howling, baying not against the moon, howling not to one another but to heaven at the thought that one of theirs could feel such pain. For he did not sound human.

The loud keening ended and was followed by the thump, the steady thump, thump, thump of Wyatt's head against the wood frame of the sweet little house he had built for Urilla. Wyatt didn't stop, not all night, not even with the dawn.

There were two coffins between the Earps on one side and the Sutherlands on the other, one for mother, one for child, and the two graves side by side tore apart the two families.

Later that day Wyatt, dressed in black still from the grave-yard, silhouetted against the blood sky, held the kerosene can before him in growing darkness. His eyes were dead as wet coals. He splashed kerosene against the house she wanted, against the walls, against the drapes and doilies, against the light and pretty things that young girls bring into dark lives of lonely men and set them all aflame. He didn't stay to watch it burn, just mounted up and rode away into the dark.

A buckboard lit by lightning splashed through the prairie mud and rain and thunder and headed into the little town of Van Buren, Arkansas. The rain poured down and off the hat so you couldn't see the stranger's face, not even with the lightning. He opened up the door and said, "Sheriff Bodeen?"

"That's right," said the sheriff, looking up from his big ledger where the names of jailed men all filled the page.

"You have a young man here who's been arrested for horse thievery." It was not a question when he said it, but then, few things ever were.

"What business might that be of yours," the sheriff said, pushing the kerosene lamp back farther on his desk so he could see the stranger's face.

"I am Judge Nicholas P. Earp. I am here to make his bail. I am his father."

* * *

The jail cell smelled like a wet dog. But it wasn't a dog they had enclosed there.

Wyatt turned and looked up into his father's eyes and saw by the look on the Judge's face how he must appear there in the jail cell, more clearly than had he been looking into a mirror.

Nicholas's best-loved son sat there, eyes red-rimmed, scab-faced with stubble, wounds, and bruises, dried mud and blood of months of barroom brawls and alleys. Lice crawled on the boy as he blinked in the dim light. He looked like James.

"Pa . . . ?"

"Horse thief," the old man said as though he'd tasted something bitter.

Wyatt looked down and then back up. He was too tired to stand without wobbling, so he sat there. "How did you find . . ."

"You wired Virgil," Nicholas said with a sigh. "Virgil's gone off . . . so has James. The telegraph people brought it to me. Did you do it? Did you steal those horses?"

There was a long silence, and then Wyatt said, "I don't remember, but yes, sir, sure."

"You don't remember . . ."

"I've been drunk," Wyatt said, and sounded more like James than ever. "For . . . how long has it been since . . ."

"Six months," said the Judge. "I've made your bail. Five hundred dollars. I've told them that I intend to defend you at your trial."

Wyatt stood and stumbled back against the wall from the blood that drained down from his brain when he got to his feet. He swayed back and then toward the bars that stood between them. "I don't want that, Pa. I . . ."

Nicholas looked around, and for the first time that Wyatt could remember, the old man looked like a conspirator, looked afraid and spoke in whispers. "There's not going to be a trial."

Wyatt just looked at him, not comprehending, as his father whispered, not soft but rasping, "You're going to run."

Wyatt's eyes grew wide, as if he'd caught his father naked in a brothel. "*You're* telling me to do that?"

His father's breath was hot upon him as the Judge leaned in close and gripped the bars. "They hang horse thieves, Wyatt. You're guilty. They'll hang you." He let that one sink in, and his voice grew not softer, not weaker, just not as hard and not as strong. "So you run. And you keep on running until you're clear of this county, until you're clear of Arkansas, and you don't come back here, and once you're out of Arkansas, Wyatt, you stop and take a look in the mirror." His pa swallowed hard. "You take a good look . . . and you . . . you take yourself in hand . . . because otherwise . . . ." He paused a long time now, then spoke with dread. "Otherwise, you're going to wind up dead, son."

"I don't care," Wyatt said like a kid who needed slapping.

His father hit him hard across the mouth, the big hand reaching through the bars, smacking him so hard it made his ears ring. Then he grabbed Wyatt and tried to shake some sense into the boy.

"You're not the first man to lose a wife! Or a child! My first wife died! My first child died! This is a hard land, Wyatt, and a hard life. It doesn't suffer fools. It will not tolerate weakness. . . . You've got to tighten up on your tears, boy," Nicholas said, and then pulled his son toward him. He put his arms around him, hugged him close, and went against his own words and cried bitter tears. Wyatt felt his father sag upon him, felt his chest heave against him, felt the old man's tears, but not his own.

Later, in the dark beside the jail, Nicholas watched as his best-loved son rode off into the storm, into the lightning and the rain, and once again into the darkness.

CHAPTER FOUR

1874. The Kansas buffalo camp was a ramshackle affair made up mainly of tents and a couple of wooden buildings. What it lacked in amenities it made up for in buffalo hunters, hides, and flies. Two hungry kids aged nineteen and eighteen, respectively, eyed the various hunters who rode into the camp with their mounds of buffalo hides piled up on rigs behind them. The two kids were brothers, and they were trying to size up who would make the best prospective employer. As the various hunters drove their rigs past them the brothers commented on their chances with each.

"What about that one?" said the younger brother, indicating a hunter driving his rig into the camp. There weren't that many hides piled up, and upon closer inspection one could see that the hunter was cross-eyed.

"Which one?" the older brother said.

"That one right there!"

"The cross-eyed one?" the older brother asked.

"Is he cross-eyed?"

"Well, he's lookin' at both sides of the street at the same time from different directions." The older brother, whose name was Ed, smiled and shook his head and then saw another

hunter ride into town on a flatbed wagon piled high with
buffalo hides. His hair was long and his face was stubble,
and he looked nothing like the drunken boy from the jail cell
in Arkansas. He was a hardened frontier hunter, a deliberate
man. Ed's eyes followed his progress down the road.

The hunter stepped into a tent saloon at the end of the street
and crossed over to a bar, which was little more than a plank
perched on two barrels. The tent was crowded with hunters,
most of them already drunk. The hunter turned to the bartender as behind him Ed and his younger brother entered the
tent.

"You got any cold beer?" the hunter asked the bartender.

"We got warm whiskey."

"How 'bout some hot coffee?"

"Friend, this is a saloon," the bartender said. "We serve
whiskey." The hunter took a dollar and smacked the coin on
the plank bar. "Why don't you brew up some coffee," he
said.

"Coffee she is," said the bartender. And he scooped up
the dollar. The younger of the two brothers crossed over to
Wyatt. Wyatt was over six feet tall, and the brothers, younger
and obviously less experienced, were both around five nine
and very deferential.

" 'Scuze me, mister," said the younger brother. "We seen
your wagon out there. Looks like you had a pretty lucky
hunt."

"Slaughtering dumb animals doesn't take much luck. Not
much skill, either," Wyatt said.

"We didn't see any skinners riding up there with you,
though." This came from the older brother, who had a very
affable way about him.

But Wyatt was not in an affable mood. "That's 'cause
there wasn't any," he said.

"He quit?" the younger brother asked.

"He's dead," Wyatt said, and looked the kid in the eye,
hoping that would be the end of it.

"Well, that's as good as quit in my book," said the
younger brother, who though short was powerfully built and
had a quickness about him that was not unimpressive. "My
brother Ed and me are lookin' for work as skinners. We're
from Sedgwick County."

Wyatt wondered what kind of a recommendation being from Sedgwick County was for those who sought employment as hide skinners. But before he could pursue that line of thought any further, a huge man, a drunken buffalo hunter, stepped up to the bar. His name was Link, and he resembled nothing so much as a very large sausage.

"Bartender!" said the sausage. "It's the end of a long, cold dry spell. Whiskey all around!"

A cheer went up as the bartender put glasses on the plank. Being right next to Wyatt, the drunk buffalo hunter named Link thought the gesture might be best punctuated by slapping Wyatt on the back.

"Ha . . . ?" the drunken buffalo hunter said, as if to cue Wyatt that it was now his turn to praise the latter's generosity.

Wyatt smiled at the non sequitur. The bartender filled glasses all the way down the line. He put one in front of Wyatt. He was just about to fill it when Wyatt covered the glass.

"No, thanks," Wyatt said softly.

"Okay," said the bartender, thinking nothing of it. But Link, the drunken buffalo hunter, was offended.

"Wait a second," Link said. "I'm buyin' . . . so drink up."

Wyatt didn't look up, just said, "Thanks, but I got some coffee comin'." Then, by way of explanation, hoping to mollify the big man, he added, "I don't do so well on whiskey."

"I don't give a pail of hot spit what you do well on. If I'm buyin', you're drinkin'."

"Fair enough," Wyatt said. "If you'd pay for my coffee, I'd be much obliged." And he thought that would be the end of it. But Link leaned over and got the bottle of whiskey out of the bartender's hand and set it down in front of Wyatt.

"Drink it," he said, slow, low, and deadly.

Wyatt took a deep breath and turned and looked at the man. He gazed at him with those pale-blue Earp eyes that betrayed no expression until it was too late.

"Mister, I been in a real bad mood for a couple of years. So why don't you leave me alone."

Link was not a naturally talkative man. He figured he'd let

his gun do the talking for him. His hand went down for his side arm.

Quick as a heartbeat Wyatt's gun was up out of its holster, cocked and pointed right into Link's ugly face. Link's own gun had not yet cleared leather.

"Drop your gun belt . . . and go away," Wyatt said, very soft and very calm. So calm that Link knew Wyatt would kill him where he stood, blow his brains out and then drink his coffee.

Link looked at the cocked gun that was pointed right between his eyes and struggled to keep control of his bowels.

"Okay . . . sure . . . You betcha," he said. "That's just what I'm doin' . . . I'm leavin' now."

He undid his gun belt and let it drop to the floor as he backed away from Wyatt, who kept his gun on him until Link was at the tent opening. "Bye," Link said, real sheepish-like, and then he turned his back and ran.

When Link was out of sight, Wyatt's eyes flicked around the room to see if anyone else wanted a piece of him. Everyone was very quiet and very respectful. Wyatt uncocked his gun slowly and reholstered it. Then he turned to the two kids. The older one, Ed, figured he was just about to tell them to skedaddle too, which was fine with Ed since this man looked as if buffalo weren't the only thing he killed for a living, when Wyatt said, "Twenty-five dollars apiece."

"Huh?" said the younger one, grabbing his older brother's shirt to keep him from running out of the tent.

"You said you wanted to be skinners. That's what I'll pay."

Ed stuck out his hand and said, "Mister, that's a deal. My name's Ed Masterson. This is my little brother, Bat."

Wyatt looked at the two brothers and held out his hand. "Wyatt Earp," he said. And the deal was struck.

When Wyatt initiated his participation in the great slaughter of the buffalo, he did so because it offered him the three things he thought he wanted as he fled the jailhouse back in Arkansas: solitude, employment, and the chance to inflict death on living creatures. It was a mistake, therefore, to hire the Masterson boys, because they awakened in him a kind of fraternal affection.

"We said we'd work for you," Ed said at the end of the season, at the end of the slaughter, when they had two wagons piled high with the dead skins of buffalo they had hunted. "You don't need to cut it no three ways. We said we'd work for wages, and we'll stick to the bargain."

They tugged at Wyatt's heartstrings, these two boys; they reminded him of his brothers, and like a levee cracking with the pressure of rising waters, the wall he had built around his emotions began to give way. He was homesick for his family and heartsick from the killing.

"Well, I'll tell you the truth, Ed, I can't rightly remember what bargain we made." And Wyatt divided up the profits into three piles, one for each of them. He shook hands with Ed, who thanked him, and he shook hands with Bat, who seemed to read his heart.

"We got room in our family for another brother, if you ever find the need," Bat said.

"I appreciate that, Bat." Wyatt's eyes looked off to the horizon in a way that would have reminded anyone who knew him of the Judge.

"I've got a brother who just got married over in Wichita. I believe I'd like to see him awhile till I can figure out somethin' else to do."

"Aside from slaughtering dumb animals?" Ed said.

"Something like that," said Wyatt, and then he added, "You boys stick together. Nothing counts as much as blood. The rest is strangers."

"You're no stranger," Bat said, "not to us. Not from here on out."

"Fair enough," Wyatt said. And he rode to Wichita to find James, his brother.

CHAPTER FIVE

There was an uneasiness in the relationship between Wyatt and James Earp now. A stiffness, a formalness that had never been there before. Wyatt was much improved in appearance, wearing a dark coat and white shirt as he walked next to James on the wooden sidewalk there in Wichita. Wyatt's hair was neatly cut, the stubble all gone and the smell of buffalo hide almost undetectable. For his part, James looked like the prosperous drunk he had become by this year of 1875. What troubled Wyatt, however, was the rumored source of his brother's newfound middle-class economic status. It was a delicate matter, since his elder brother had offered him a place to stay until he could find suitable employment. Nonetheless, Wyatt felt obliged to raise the matter in a forthright manner. He took a breath and plunged into the breach.

"James, I appreciate you givin' me a place to stay and all," Wyatt said, "but there's just one problem."

"Your mattress lumpy?" asked James, seemingly with genuine concern.

"No, no, it has nothing to do with mattresses. Well, not with *my* mattress at any rate."

"We're brothers," James said, as if that needed to be

stated. "What's the problem, Wyatt?" he said, just as even-tempered as could be.

There was a pause, and then Wyatt said, "It's Bessie . . ."

"Bessie?" said James, as if the name were only vaguely familiar.

"Right, James," Wyatt said.

"My wife Bessie?" asked James.

"Yes," said Wyatt definitely.

"What about her?" James asked, betraying no sense of suspicion at his brother's query.

Wyatt cleared his throat and spoke with obvious difficulty and discomfort. "I haven't been here long, but I've heard."

"Yes?" said his older brother.

"Well . . . She's . . ." Here, Wyatt could hold it back no longer. "She's a whore, James."

The news seemed to come as no surprise to Wyatt's older brother. "Yes she is, Wyatt," he said, and then added with an unmistakable touch of pride, "And a hardworking one at that."

Wyatt could not believe his ears.

"I . . . I . . . don't understand, James," he sputtered.

James looked at him as one would look at a slow-witted child and then set out to explain. "Well, it's pretty simple, Wyatt," he said. "Fellas pay her money and she shows 'em a good time. It's not too complicated."

Wyatt reddened, both at being taken for a dimwit and at having to discuss the topic more in depth. "What I don't understand is . . ."

"Is what?" said James, beginning to sound just the tiniest bit testy now.

"Is what you're doin' with her!" Wyatt blurted.

"I'm doin' the same thing everyone else is doin' with her, Wyatt," said James, the exasperation beginning to be heard in his tone of voice. "The only difference is she doesn't charge me."

"And it doesn't bother you?" the younger Earp asked in shocked disbelief.

"That she doesn't charge me for it?" James asked in equal disbelief. "Why no, Wyatt. Truth to tell, I'm rather fond of the arrangement. Why, on a good day," he added, "I can even get her to cook and clean a little."

Wyatt just shook his head. "I—I'm not new in the woods James, but . . ."

"But what?" said James, beginning to tire of the subject.

"But I still don't get it," Wyatt said.

"Well, I have no doubt about that, Wyatt. It's because you're too dour. You're no fun," James said, looking his brother in the eye. "Maybe you ought to start payin' for it and then you'll get it for sure."

There was an uncomfortable silence between the two brothers, and then James broke it by adding, "In fact, you mention my name and you'll get a discount. It's one of the advantages of having a harlot in the family."

Wyatt threw his hands up in moral surrender.

"Okay . . . Okay," was all he could say.

But now it was James's turn to push the conversation forward. "Okay, okay what?" he said.

"If your 'arrangement' doesn't bother you, I guess it doesn't bother me," Wyatt said, giving in.

"Well, that's sure a load off my mind," said James, with no small degree of sarcasm. "I was really losin' sleep, Wyatt, worryin' about whether or not my arrangement bothered you. Whew!"

There were a number of things about Wichita that took some getting used to, and Wyatt encountered them all in those first few weeks. Out of lack of gainful employment he joined the local constabulary. He would later maintain that he felt no special calling for law enforcement. Quite simply, he needed a job and they had one. Also, he may have felt that as a policeman he would be able to keep his brother's wife out of jail. Not that prostitution was illegal in towns like Wichita, but failure to pay the proper tax and licensing fee was indeed punishable by incarceration. Bessie Earp's moral looseness was not confined to the bedroom. She was just as free and easy with the tax man and his regulations as she was with her customers. She was determined, as she put it plainly to Wyatt, to screw them both.

Towns like Wichita existed because of the cattle trade, or more specifically, they profited from the money spent by cowboys blowing off steam. The cowboys would come in off the range at the end of a cattle drive. They wanted to come to town, get drunk, gamble, and brush up against something softer and sweeter-smelling, though not by much, than their horses. And they would pay good money to do it. Such towns as Wichita existed off their trade.

The problem was that towns like Wichita had to walk a fine line in keeping those same drunken cowboys from killing not only one another but their local shopkeepers, without discouraging them from coming in to their fair cities to spend their money.

Thus was born the notion of the Deadline. It was in fact an actual line that ran through such towns as Wichita, beyond which no firearms were allowed, but beyond which drinking, gambling, and whoring were not only allowed but encouraged. The philosophy was: separate the drinking from the firearms and the local burgher would be able to separate the cowboy from his money without getting shot in the process. The problem, as Wyatt was about to find out, arose when the cowboy crossed the Deadline with his firearm still on.

Wyatt was taken under the tutelage of Sheriff Mike Meagher, a big man in his mid-forties with whom Wyatt found himself on patrol in the sporting district of Wichita, Kansas, on this particular night in 1875. As the two men with badges on their breast pockets walked up the street, two drunken cowboys staggered out of a saloon up ahead some distance away. Though the light was dim, it was sufficient to make out the gun one of the drunken cowboys sported on his hip.

"What do you expect we ought to do with them, Mister Earp?" Sheriff Meagher said.

"Disarm them, sir?" Wyatt answered.

"Sir," said Sheriff Meagher appreciatively. "I like that . . . very polite, very well mannered. No, disarming them is not first on our agenda."

The distance between Meagher and the cowboys had now closed considerably. As he passed close to the armed cowboy, Sheriff Meagher gently moved Wyatt off to his left side so that the cowboy would be on his right. Then, quick as a snake, Meagher pulled his own gun out of its holster and whacked the drunken cowboy over the head with it, sending him bleeding to the street.

Meagher then whirled his gun on the cowboy's friend to

make sure he didn't try anything. He reached down and pulled the gun out of the fallen cowboy's holster. He spoke matter-of-factly to Wyatt, like a master to his apprentice.

"First you knock him over the head," he said. "This is known as buffaloing him," he said calmly, rolling the unconscious bleeding cowboy onto his back and patting him down for additional weapons. "Then you disarm him. The theory is that an unconscious cowboy is much less likely to shoot you. You may then inform the cowboy that he is under arrest."

Sheriff Meagher looked down at the unconscious cowboy. "You're under arrest," he said. Then he looked over at the cowboy's friend. "Your friend's under arrest."

"Yes, sir," said the cowboy's friend, just as meek and cooperative as you please.

"You can pick him and his gun up at my jail in the morning," the sheriff said, as Wyatt looked on, dumbfounded at the sudden bloody violence.

When Sheriff Meagher closed the jail door on the knocked-out drunken cowboy, Wyatt was there next to him.

"Now, then, did all of that seem cruel to you?" asked Meagher.

"It did," Wyatt said quietly.

"It did?"

"Yes, sir."

"Well," the sheriff sighed, "maybe it is. But it seems to me that it's less cruel than having that same cowboy get shot in the guts or seeing him do the same to somebody else and then start a riot. And if the cowboys know that that's what you're going to do if they break the law, then they'll tell their friends that it's a big mistake to take their firearms past that Deadline, and pretty soon they won't."

Wyatt said nothing.

The sheriff continued, "If you cannot accept that and you continue as a constable, it is only a matter of time until you are murdered by a drunken cowboy with a firearm."

Thus, Wyatt learned the dangerous art of law enforcement as it was practiced in frontier cattle towns. He proved himself an able deputy under Sheriff Meagher, who was mighty sad to see Wyatt accept what on the face of it seemed less lucrative employment, as a Dodge City deputy marshal, the following year. But Wichita was quieting down, and Wyatt rightly saw the move as one that would advance his financial projects, even though the position of deputy city marshal of Dodge City, Kansas, did not at first pay a salary. The job in fact paid $2.50 for every drunken cowboy he could disarm on the wrong side of the Deadline.

The two dollars and fifty cents was, by the way, the same pay a cowboy got for breaking a wild horse.

It was a testament to the characters of Dodge City, Kansas, and Wyatt Earp that during his first month of employment at $2.50 a head, Wyatt neatly cleared one thousand seven dollars and fifty cents.

CHAPTER SIX

Wyatt walked down Front Street in the company of Bat and Ed Masterson. Bat and Ed had come to Dodge City, Kansas, in 1877, having grown tired of the stench of dead buffalo and the flies that swarmed constantly around them. They had come to Dodge to drink and gamble and find a sporting woman who would give them a discount because they were brothers, but they had found Wyatt instead. He had disarmed them nonviolently when they were drunk, and when they sobered up, he offered them jobs. As they walked down Front Street, Wyatt wore the long dark coat and white shirt, string tie, and broad-brimmed black hat that later would become his trademarks. Bat all but mimicked him in his dress, whereas Ed looked much more the slicked-up dude. He wore a vest and three-piece suit and derby hat. Two things they all had in common, however, were the little metal scroll badge that indicated their positions as policemen and the Colt New Model Army Frontier pistols, which would later gain fame under the name Peacemaker. The sound of music and drunks rolled out of the various saloons and bawdy houses on Front Street. Coming down the street toward them were two cowboys who had just come out of a saloon. They were drunk and they were armed. Wyatt looked over at the Masterson brothers, who both seemed a little nervous.

"Well," he said, "you might as well get broke in sometime. Why don't you two boys handle this."

Ed and Bat stole a look at each other as the two drunks approached them. Ed smiled to both of the cowboys and even tipped his derby. Wyatt stepped quietly off to the side, into the shadows.

"Evenin'," Ed said, just as friendly as you please.

"Yeah, right," said the first cowboy, who ignored Ed and kept on walking.

"Looks like you two fellas been doin' some drinkin'," Ed said, trying again.

The second cowboy let out a huge, wet belch. "What makes you say that?" he said.

Ed smiled and said, "Oh, just intuition, I guess. Anyways, I'm glad you two are havin' a good time, but you know there's a city ordinance against wearing firearms in this part of town."

You might have said that at that point the first cowboy turned ugly, except for the fact that he was probably born that way. "Oh yeah, says who?"

Bat spread his feet to get a good stance and then let his hand slip down to his pistol grip. "Says the law, that's who."

But Ed turned to Bat as the two cowboys stepped back a pace as if they are getting ready to fight. "Now, Bat," he said, "you're bein' about as sociable as an ulcerated back tooth. These here boys are just tryin' to have a good time, and—"

Ed's speech was cut off as Wyatt sprang out of the shadows and whacked first one and then the other of the two drunken cowboys over the head with his gun barrel, splitting the skull of one of them in the process.

Ed just stood there, shocked, not knowing what to say or do, though Bat had moved with alacrity. His gun was out, cocked and pointed at the two cowboys to cover Wyatt's actions.

"Gee-minney Christmas, Wyatt!" Ed said.

Wyatt bent down and unbuckled the bleeding cowboy's gun and relieved him of it. He looked up at Ed tight-lipped, as his father used to get when one of his sons had failed him.

"You talk too much, Ed," Wyatt said.

"You didn't have to do that, Wyatt," Ed said, looking at the bleeding cowboy. "You had no call to knock 'em ass over teakettle like that!"

Wyatt didn't answer. He just moved to the second cowboy, who was also unconscious. He rolled him back and pried open the cowboy's hand, in which there was a small-caliber pistol.

"Hmph," Wyatt said to himself, somewhat surprised.

Ed let out a low whistle and said, "I'll be a son of a . . ."

For his part, Bat was still holding his gun on the cowboys, covering every move Wyatt made. "How'd you know he'd already pulled a gun, Wyatt?" Bat asked. "I was standing right in front of him and I didn't see it."

"Neither did I," Wyatt said. "Put your gun away, Bat. It might go off."

Bat held the jail cell door open as Wyatt put one unconscious cowboy onto one bunk and Ed put the other on the other. They had gotten a bandage on the one fellow and his bleeding had stopped.

"Guess I didn't make too spectacular a debut, huh?" Ed said, laughing at himself and shaking his head.

Wyatt gently pushed Ed out the door. He closed it and locked it and walked with the Masterson brothers into the office. He put the keys back into the desk, then took out a booking report and started filling in the blanks.

"You know," Ed said, "that one fella could have gone for his gun after he saw you put the dent in his friend's head."

"Yes, that's true," Wyatt said without looking up.

"All I'm sayin' is, Wyatt, I don't think we were in . . . 'mortal danger' exactly, you know?"

"Mebbe not," said Wyatt without looking up.

"I mean," Ed said, "those two was so drunk they couldn't have found their own butts in an outhouse."

Bat chuckled and shook his head. Wyatt said nothing. But a chuckle to Ed was a sure invitation to keep right on talking.

"Well, it's true, Wyatt," said Ed. "That one fella was so drunk he couldn't have hit the ground with his hat in three tries. I don't believe they could have hit a bull's ass with a banjo."

There was no sound in the room except Wyatt's pen scratching his report into the ledger.

"Could be," said Wyatt, still not looking up.

But Ed Masterson was just a naturally talkative fellow. Wyatt could have broken wind and Ed would have taken that as Wyatt's side of the conversation. "They were just havin' a good time, Wyatt, that's all, and I don't know if it was necessary to crack 'em upside the head with a gun barrel just to get their attention." Then Ed took a deep breath and said, "I believe I could have talked those guns off 'em."

Wyatt finally looked up.

"Ed . . ." he said, putting down his pen. "If I were you, I'd look for another line of work . . . politics maybe."

There was a silence in the room, and Bat felt it most heavily upon him, felt he had to say something to defend his brother. "Ed's just got a different style is all, Wyatt."

Wyatt cut them both off quiet and quick.

"You could get killed in this line of work, Ed," he said. "You could get people around you killed."

Though he was younger than his brother, Bat was the one who always felt protective. "Wyatt," he said, "it's just our first night."

Wyatt stood up behind the desk and closed the ledger.

"I know," he said, getting ready to pass judgment in the manner of his father. "But when I hit that fella, your first instinct was to pull your weapon and cover me," he said to Bat. Then he turned those cold, expressionless eyes on Ed and said, "This is a hard land, Ed. . . . It doesn't suffer fools."

"I'm not a fool, Wyatt."

"No, you're not," Wyatt said. "But you are not a deliberate man. I do not sense that about you, Ed. You're too . . ." Wyatt searched for the word and then found it, and when he said it, it was not a compliment. "You're too . . . affable."

Fort Griffin, Texas, was another ramshackle camp town made up of hunters, outlaws, cowboys, gamblers, and whores. Wyatt, dusty and dirty from the trail, rode into town and craned his neck as he saw a sign on a saloon that proclaimed that this place was known as "Shanssey's." Wyatt dismounted his horse and entered the drinking and gambling emporium.

John Shanssey, the saloon's proprietor, was a big, tough Irish pug, an ex-fighter. He was behind the bar as Wyatt walked into this very tough saloon full of all the frontier types, some of whom were trying to decide if this was as good a day as any on which to die.

"John . . ." Wyatt said, looking at the bartender. "John Shanssey?" Shanssey turned around and looked at Wyatt a second or two before it registered and then he stuck out a big ham hock of a hand.

"Well, I'll be . . ." he said, pumping Wyatt's hand. "Wyatt . . . How the hell are you?"

"I saw the name out front," Wyatt said. "But I didn't think it could be the same John Shanssey."

"My gosh, it's good to see you," Shanssey said, the brogue rolling out and across the room like a wave lapping at the shore. "What are you doin' in these parts? I thought you was deputy marshal in Dodge. What would you say to a cold beer, lad?"

"I'd say long time no see," said Wyatt, and ran his tongue across his teeth and felt the trail dust grit that washed away with the first cold gulp of the beer Shanssey set in front of him.

"This is a long way from Dodge," Shanssey said.

"Well, I am no longer employed as their deputy marshal," Wyatt said, taking another gulp. "I was till the city fathers forgot to renew my contract. Guess they figured I was too much of a hard-ass."

Shanssey let out a laugh. "Well, you are, Wyatt, everybody knows that. I hear they've elected themselves a new city marshal, too."

"Yup," Wyatt said, setting the empty glass on the bar. "Fellow named Masterson. Ed Masterson," Wyatt said, and fished a coin out of his pocket and put it on the bar.

"What's he like?" asked Shanssey as he slid the coin right back to Wyatt.

Wyatt smiled at the gesture in appreciation, then spoke in a voice growing very dry despite the beer. "Affable. Very affable. You got an office or some place where we can talk?"

In Shanssey's office Wyatt pulled out a reward poster with

a likeness of one Dave Rudabaugh on it. Rudabaugh was wanted for train robbery.

"I'm working as a detective for the Sante Fe Railroad on this, John," Wyatt said, handing him the poster. "They're offering three thousand dollars' reward for any information leading to the arrest of Dave Rudabaugh. He's robbed three of their trains, and they'd like to put a stop to it."

Shanssey set the poster down and looked up at Wyatt. "He's been through here, Wyatt, but where he went, that's another matter." He slid the poster back across to Wyatt.

"Anybody around here you think might know?" Wyatt asked, folding the poster back up along its creases and putting it in his pocket.

"Any number of people *might* know," Shanssey said. "But there aren't too many of them that wouldn't be too scared to tell you."

"Gotta be somebody."

Shanssey leaned back in his chair and smiled. "Doc Holliday . . ." he said. "He's here. He'd know, and he's not scared of Rudabaugh—or anyone else, for that matter."

"Holliday?" Wyatt asked. "He's a killer, isn't he?"

"He hasn't killed anyone around here, Wyatt, least not today."

Wyatt just looked at him. Shanssey took out his pocket watch, opened it, and glanced at the hour. " 'Course, it's only noon."

Wyatt didn't even crack a smile.

"That was a joke, Wyatt," Shanssey said.

"And a very humorous one, too, I'm sure," Wyatt replied without smiling. He leaned in toward Shanssey. "What makes you think a man like Holliday would give any information to a lawman?"

Shanssey looked at Wyatt realizing the man had no sense of humor whatsoever, but he was in a land of Protestants and had learned long ago that it was a scarce commodity on the frontier.

"Holliday is no friend of Rudabaugh's, and he does owe me a couple favors. In fact, that may be one of Doc's finest attributes. For a drunkard he is amazingly loyal to his friends."

For his part, if Wyatt had a religion it was loyalty.

"What else can you tell me about him?" he asked.

"Well," said Shanssey, "he travels with a woman named Big Nosed Kate. She's a whore, but he's not her pimp."

Shortly thereafter, Shanssey and Wyatt walked down the very bare street of this camp town and entered a tent saloon. Once inside, they walked over to a table where a pale, consumptive-looking man in a nicely tailored jacket and vest, with deep-sunk eyes and sallow complexion, sat with a water glass full of whiskey. The bottle beside him was half empty, and he was playing solitaire. He looked up when Shanssey said, "Doc." It was a very dangerous look, and it had nothing to do with anything other than the fact that he was a very dangerous man.

"John . . ." Doc said, smiling.

"I'd like you to meet someone," Shanssey said. "A friend of mine from Wichita."

Doc looked over at Wyatt.

"Wichita?" he said, and took a drink. "Nasty little town, as far as I recall. They had some local constable there who walked around like he had a cob up his butt . . . name of Burp or Slurp or some damned thing." He started coughing, mildly at first and then it turned into a hacking spasm.

"Earp . . ." Wyatt said. "Wyatt Earp. How do you do, Doctor Holliday."

"That *was* you, wasn't it?" Doc said, taking another drink, which seemed, momentarily at least, to quiet his cough. "You're the one who liked to beat up drunken cowboys?"

Wyatt said nothing, just looked at him.

The Doc continued in a languorous, elegant way.

"Speaking as a drunkard myself," he said, "I can tell you that I take offense at stories I've heard of you, sir. I have in fact heard that you are a prig and a bully."

Wyatt's eyes were on the Doc's hand and the six-guns that he wore inside his coat. He had heard that the Doc was a good man with a knife as well, and assumed a knife must be inside his boot.

"Doctor Holliday," he said. "I need information about Dave Rudabaugh. There's a reward if that information leads to his arrest. If that's of interest to you, we have reason to continue this conversation. Otherwise I'll leave you to your game."

The two men stared at each other, each one taking the measure of the other.

"You keep callin' me Doctor, not Doc. I *am* a dentist, you know. That's not a nickname. I have a degree."

"So I understand," said Wyatt.

"It was just that I got tuberculosis and people didn't tolerate my coughing with their mouths open. So I, uh, took up gambling instead," he said and laughed, then coughed again and again. It was mild at first and then he really started hacking, covering his mouth with his right hand. He reached for the bottle of whiskey and poured the empty water tumbler full, then downed it. Once again it stopped the cough.

"Well . . ." Doc said, lowering the glass. "You want information about Rudabaugh, I'll get some for you. . . . You've got yourself a deal." He coughed once again into his hand and then stuck it out to Wyatt. "Shake," he said, smiling right into Wyatt's expressionless eyes.

Wyatt looked down at the proferred hand and then shook it, returning his gaze, straight into the dentist's eyes.

Then Doc laughed so hard that the coughing started again, and when it finally quieted, he said, still smiling, "Maybe you don't have a cob up your butt after all, Wyatt!"

Wyatt walked out of the tent saloon, wiping his hand on his pant leg, shuddering.

There was a telegram waiting for him at the Western Union office. It read as follows:

TO WYATT EARP, CARE OF SANTA FE RAILROAD HEAD OFFICE, STOP. MARSHAL ED MASTERSON KILLED BY DRUNKEN COWBOYS, STOP. LAWLESSNESS NEAR RIOT PROPORTIONS, STOP. REQUEST YOU RETURN IMMEDIATELY TO DODGE CITY, STOP. WILL RENEW YOUR PREVIOUS CONTRACT AS ASSISTANT CITY MARSHAL AT DOUBLE SALARY, STOP. SIGNED JAMES KELLY, MAYOR.

A sign was posted in Dodge City that stated that the carrying of firearms north of the line that ran along the railroad tracks just south of Front Street was strictly prohibited by city ordinance and that those who did so were subject to immediate

arrest. The entire area of Front Street north of that line and
its sign of warning was filled with drunken cowboys, almost
all of them armed, almost all of them shooting their weapons
off at one thing or another. Windows were being shot out.
Sporting women were heard screaming. The town was in the
grips of drunken cowboys with guns a-blazing.

At the city marshal's office, Wyatt assembled his lawmen.
He had sent for his brother, Morgan, and Bat Masterson had
sent for his brother, Jim. There was Luke Short and Charlie
Bassett and Bill Tilgham. All the law officers were grim-
faced as Wyatt looked up and said, "Let's go."

On Front Street, drunken cowboys were carousing in the
streets and on the sidewalks, breaking out windows and fighting one another, when out of the shadows walking resolutely
toward them from both sides of the thoroughfare were Wyatt
and his newly assembled deputies. Without words or warning
they systematically beat into unconsciousness any cowboy in
their path wearing a gun. They then picked up the guns of
the unconscious cowboys and put them in a gunnysack Jim
Masterson carried.

The Long Branch Saloon was ransacked. Furniture was
broken and the piano player, trussed up like a pig at Christmas, was suspended upside down from the chandelier. The
cowboys' wild revelry was, however, interrupted by the roar
of a shotgun blast. All eyes turned toward the door frame
filled by Wyatt Earp and his double-barreled scattergun. Morgan, Bat, Jim, Charlie, and Luke entered from various portals, coming in out of the darkness with the promise of swift,
sure death. There was another blast from Wyatt's scattergun,
and then all was quiet save the voice that called out, in deadly
calm, "My name is Wyatt Earp. It all ends now!"

The following morning, a buckboard wagon drove into
town past broken windows and a line of cowboys. The cowboys proceeded like prisoners of war under the gaze of Morgan Earp and Luke Short, who held shotguns on them as
they literally marched them out of town. The driver of the
buckboard was a dentist known more for his skills as a card-
sharp and killer than as a practitioner of the healing arts.

"What the hell happened here, anyway?" Doc said as he
looked at a mournful cowboy in the prisoner-of-war line who
looked back up at him.

"Wyatt Earp," said the mournful cowboy. "That's what happened."

Doc thought about that one. Most people who knew him believed Doc to be fearless. But the reason for that was that Doc had nothing to fear. He knew for a fact he would die young, and the circumstances of that impending death did not matter. In fact, the more he could take with him the merrier a send-off it would be. But in Wyatt Earp, Doc saw a man who was in apparently good health, not mentally incompetent, and yet seemingly as unaffected by a fear of death as he was. The dentist considered that Wyatt Earp might well be the first truly brave and honorable man he had ever met since leaving his father's house. He was certainly the only one who had offered both the respect to which Doc believed his education and breeding entitled him, and a hand extended in friendship. All his life John Holliday had dreamed of having an older brother, a beacon to emulate and a pal, one who would not judge him but stand by him. It dawned on him that perhaps this person might well turn out to be Wyatt Earp.

Doc surveyed the effect of this one man on an entire lawless town. He turned to his companion, a well-known whore named Big Nosed Kate, and smiled. "You got to love a guy like that," he said.

"Only if he pays me," Kate replied in a slight lilting Hungarian accent.

Doc laughed till the hacking cough shook his frame, only to be quieted by the generous draft he took from his flask.

"Oh, Kate! Darling Kate," he said. "You're one in a . . . dozen or so, give or take."

Doc shook the reins, and the buckboard moved down Front Street. Kate was the one at his side, but the one he would come to love enough to kill and die for was Wyatt Earp.

CHAPTER SEVEN

Wyatt, wearing his dark coat and string tie, walked down Front Street. Shopkeepers were repairing windows, children played on the sidewalks, and women, feeling the streets were safe once again, took to the promenade. To each and all Wyatt tipped his hat, and everyone was happy to see and greet him as well. The town was safe and Wyatt was a hero.

Those were the salad days. That summer of 1878, Wyatt and his deputies became legends throughout most of the frontier as the local papers spread the stories of Dodge City and her lawmen. Tricky thing, though, the legend business. The problem is, you get a reputation and there's always someone who wants to test it. That's what happened with a fella named Clay Allison. They said he'd killed thirty men or something like that.

Clay was tough as they came and crazy as popcorn on a hot skillet. And he had decided to see just how tough this Wyatt Earp was. So he sent word he was coming into town to kill him and that, moreover, he intended to do so while drunk and bare-assed naked.

Aside from the boots on his feet and the gun on his hip, he was indeed naked as a cherub when he rode through the town, down Front Street, a bottle of whiskey in one hand and a Winchester in the other, making what came to be known as Clay Allison's "Lady Godiva Ride."

He randomly shot out newly installed windows as his horse pranced its naked rider up the sporting district's main thoroughfare.

"Earp!" he bellowed. "Earp, you dour do-gooder cowboy-clubbin' son of a bitch! Show your face so's I can put some daylight through it! A little ray of sunshine clean through your skull! Earp! Do you hear me!?"

He punctuated this speech with rounds fired from the Winchester. Brave men took cover, horses stampeded, windows shattered, and gentle ladies hid their eyes and their children in shock and horror as he rode naked through the town. On the other hand certain other ladies, most prominent among them being Big Nosed Kate, looked out through the window of the boardinghouse at Clay and judged his assets with an appreciative nod of the head.

Clay rode up and down the main street shooting and drinking from his bottle. When the bottle was empty he threw it up in the air, drew his six-gun, and blew it to pieces. He placed his Winchester in the scabbard, dismounted, and entered the Long Branch, which all things considered was as poetic a choice of venue as he could have chosen.

"Eaaaaarrrrrrrppppppp! You're all gurgle and no guts! You're as yella as mustard without any of the bite! You hear me, Earp!?" There was no reply as he entered the saloon and walked over to the bar, dangling his various weapons.

The bartender's back was turned to him as the naked gunman yelled, "Bartender! Whiskey!"

The barman, however, instead of turning to Clay with a bottle in his hand, held a shotgun. Clay thought through his drunken stupor that this was the most dangerous-looking barkeep he had ever seen.

"Hi . . ." said Wyatt, cocking back the hammers on the shotgun he held on Allison. "Were you looking for me?"

"Earp?" was all Clay could say.

"I'm filling in for the usual bartender," Wyatt said, and then, not unkindly, added, "I bet that gun belt chafes. Why don't you take it off."

Clay stood looking at Wyatt and Wyatt stood looking at

Clay, though making sure that his gaze was directed at the cowboy's eyes. Clay for a moment considered what the odds were that his hand could reach his pistol, draw it, and fire before Wyatt could squeeze the scattergun's trigger. It must be assumed that he did not favor the odds, since the only sound to be heard shortly thereafter was that of his gun belt clattering to the floor.

Then Wyatt said, "And since I don't appreciate you pointin' the other thing at me either, why don't you just turn around, show me your better side . . . and leave."

Back out on Front Street, still naked but without his six-gun, Clay Allison mounted up and rode slowly in the direction from whence he came.

Wyatt stood at the saloon door following Allison through his shotgun sights, just to make sure the naked gunman tried nothing desperate.

And from her vantage point in her window, like a medieval princess in a castle's turret, Big Nosed Kate leaned down and shouted out to Clay. "Hey . . . stranger," she said in that lilting way. "I'm glad to see you're still armed."

If he had had a hat, he would have tipped it. "And dangerous, ma'am," he said, smiling.

And the naked cowboy rode away.

CHAPTER EIGHT

Doc Holliday sat at a table playing poker. Kate sat in on the game, smoking a cigar. The summer had given way to the first chill days of autumn, and there was a hubbub outside as citizens of Dodge marched through the streets carrying torches. Seeing as how the problem of drunken cowboys rioting in the streets had been quelled by the arrival of Wyatt Earp, Doc wondered as to the nature of the commotion. He crossed over to the window and looked out. Then he turned back to his poker companions, one of whom was an itinerant salesman who answered to the name of George, and the other the proprietor of a tannery by the name of Ben.

"Very colorful," Doc said, indicating the throng that noisily made its way up the street. "Are torchlight parades a regular feature of the cultural life here in Dodge? It seems positively Teutonic, if you ask me."

George looked up from his cards and said, "What? Oh, that. . . . No, I expect that's just some of the gentry who are worked up about this fella Johnny O'Roarke, the one they call Johnny Behind the Deuce."

"What about him?" asked Doc as Kate belched and motioned with her hand for another beer.

"Nothin' much," George said. "I expect they're just gonna hang him, is all."

Kate took a thirsty gulp off the newly arrived lager. "Thank God," she said. "I was afraid maybe it's something serious like a temperance movement or the wives marching against prostitution."

Doc solicitously patted the shoulder of his paramour. "Now now, my dear," he said, trying to reassure her. "It appears to be little more than a lynching, so we're both safe." He sat back down at the table and picked up his cards once again, adding as an afterthought, "Though I doubt that they'll get their little parade past the village constabulary."

"Ain't no constabulary left in town to speak of aside from Earp," said George.

"What do you mean?" This from Doc.

The one called Ben peered above his cards and his spectacles, looking like a fat owl too well sated to be troubled with pursuing further rodents. "The Masterson brothers and Earp's brother and Bassett and Tilghman and the rest went up to Fort Leavenworth to bring back those seven Indians from Dull Knife's raiding party to stand trial. So Wyatt's the only one left in town."

Johnny O'Roarke was singularly aware of that fact as well. In his cell he stood on his bunk and looked out the barred window at the crowd and their torches moving down the street toward him.

"Earp!" he yelled. "Marshal Earp! They're comin'! Must be close to a hundred of 'em. Earp, you got to give me a gun!"

Wyatt, who was calmly loading a shotgun in his office at the time, called back, "Can't do that, Johnny. You're an outlaw."

Wyatt then put an extra six-gun in his belt so that now he was armed with two pistols and the twelve-gauge scattergun.

The lynch mob meanwhile came down the street toward the jail, headed by a heavyset man named Dick Garth. Just then the jail door opened and out stepped Wyatt Earp, holding the shotgun in his hand, his jacket off so that his six-gun and the extra one in his belt were plainly visible to the approaching mob.

"Hi . . ." Wyatt said as if greeting lynch mobs outside his front door were what he did every evening. "Nice mob you got here, Mister Garth."

Garth's face was bloated and blotched with burst blood vessels, which gave him a deceptively rosy-cheeked appearance beneath his little piggy eyes. "We want Johnny O'Roarke," he said.

"Get set for disappointment, then," said Wyatt.

Garth let fly a skinny stream of whiskey-soaked tobacco juice between his teeth and said, "He killed one of my men."

"And that's what he'll stand trial for."

"Maybe," Garth said, not so much to Wyatt as to his mob, playing to their basest instincts. "Maybe we'll just save the county the expense of holding a trial." A cheer went up from the mob.

Wyatt betrayed no sense of intimidation, however. "You can try, but then the county will have to reimburse me the expense of shotgun shells." It was as close as Wyatt had come in several months to making a joke, and for his part, he thought it was a humorous one. But it served only to inflame Garth further.

"Why, you arrogant son of a bitch," he said. "You think you can stop all of us?" He raised his hand to urge the mob forward, when there was heard a whiskey-soaked though nonetheless elegant voice ringing out.

"That's tellin' 'em, fatso," came the voice of John Holliday, D.D.S.

The crowd turned to see who was talking and out stepped Doc, his coat back behind his two guns. Wyatt turned and looked in amazement at the Doctor as well.

" 'Course, he can't stop all of you," Doc said as he moved to the side of the crowd, taking what shootists referred to as "position." I figure five or six at the most will go down from that scattergun, and taking up as much space as you do it would be difficult not to hit you, Mister . . . Girth was it?"

"Garth . . . the name is Garth."

"Mine's Holliday . . . I'm a dentist," Doc said, and smiled a perfectly lovely, deadly smile. A murmur went up through the crowd as they realized that this was the legendary killer.

Doc was warming to his subject now, and shared with them his glimpse at their chosen fate.

"Twelve more will die from Mister Earp's side arms, and twelve more from mine. So what are we saying, then . . ." He seemed to be adding up the corpses in his mind. "Only thirty of you will grace the obituary pages. What the hell . . . sounds right to me."

The smile flashed again in the darkness, and then an awful calm, as everything human seemed to drain from his face like the devil sitting down to do accounts. "Let's get started. What do you say . . . who's first?"

One edgy cowboy was sure Doc was bluffing. His hand moved inside his coat pocket and came out with a gun that he almost had a chance to fire, had it not been for the fact that Doc drew, cocked, fired first, and killed him where he stood.

"Okay," said Doc. "Who's second?"

The mob, faced with their own mortality, changed from a mob and turned into individual men whose fear burned through the alcohol they had consumed. They looked at each other and wondered if this appointment with the man they called "The Doctor of Death" there in the street was worth the price.

"Come on, you syphilitic pimps," Doc said, like a degenerate Pentecostal. "You sons of whores, you walking pustules, you sty-ridden scum suckers! Come on, you heroes! I've got consumption! I'm dead anyway. . . . Which of you is comin' with me!?"

And there it was, an open invitation to a moonlight dance with a dead man. The crowd backed off as one.

"Don't worry, Johnny m'lad," Doc called out to the dark barred window. "The candlelight choir are all going home."

The mob had receded into the darkness like so many cockroaches when the light comes on. Then Doc turned to Wyatt.

"You're a brave man, Earp," he said. "I admire that."

Wyatt slowly put down the shotgun, scratched his head, and looked at Doc. "You're a . . . piece of work yourself, Doc."

CHAPTER NINE

Mattie Blaylock was not a beautiful woman. She was not even what you would call pretty. Attractive possibly, if you were a lonely man, if you weren't particular, and if you were just looking for any port in the storm, or if perhaps you were just looking to rent a moment's respite, a bit of warmth on a cold night for which all you had to pay, you thought, was money.

Mattie was in bed. Wyatt stood by her dresser tucking his shirt into his trousers. Mattie Blaylock was much enamored of Wyatt Earp.

"Do you have to go?" she asked. It was what she always asked.

"Yes," said Wyatt. "I have some paperwork that needs to be done."

It seemed there was always paperwork. It sat on his desk, she imagined, like livestock waiting to be fed.

Wyatt took some money out of his pocket and put it, very respectfully, on her dresser top. Mattie watched him sadly.

"You don't need to do that, Wyatt. I told you that before."

Wyatt stood before the dresser with his back to Mattie. He looked at the money he had slipped beneath her doily and

wished she would just take it and be done with it, wished
he had never started coming to see her, wished he didn't
occasionally feel the need. When he spoke, it was with difficulty.

"Well, I . . . I appreciate that, Mattie, but uh . . ."

She leaned forward in the bed, rising up onto her knees,
reaching out to him.

"I care about you, Wyatt," she said, reaching out to take
his hand. "It's not like it is with anybody else. I care a lot
about you."

Wyatt did not know what she wanted of him. He never
knew what women wanted. He had supposed with a whore it
was money, only to find that he knew even less what was
wanted. "I'm very . . ." he searched for the words, ". . .
fond of you too, Mattie," he said.

"I could make you happy, Wyatt," she said, grabbing at
his fingers, pulling him toward her. "If you'd give me a
chance . . . I know I could."

Wyatt stood there looking very confused. She had his hand
and he wanted it back.

"I . . . I don't know what you want me to say, Mattie. I
. . . I . . ." He was trying to think of a thing to say that
would compliment her, mollify her, and allow him to take
his hand back unobtrusively and leave. "I look forward to
seeing you, but I . . . I won't tell you things that aren't so."

She held his hand even tighter, saying, "We could leave
here, Wyatt. You could get a job anywhere. You're so smart
you could do anything you set your mind to, and I could be
a wife to you." She pulled his hand into her bosom. "I could
be a real wife, a helpmate. I could give you children, Wyatt,
and . . ."

Wyatt was torn between trying to pull his hand out of hers
and wanting to comfort her as she began to cry.

"I swear I love you, Wyatt," she said, weeping. "I swear
I do."

He dreaded the thought of her tears.

"Mattie," he said, stroking the back of her head gently
with one hand while trying to disengage the other, "I don't
want to cause you pain. I'm very fond of you, and if seeing
me causes you pain I . . ."

"No, no," she said, looking up at him and sniveling miserably, letting loose of his hand to run her own underneath her nose and wiping away at her tears. "You're about the only thing in my life that's not painful to me, and I'll be anything you want me to be, Wyatt, only don't leave money on my dresser, please." And he was about to cross to it and take the bills from underneath the doily and vow silently never to return, when she added, "Unless it's 'cause you want to take care of me. Is that what it is, Wyatt?" she said, looking up at him hopefully. "Is that how you mean it?"

And he wanted to say, no, that's not what I mean, he wanted to say, I'm trying to buy something, take the money and don't back out on the bargain I thought we had made: brief warmth for dollars hard earned—fair, straightforward, and simple. And he wanted to say, if you can't accept it that way I'll be done with you and come no more. Instead he said, "Sure, Mattie, sure. That's how I mean it," just so he could get out of the room.

Exiting the boardinghouse where Mattie lived, Wyatt shuddered like a child in a graveyard.

Halfway down the street there appeared at Wyatt's side a portly gentleman of middle age in a vested three-piece suit and derby hat.

He was a large gentleman, obviously from the East by his dress but not weak in appearance, nor soft; sharklike was more like it. "Excuse me," he said with a flourish. "Mister Earp? *Correction*, Marshal Earp?"

"Yes," Wyatt said, eyeing the easterner.

"Marshal Wyatt Earp?" he repeated.

"That is my name, Mister . . . ?"

Wyatt looked him up and down, trying to size up what manner of man stood before him.

"Judson," he said by way of explanation. "Edward Zane Caroll Judson. The name is not familiar to you, I take it."

"No," Wyatt said, stepping down from the wooden sidewalk and into the dusty street, "can't say that it is."

"That is because, dear Marshal Earp, I am better known by my nom de plume, as it were." He hopped along beside Wyatt like a large marsupial. "Let me ask, sir, if you are acquainted with the name . . ." He paused as if unveiling a great and hidden treasure. ". . . Buffalo Bill Cody?"

Wyatt stopped dead in his tracks and looked at the man with new appreciation. "You're Buffalo Bill?" he said with unabashed admiration.

The stranger smiled like a department-store Santa to a wide-eyed child upon his knee.

"In a very real sense, an almost, if you will, transcendental sense, may I say, I am indeed," he said, lowering his eyes with a manly show of modesty, and then looked up and with a flourish of hand and wrist continued, "just as I am Wild Bill Hickock, or any of the literally hundreds of other characters about whom I have written. I am, sir, Buntline. Ned Buntline." He said it with obvious pride, as if the unmasking of his true identity were the final treasure revealed.

Wyatt, however, just looked at him blankly. "Well," he said, "well, pleasure to meet you."

But Ned was not crestfallen at this lack of recognition. "Marshal Earp," he said with a kind of noble flourish. "May I buy you a drink, sir?" he said gravely.

"Well, Mister . . ."

"Buntline," said Buntline.

"Well, Mister Buntline," said Wyatt, "I don't drink."

Ned feigned a swoon. "The western hero doesn't drink, oh be still my heart," he said. "Coffee perhaps . . . lemonade . . . something . . . a cup of cheer over which we may discuss business and at which I can present you with a small gift I have commissioned to be made for yourself and Bat Masterson?"

It was harder to get rid of this man than to get your hand back from Mattie Blaylock's bosom. Thus, Wyatt found himself sitting next to Bat Masterson across a table from Ned Buntline in the Long Branch Saloon.

Bat tilted back in his chair and eyed the survivor of a thousand duels, which is how Buntline billed himself on his visiting cards. "Let me see if I got this straight. You want us to come back east with you and be in some kinda sideshow."

"Sideshow?" said Buntline in horror, waving his hand back and forth as if to stave off something vile. "Sideshow? Perish the thought! Sideshow connotes cheap hucksterism and fakery. No, sir, I am talking about an historical drama, a western *Henry the Fourth*, an *Iliad of the Frontier*, if you will. The saga of Dodge City and her lawmen." He looked from Bat to Wyatt and back to Bat again, then leaned in as if to share a secret. "Buffalo Bill starred in a drama with me only last season. He made a fortune, gentlemen, an absolute fortune. And Hickok assigned to me the rights to his exploits to be written in novella form, another fortune, gentlemen." He leaned back in his chair, and his voice rose in the kind of dramatic presentation that heretofore Wyatt had seen only in traveling shows on stage. "And neither of them," said Buntline, "let me say it now, neither Hickok, nor Cody, is possessed of the same charismatic personae that you two magnificent paladins possess in such abundance."

There was dead silence as Bat and Ned and Wyatt regarded one another. Then Wyatt spoke, tentatively.

"Mister . . ."

"Buntline," said Buntline.

"Mister Buntline," said Wyatt.

"Yes, Marshal Earp?" said Buntline.

There was a pause and then, "Thanks for the coffee," Wyatt said and got up to leave.

"That's it?" exclaimed Ned. "Thanks for the coffee and good-bye. You won't even consider my offer?"

Wyatt considered for a moment and then said, "I already have, sir."

But the survivor of a thousand duels remained unfazed.

"Ah, yes," he said, "well. Nor can I blame you. For you do not know me, but perhaps this will speak for me, a token for you both. Nay, more than a token—a mythic weapon . . . no less destined to become part of your legend than Excalibur was to King Arthur. To wit . . ."

Buntline reached underneath the table and pulled out two long cases, regarding each as Merlin must have regarded the sword plucked up from the stone. He handed one to Bat and one to Wyatt, and continued.

"Two magnificent revolvers, each with a barrel twelve inches in length designed by me and engraved with my name—Ned—on each." Wyatt and Bat opened the cases and saw the two revolvers, what legend would come to call Buntline Specials.

"An invention of my own creation," Ned said. "Made for me to my specifications by the Colt Firearms Company. The

Buntline Special. The perfect modern-day sword for two knights-errant of the frontier. No strings attached. Accept them as tokens of my esteem."

Shortly thereafter a stagecoach stood outside the Wells Fargo office. Ned was getting aboard it, saying good-bye to Bat and Wyatt.

"I'm sorry we couldn't do business, gentlemen," he said. "Let me know if you change your minds."

"We certainly will, sir," Bat was quick to say. "And thanks once again for the guns."

"Not at all," said Buntline. "And when you fire them at some desperado, think of Ned. Adieu."

He hoisted himself into the stagecoach and was gone.

Bat and Wyatt went back to Hawkins' Blacksmith's Shop, where Bat put his new gun in a vise and began cutting the barrel down with a hacksaw.

"Well," he said, "what the hell, a free gun's a free gun."

The hacksaw cut through the metal and the extra-long piece of barrel fell to the ground, leaving a normal-size revolver. Bat loosened the vise and looked at his handiwork. "Want me to do yours?" he said to Wyatt.

"I don't know," Wyatt said. "I think I'll leave mine the way it is."

It was but a few weeks later that Wyatt found himself riding shotgun on a stagecoach that was being pursued by six masked highwaymen. Wyatt shot and the robbers fell. Wells Fargo had offered Wyatt the princely sum of seventy-five dollars to ride along as security guard on one of their shipments of gold.

By the time the coach arrived at the first way station it was riddled with bullets, the driver was wounded, and Wyatt had twice nearly been killed. The station manager was the type of fellow who makes the village idiot look gifted. His name was Lucas, and there was a newspaper sticking out of his back pocket. Wyatt hopped down, helping the driver and shouting to the manager, "We been hit, Lucas, twice!" The driver's arm was around his shoulder as he took the man inside. "I don't know what the hell's goin' on out there."

"I expect," said Lucas in a high, whiny voice as he scratched at his long johns, "I expect you'll be hit a few more times too 'fore you reach Topeka."

"What are you talking about?" Wyatt asked, setting the driver on a stool and ripping open his shirt to inspect the wound.

Later, when the wound was dressed, Lucas pulled out his newspaper and showed it to Wyatt. There was a full-page ad, which Wyatt read to himself in growing disgust.

"Ship your valuables," it said, "with confidence. Our Overland Stage carrying mail and *GOLD BULLION* will be guarded personally by none other than the famous Western hero, Dodge City's own Assistant City Marshal, Wyatt Earp!"

"Judas Priest!" Wyatt exclaimed.

When the coach rattled into Topeka, Kansas, at a gallop, its canvas skin was in shreds. Wyatt was filthy, and both he and the new driver had been wounded. In a cold fury, Wyatt jumped stiffly down and strode over to the Wells Fargo office.

He entered the office still carrying his rifle.

"My name's Earp," he said. "I just delivered your freight."

Then he pulled out the newspaper Lucas had given him and tossed it onto the station manager's desk.

His voice was barely above a whisper as he said, "We got hit eight times because of this." And then he banged his fist down onto the desk. "Eight times on one run!"

The station manager thought that Wyatt might kill him. Wyatt, for his part, could think of nothing further to say and so started out the door. Then he turned back and said in a very hoarse voice, "You owe me seventy-five dollars."

Back in Dodge City, Bat looked up smiling as Wyatt walked in with his saddlebags.

"Read about you in the paper, Wyatt," Bat said in a good-natured way.

There was a jocularity with which brave men of that time treated one another's bravery, but to Bat's surprise Wyatt was not in a jocular mood.

"Tell the mayor I quit," Wyatt said, taking off his badge.

"What?" Bat said incredulously.

"I've had it with the law business, Bat," said Wyatt, crossing to his desk to clear out his things. "I've had it with bein' famous. I've had it with Dodge and I've had it with the whole state of Kansas."

"Yeah, but . . ." Bat sputtered.

But Wyatt waved him off with a free hand. "I'm gettin' out of all of it, and you'd be smart if you did too." Wyatt took a deep breath as if he had passed over a particular Rubicon of the mind and then said, "I'm gonna settle down. I'm gonna take a helpmate. I'm gonna open up a nice quiet saloon or somethin' and move someplace where nobody wants to shoot at me anymore."

"Yeah?" said Bat. "And what place is that?"

"Arizona . . ." Wyatt said, filling his saddlebags with his few possessions. "Lot of money in Arizona, Bat, lot of opportunity. A man can make a handsome living in Arizona. My brother Virgil's already there." And then Wyatt got the same kind of look in his eye that Nicholas Earp would get when he talked about the El Dorado—like state of California. It was not a place that drew them, but a dream, a dream the likes of which he had not permitted himself in many years, a dream of family. "I'm gonna get James. Gonna get Morgan. We'll all go." Then he sighed, and said, "I'm just tired of gettin' shot at and not havin' anything to show for it. So good-bye, Dodge City, Kansas, and good riddance, and hello, Tombstone, Arizona."

"Tombstone, huh?" said Bat. "Well, it does sound quiet, I'll give you that."

PART TWO

Tombstone

CHAPTER TEN

Wyatt, Virgil, Morgan, and James went out to Tombstone, Arizona, in 1880 with the idea of starting up their own stagecoach line. The problem was, though, all the routes were already taken and Wells Fargo wasn't interested in giving Wyatt a contract, just a job if he wanted it. Still, Tombstone was a silver-mining boomtown, a land of opportunity. That was just what Tombstone's mayor, Alder Randall, was calling it as he addressed a group of Tombstone's finest businessmen who had gathered at the Maison D'Oree Restaurant.

The furnishings of this establishment were of the finest caliber. The service and silver were the best that money could buy. Waitresses in starched, French-styled blouses and black skirts slid silently between the men, refilling cups of coffee as the mayor at the head table, flanked by his city councilmen, delivered his address. The handsomest of the councilmen by far was a distinguished-looking man in his fifties whose bearing marked him as one of a rare breed, for he was a former lieutenant in the Texas Rangers. Mike Gray was a leader of men who had come to Tombstone like other former lawmen to seek his fortune.

Behind the dais was a banner that proclaimed, ''Welcome to the Mayor's Fourth of July Breakfast.''

''Opportunity,'' the mayor proclaimed, ''and not just any opportunity, but the opportunity of a lifetime. That, after all, is the gift of the West to the rugged individualist, freedom to pursue opportunity bounded only by the limits of one's own ambition.''

As the mayor spoke, another group of rugged individualists in search of opportunities approached the town from out of the desert. The road into Tombstone was hard and dry, hot and dusty with mesquite bushes and crown of thorn bushes competing for what moisture they could suck out of the dust. Several vultures fed upon the carcass of a wild dog lying, evidently run over, in the middle of the wagon track. The sound of horse hooves clip-clopping toward the desert metropolis announced the approach of another wagon. The vultures looked up lackadaisically. The carrion birds took off into the air at the very last moment as a wagon drawn by a team of four horses ran across the carcass of the dead dog. Thump, thump over the broken animal, the dust swirling; then the wagon rode off into the distance. The vultures circled and returned, landing to rip more meat from the body.

The wagon in question was not used for carting typical pioneer provisions, despite the fact that it was of the usual Conestoga shape. Inside the wagon were six shapely French whores, complaining about the dust in their mother tongue and excited that they were soon to reach their destination. On the side of the wagon there was a sign that featured a drawing of a young belle in a low-cut gown with a graceful arm holding a bunch of grapes about to be plucked off the dangling stem.

Under the portrait there was the caption: ''Mme. LeDeau's. Our Recommendation—Ask Any Man.''

The wagonload of whores was rolling down the road toward Tombstone while Mayor Randall extolled the virtues of the free-enterprise system to the assembled pillars of Tombstone's society.

''The opportunity of which I speak can be found in the mineral wealth of the land and in the freedom to exploit it unfettered by the bonds of eastern tradition. These three words should be our city's motto: Freedom, Opportunity, Ambition.''

Madame LeDeau's wagon cut a majestic swath down the length of Allen Street, the main drag of Tombstone, Arizona. Beginning at First and Allen and running to Third and Allen was what was known as Hoptown, Tombstone's thriving Chinese district. By 1880, fully half of Tombstone's population was made up of Celestial laborers. As the wagon rolled down the road the French girls pointed and poked one another with laughs and giggles at the sight of this exotic city. The signs were almost all in Chinese as well as English. There were Chinese joss houses, mercantile stores, herb stores and laundries, restaurants and grocery stores. The Chinese were in traditional dress, with the long pigtails and fezlike caps. The women who scurried back and forth subserviently had bound feet, traditional in their culture.

Here and there people squatted over coal stoves preparing pungent-smelling meats, while dumping dough hung like laundry on long lines and various Celestials screamed at one another at the top of their lungs in a variety of dialects, though most of them were from the Sam Yap and Sze Yap areas of the Chinese empire.

The district's main joss house was flanked by carved dragons that stood watch over large mahogany doors and ornate jade carvings.

The wagon bearing Mme. LeDeau's latest imports moved now through the business district of downtown Tombstone. Mayor Randall looked up through the lace-curtained window of the Maison D'Oree and saw it pass.

"This is no Garden of Eden where the fruit falls into our mouths from off the tree," he said as the wagon proceeded outside, past the Oriental Saloon, the Occidental Saloon, the Longhorn and the Alhambra, the Crystal Palace and the O.K. Corral. The wagon passed beneath two festive banners hung across the street, one of which proclaimed, "HAPPY FOURTH OF JULY!!!" and the other of which said, "CHINKS GO BACK TO CHINA! JOHN CHINAMAN MUST GO!"

The business center gave way to the red-light district, which even now was alive with ladies extending invitations to drunks from their windows and doorways. Some of these

establishments were wooden structures, some just tents.
There was May's place, Rose's, The Boardinghouse, Marie's
Parlor, and the crème de la crème, Mme. LeDeau's, with its
trademark sign advising one to "ask any man" out front.

The wagon pulled up in front of Mme. LeDeau's and the
girls alighted to the boisterous shouts of approval from the
midday patrons.

At about this time Mayor Randall's speech was approaching its climactic raison d'être. "This, rather," he said,
stretching forth his arms, "is a land of opportunity where the
virtue of honest labor and the sweat of one's brow brings
forth the fruit of just reward."

Willard Elkins looked from the mayor out the window to
the greeting the girls were getting down the street. "What do
you think about that," he said to Mr. Watt of the Watt &
Tarnball Undertaking and Embalming establishment. "Six
new whores all the way from Paris, France." Mr. Watt, who
was not a lively man, said, "Shhhh," as from the dais Mayor
Randall continued.

"Tombstone has gone from mining camp to town, from
town to fastest-growing city west of the Mississippi," said
the mayor, as Willard shouted out, "And the richest too,"
and Mr. Watt said, "Shhhhh," again.

Mayor Randall cast a disapproving glance at Watt and
continued waxing to his theme.

"Rich not only in silver but in the democratic spirit of its
citizens."

"Hear, hear! Hear, hear!" was heard all around.

"Now," said the mayor, "you are all invited to the fireworks display this evening, where in addition to pyrotechnics
there will be several interesting and informative speakers
addressing the problem of the Chinese menace in this city."

And again the murmured hear-hears echoed, though less
lively than before.

"And I can think," Mayor Randall said, "of no more
appropriate holiday for such a discussion than this, the founding of our nation. Our nation—not theirs! So eat up, Happy
Fourth of July, and God Bless America!"

"God Bless America," echoed all those in the room.

CHAPTER ELEVEN

"Brilliant speech," Mike Gray said, pumping Alder Randall's hand as the mayor stepped away from the head table of the Maison d'Oree's dining room while the waitresses cleared the tables. "Inspiring, Mister Mayor, absolutely inspiring."

"Thank you, Mike," said the mayor graciously. He was about to move on to work the rest of the room, which had not yet begun to empty out, when he felt his arm squeezed in the firm grip of Mike Gray, who leaned in and whispered, "We don't have time for this, Alder. We have business."

The business of which Gray spoke was waiting for them even now out at the Clanton Ranch, along with sides of beef roasting on spits over open flames as Chinese cooks poured on plenty of barbecue sauce and other Chinese pulled corn bread from outdoor ovens. These particular cowboys had slicked their hair down and were trying to look their best. There was a long table set with a long checked tablecloth, and it was piled high with the bounty of the prairie: steaks, ribs, corn bread, beans baked bubbling with brown sugar, fruit pies with flaky crusts and fresh-baked cakes and plenty of cold beer waiting in buckets for thirsty dinner guests.

Mexican and Chinese servants scurried around, setting out

the feast. At the center of all this activity, of this wholly male dominion save for the occasional female servants, there was an imposing figure of a man. He was thickly whiskered and appeared to be in his late fifties or early sixties.

Indeed, he resembled no one so much as Nicholas Earp. He wore a vest and suit and a gold watch chain. He was a dignified man, obviously revered by the three young men who called him Pa with no small amount of respect and no small amount of fear. The youngest of the boys was his father's obvious favorite but was not called Wyatt or Morgan or Warren. His name was Billy and his father was Newman Clanton. Billy and his brothers were all in their early twenties. The patriarch of the family turned now to his youngest son.

"Are there enough places set, William?" he asked in a baronial manner.

"Yes, Pa," the boy said respectfully.

"You sure?" said Newman, knowing that his youngest son could sometimes overlook the small details. "You counted?"

"Yes, Pa," the boy said again.

"Isaac," the elder Clanton said to yet another son. "Straighten your tie."

The one whom his father called Isaac shot a glowering look back at his pa.

"Straighten your tie," Newman said again, not to be put off by a surly child. "These are important men," he said. "They have to know that we're not some sort of bumpkins. They have to know that we can be businessmen together. They have to respect us."

Just then another of the boys, the one called Phinn, pointed off at the buckboard approaching through the ranch gate.

"Look, Pa!" he called, and Newman looked at the buckboard and then at the watch that he had pulled from his vest pocket.

"Look at that," Newman said, looking at the watch, which he had plucked only the week before from the dead Mexican whose skull he had split with his rifle butt. "You could set your watch by their arrival," he said, beaming. "*Those* are businessmen. Great things can come of this . . . great things."

The one whom he had referred to as Isaac, who preferred to be called Ike, spoke out of the corner of his mouth.

"My ass," he said.

Newman looked at this son for the tiniest moment and then, by way of reply, picked a burning log out of the fire and hit Ike square in the side of the head with it, sending Ike sprawling and screaming in pain just as the buckboard pulled up.

Mayor Randall and Councilman Gray, along with Dixie Lee Gray, Mike's rather frail and limping twenty-year-old son, alighted from their buckboard. They looked aghast at Newman's sudden violence against one of his own offspring.

Newman himself was embarrassed and tried to cover that embarrassment by sharing his philosophy of child rearing.

"Spare the rod," he said, "spoil the child."

There was an uneasy silence, which Newman tried to break by proclaiming with forced joviality and genuine pride, "Well, the Chinks have prepared a hell of a meal. Let's eat."

The guests and the cowboys repaired to the banquet table spread out before them, beneath a backdrop of the stunning Arizona sky. Newman stepped forth to make the introductions.

"I'd like to, on behalf of my sons and myself . . ." he said, looking around sternly at the still-whimpering Isaac, who rubbed the growing welt on his temple where the hair had been singed by the burning log, "I'd like to welcome our guests to our ranch, Mayor Alder Randall and Councilman Mike Gray . . . formerly Lieutenant Gray, I might add. We bid you . . . *bienvenido*."

A handsome young cowboy by the name of Johnny Ringo looked up. "Little old to be a lieutenant in the Army, if you don't mind the observation," he said.

"Not at all," said Mike Gray, looking at him with eyes as cold as Wyatt's. "I was a lieutenant in the Texas Rangers."

Looks went back and forth between the cowboys, looks of betrayal at the presence of a Texas Ranger. There was a dangerous silence. Tension was palpable between the two factions, and Newman had a sense that his vision of this newly forming alliance could fall apart at any moment. Then Johnny, who looked to Mayor Randall like a decent enough sort, continued in an embarrassed tone.

"Uh . . . we've killed a number of Texas Rangers," he said apologetically. "I hope that's not gonna be a problem."

"Business is business," said Mike Gray with a shrug.

"By God, that's what I say!" said Newman, clapping his hands together joyfully. Great things could come of this.

Alder Randall, Mike Gray, and Dixie Lee stood on one side of the table getting their food chuck-wagon-style, while the Clantons and the others stood on the other side a ways off, getting their fixings. Randall leaned in and whispered to Mike Gray.

"Those two hyenas are Frank and Tom McLaury," he said, indicating two more of the cowboys. "The one who spoke up before is Johnny Ringo, and that one over there who looks like he's a homicidal maniac *is* one—Curly Bill Brocious."

Mike nodded his head and said, "Who are the other three degenerates?"

"Old Man Clanton's kids," said the mayor. "Ike, Billy, and Phinn Clanton."

"Well," replied Gray, "there is something to say for breeding."

He looked up and smiled over at Old Man Clanton and his faction.

For their part they stared over at Mike, Randall, and Dixie Lee. Curly Bill snarled, sadistically sotto voce, to Newman Clanton, "Who's the cripple?"

"That," said Newman, "is Gray's gimpy kid, Dixie Lee."

The three of them smiled carnivorously over at Mike, Randall, and Dixie Lee.

Later, at the table, all the gents were in mid-meal with more buckets of beer being brought up when Mayor Randall said, "These steaks are first-rate . . . really wonderful."

"They ought to be," said Curly Bill, the homicidal maniac, smiling at Mike Gray. "Those weren't from Mexican steers. We stole those in Texas."

Newman spoke quickly to cover the faux pas.

"Not from any of your ranches, I trust, Mister Gray," he said.

Mike waved him off with a fork of red, dripping meat. "I'm out of the ranching business, Newman. Got tired of shooting rustlers."

There was a silence and a showdown, and then laughter, and Newman thought men of common purpose could overcome their pasts after all.

Later still, as the men ate pumpkin pie, a Chinese servant came around with coffee.

"None for me, thanks," said Mike, "I'm full. Well, shall we get down to business?"

"Sounds good to me," Curly Bill said, throwing his napkin down and leaning forward in his chair. "What's this crap about I can't kill Wyatt Earp? I want to kill Wyatt Earp, and I don't see how it's any business of yours."

Mike turned to the Chinese servant and said, courteously, "Maybe I will have just another slice of pie. It's awfully good. And some more coffee, please." Then he turned to Curly Bill. "I'm sorry," he said. "You were saying . . ."

"I was saying I want to kill Wyatt Earp, an' I don't see what business it is of yours!"

Mike looked over to Tom McLaury and asked, "Could you pass the sugar, please?"

Tom passed it and said, "Here you go."

"Thank you," Mike replied.

Then Newman leaned forward and asked solicitously, "Would you like some milk in that, Mike?"

"Yes, please, thank you," said Mike.

"Okay, how 'bout you have your coffee and pie and I'll kill Earp, and we'll just go on to the next item of business," said Curly Bill, about to shit or bust.

"In answer to your question, Curly Bill . . ." said Mike evenly. "Do you mind if I just call you Curly?"

"Mister," said Curly Bill, getting deadly, "you're startin' to rub me the wrong way."

"In answer to your question," said Mike, unfazed, "about what business it is of mine as to who you kill . . . I am here proposing that we become partners. If we are partners in business, then what you do affects me."

Curly Bill had flecks of spittle gathering on his lip. "Well, my business is stealing cattle and robbing stagecoaches." His eyes grew wide and crazy. "And that S.O.B. Earp rides shotgun on those stagecoaches. And as long as he's riding shotgun, my people are ascared to hold it up. So I want to kill him, and I don't see what the big deal about that is."

He turned and looked at his compañeros, holding his arms out wide for all of them to see the justice and logic in what he had just said.

It was precisely this that Newman Clanton feared. He leaned forward to nip this in the bud. ''The big deal is,'' he said, ''you kill Wyatt Earp and you've got James and Morgan and Virgil Earp to deal with . . . *and* Doc Holliday, and you've got yourself a nice little war.'' War obviously was the last thing that Newman Clanton wanted. There was no money in it.

''Old Man Clanton is right,'' Mike said, helping himself to another forkful of pie. ''Now we have business, Bill, big business, important business—too important to be disturbed by starting a range war with men who are so dangerous that one of them with a shotgun keeps a whole gang at bay.''

Curly Bill took that as a slight, and he didn't care who knew it. ''Mister,'' he said, ''I ain't seen a dime from your business yet. I know what robbin' stagecoaches brings in. All I heard from you is talk.''

Mike leaned back and let his hand slip unobtrusively to his gun. If it came to that, he'd kill Curly Bill first and then the one called Ringo. But perhaps logic would prevail. ''How much money can you get in a stagecoach robbery, Bill?''

''If it's got a mine payroll on it,'' Curly Bill said expansively, ''shoot . . . ten, fifteen . . . could be as much as twenty thousand dollars,'' as if there was no way to top that.

He had taken the bait, and Mike Gray was about to set the hook and reel him in.

''Well, the business I'm proposing, gentlemen,'' he said, ''is worth four, six . . . maybe as much as ten *million* dollars . . . maybe more.'' He finally ate the forkful of pie.

The cowboys looked from one to the other as Newman Clanton smiled and said, ''Great things, boys . . . great things.''

Mike Gray turned in a conciliatory way to Curly Bill. ''We'll find a way to get Mister Earp off your stage, Bill, without disturbing our plans,'' and then he permitted himself a smile. ''Maybe we can offer the proper hint and Mister Earp will learn to take it.''

''A bullet through the brain's a hint in any man's language, far as I'm concerned,'' said Curly Bill, who was not inclined in the least to smile.

''Think big . . . Curly,'' said Mike. ''The Earps are small change.''

CHAPTER TWELVE

The Earps had come to Tombstone, and the brothers and wives together now gathered to celebrate the anniversary of the nation's birth as one big happy family. Virgil's house was on one side of the street and Wyatt's on the other, and catty-corner to that was James's, just a little way down from Morgan's. The houses were all pleasant, with front porches and backyards, each of them protected by a picket fence. The location was a good one, being only two blocks from the central business district and a block from a good livery stable, called the O.K. Corral.

"Uhhh . . . I'm lookin' for Mrs. Earp," said the redheaded twelve-year-old boy carrying the two buckets of beer, as he stood on Virgil's front porch. The boy stared up at the imposing woman not knowing that once she had been a painted lady, for without the paint and nothing but respectability for makeup, she was very plain indeed.

"I *am* Mrs. Earp, boy," said Mattie. "There's four Mrs. Earps in this house today. . . . Which one do you want?"

The twelve-year-old was understandably intimidated. "Uh . . . well . . . the one what's gonna pay for the beer, I guess."

Mattie turned and yelled into the house for her sister-in-law. "Allie, it's for you!" she called.

Allie Earp was Virgil's wife. She was a large, friendly-looking woman who reminded one of a favorite aunt. She suffered no pretense and typically gave as good as she got.

She was followed into the parlor by Bessie Earp, James's wife, who since coming to Tombstone had given up prostitution to take on the new air befitting a middle-class matron. And finally, trailing behind the two older and more imposing women, was Lou, Morgan's pretty young wife, who was terrified, often to the point of tears, of her formidable sisters-in-law.

"What do you mean it's for me?" Allie said. "It's beer for the boys."

"He asked for you," said Mattie, her hands on her hips.

"Like you're too respectable to hold a bucket of beer?" asked Allie as she crossed to the boy and took the buckets.

"No," said Bessie, "just too cheap to pay for one."

Lou as usual said nothing, just plastered herself up against the wall to get out of the way of her sisters-in-law and the beer coming through.

There were two tables set up in the backyard. One had a tablecloth on which the Earp women had spread fried chicken, sweet potato pie, fresh-baked corn bread, and Mexican chili. The other table had food for thought. Ledgers were spread out on it, around which were gathered the four men, all in their shirtsleeves. James, Virgil, and Morgan were intent upon Wyatt, who held the ledgers. The men spoke quietly of money. Lou crossed over to her handsome young husband, Morgan.

He and Wyatt were by far the best-looking of the Earp brothers, with Morgan's features being at the same time more delicate and somehow more dashing than those of his older brother, who from but a short distance could still have passed for his twin. Lou sweetly put her arms around Morgan's shoulders from behind and pushed in close up to him. "Morg honey . . ." she whispered, "supper's ready. Come on, sweetie," and kissed the back of his neck.

"I'm gonna spit up," said Bessie.

Morgan turned to his bride and said somewhat apologetically, "Be right there, Lou darlin' . . . we got business."

"Virg . . ." Allie said with no trace of the blushing bride in her commanding presence.

"In a second, Allie." This from Virg, who waved her off and traced down the column of expenses over his brother's shoulder with his index finger.

"To hell with them," said Bessie. "I say we eat."

"That's my girl," said James, reaching for a drink.

For her part, Bessie reached for a piece of chicken and Allie slapped at her hand, but it was Mattie's voice that was the sharpest, that could chop through conversation like an axe.

"Wyatt," she said, "the food's on the table." Wyatt looked up. He did not like being spoken to in this fashion before his brothers. The tone of the voice highlighted the strain in his relationship with Mattie.

"Good, Mattie," he said. "That way we'll know where to find it when we're finished." And there was in his tone the unmistakable message that the conversation regarding food and tables was now over. He turned to his brothers, having dealt with this minor, albeit ongoing irritation, to discuss with them the family's finances, a good deal of which were tied up in the mining of precious and semiprecious metals. Anyone who had spent more than a day in Tombstone, it was said, had filed a claim on some piece of land, and the Earps were no exceptions. It was like a kind of lottery that they had from the beginning decided to play.

"All right," said Wyatt to the men, "in mining claims we have the Mountain Maid Mine, the Earp Mine, the Grasshopper, the Dodge, the Mattie Blaylock . . ."

"Morg honey," Lou said in a girlishly seductive way, "how come you never named a mine after me?"

"They will," Bessie said. "They'll call the next one the idiot."

"Bessie, damn it," said Morgan, who knew that now his wife's look of affection would turn to a pout.

"Shut up, Bessie," said James, passing her his bottle. "Have a drink."

"Go ahead, Wyatt," Virgil said.

"The Mattie Blaylock," Wyatt continued, "the Comstock, Rocky Ridge, and the Long Branch. Of those we're just about fifty-fifty with mines that are producing as we are with mines that are . . .''

"Worthless," said Allie with a shake of her head.

"That are not yet producing," Wyatt corrected her.

James looked up, and after he swallowed said, "In other words, we ain't seen a dime's profit out of the mines."

"Not in other words, James . . . those are the words," said Bessie, holding her hand out for the bottle's return.

Wyatt turned a page in the ledger. "In liquidity," he said, "we have Virgil's pay as deputy federal marshal for Southern Arizona, my pay from Wells Fargo, James's pay as a bartender . . ."

Mattie broke in with a self-righteous look at her in-law. "Which he drinks up before any—"

"Oh, why don't you just . . ." said Bessie, not letting her complete the insult.

"Quiet, the both of you," Allie said in a tone befitting her position as hostess of this soiree. "They're talkin' about money now," she said reverently.

Wyatt went on. "And Morg's down working the claims, so . . . that's that. In addition, we own one whole Faro game and a quarter interest in a Faro bank at the Long Branch, and we have five thousand dollars to invest."

"Why can't we just split it up," Bessie said, "and each do what we want."

Wyatt ignored her. "What we have to decide," he said, "is how we invest it."

But Bessie was not a woman to be put off or intimidated. She had seen too many men with their pants off to be impressed by Wyatt with his on. "Is that why you got no sense of humor, Wyatt?" she said. " 'Cause you're deef? I said why don't we just split it up. We got things we need, James and me."

"And the truth is," Lou said, linking her arm through Morgan's and resting her head on his shoulder, "I got a feeling we might need to add on to our house in a while."

"Lou . . ." Morgan said excitedly. "You mean . . ."

"Well, not yet," said Lou, blushing, "but we're tryin' all the time, aren't we, honey?"

"I *am* gonna spit up," Bessie said, and belched demurely.

"Well, what about it, James . . . why don't you just ask for our cut?"

"Bessie . . ." he said, shooting her a look. "It's not that simple. It's . . ."

"Then I'll ask for it," said Bessie, pulling herself up. "Or to hell with that, we ought to just take it."

Virgil turned to her. "We didn't all come out here to split up stakes, Bessie."

Morgan turned and stood next to his brother. "We came out here to stick together."

Bessie now found herself on the outs suddenly with all of the men, having committed the ultimate transgression in this circle. Hoping to find at least one ally among the women, she pushed on as if in their names. "Why!? Huh?!" she said. "That's what I want to know! Why?! Why's it always got to be the brothers this and the brothers that." Then she turned to James, and while she did not adopt a seductive tone, it was nonetheless plaintive. "James, why can't it just be you and me?"

James did not answer, so she gestured to the other Earp women.

"They might not be sayin' it, but the others think the same as me . . . we're your wives. Don't we count more than the damned brothers!?"

"No, Bessie," came Wyatt's quiet voice. "You don't."

There it was, plain and simple. Silence fell. Wyatt turned to Bessie with dead-cold eyes.

"Our father once told us," he said, "that if we stuck together we'd always have one advantage over everybody else we'd ever meet. Each of us would always have at least three other people he could trust with his life. Up till we all came here together a year ago we all, each of us, went his own way . . . and what'd we have to show for it? Nothin', that's what, not a home, not a scrap of land, not a bucket nor a window to throw it out of. Now we're together . . . like Pa said. We got a chance here. We can make our fortunes here. But not if we piss it away . . . only if we stick together."

He said this to the brothers.

"We're still your wives," Bessie said to her husband, but it was Wyatt who answered.

"Wives come and go, Bessie," he said. "That's the plain truth of it. They run off . . . or they die."

He looked down as a wave of sadness came over him. Mattie averted her eyes, shook her head, and then went back into the house crying.

Allie watched as Mattie left. "You're a cold man, Wyatt," she said. "God forgive you . . . you are cold." She went into the house after Mattie. Wyatt took a breath, then looked back up at his brothers.

"We have five thousand dollars to invest," he said, though his voice was now hoarse. There was a silence, and then Virgil spoke.

"Well . . . I think we ought to buy land. Lot prices are goin' up to almost two thousand dollars apiece."

From inside the house he heard Allie say, "They're out back, Doc. You and Kate go on out there."

"I don't know about real estate," Wyatt said. "To me that land speculation is just plain risky. I think we ought to stick with something more conservative, like maybe buy another Faro bank. Gambling's always steady income."

Just then Doc's voice rang out. "Wyatt, you cob, it's a holiday . . . quit talking about money." Doc stepped out into the backyard as if making an entrance at one of the antebellum-plantation garden parties of his youth. Big Nosed Kate was next to him and mentioned, "What's Mattie cryin' for . . . her lost youth? Doc honey . . . get me a drink, yeah?"

Morgan turned to Doc, trying to be tactful. "Uh . . . we were just talking about family finances, Doc, so maybe . . ."

But Doc just smiled. "Well, if you want my advice," he said, "you'll open a brothel. It's what my darling Kate here did, and I for one have never regretted it for an instant."

Lou blushed as Morgan, who truly loved Doc's sense of humor, belly laughed. Doc picked up a bottle of whiskey, poured two water glasses full, handed one to Kate, and drained the other.

"*A votre sante,*" said the Doctor, who knew only too well the value of good health.

Later, while the others were eating, Wyatt went into the house to find Mattie. She was sitting by the window, weeping. He crossed to her quietly. Her tears had less of an effect on him now, but he still hated it when she cried.

"I'm sorry if I hurt you, Mattie, with anything I said. It wasn't my intent."

She turned to him and spoke with sudden urgency. "Let's have children, Wyatt. . . ."

"Mattie," Wyatt said, trying to stop this conversation before it got started. But Mattie clutched at him. "You're always talkin' about family, ain't ya?"

"This isn't the—"

"Then let's have children of our own," she pleaded. "If family's so all-fired important, let's have a family . . . our family . . . our children, Wyatt, yours and mine, before I'm too old for it, before I dry up inside. I can feel it, Wyatt, inside of me . . . drying up and dying. I want to have your children." She said it looking straight into his eyes, demanding an answer, not willing to be put off.

"Children aren't part of the bargain, Mattie," Wyatt said in a voice that betrayed no emotion. "They never were."

Mattie wept. After a while, Wyatt left the room.

CHAPTER THIRTEEN

At forty years of age, Johnny Behan was a bandy little Irishman, a dapper gent who fancied himself a lady-killer. He was a bit drunk as he fiddled with the box camera.

"Why don't you just . . . take your hair down, Josie," he said. "Take it down, love."

Josephine Sarah Marcus was a petite girl from a good family. Just nineteen and unbelievably beautiful, she had perfect skin, huge dark eyes, and a surprisingly good education for a girl of that period. Her parents had lovingly paid for her to attend one of the best private schools in San Francisco. Her family had come there by way of New York from Europe and had established themselves as prosperous merchants. Nothing had been too good for their daughter, who, having been raised in the freedom of America, longed for even more of it. So one morning she left for school in her schoolgirl skirt and blouse and never came back. She joined a traveling troupe of players who performed Gilbert and Sullivan operettas in the mining towns and camps of Arizona and one night met a frontier dandy named Johnny Behan, who swept her off her feet and stood before her now, behind the box camera.

Josie wore only a diaphanous dressing gown. She unpinned her lustrous, dark hair and let it fall down below her shoulders.

"Johnny," she said, "I don't know why you want to . . ."

" 'Cause it's fun . . . ain't it?" he said, lifting his eye from off the borrowed camera. "I think it is . . . 'sides, I want a picture of you, darlin'."

"Then why couldn't I just go to Fly's studio and let him take the picture?" Josie asked. "Why'd you have to borrow the camera and . . ."

"Josie honey," Behan said in his honeyed brogue, "we're gonna be married, we're gonna be man and wife. . . . I want the kind of picture from you that . . ." And he smiled the kind of smile he smiled when he wanted to go to bed.

"That what?" she said.

"That only a husband ever sees of his wife," said Johnny, taking the moral high road.

She arranged her hair over her shoulders and looked up at him. But something was obviously troubling her. "Johnny . . . I'm scared . . ."

"Josie honey . . . it's just a picture," he said.

"No," she said, looking at him as if he was a fool. "I'm not scared of that . . . I'm scared of tonight."

"Tonight?" said Behan, giving off a laugh. "Tonight's just gonna be a speech, that's all . . . just a political speech," he said, and slipped the photographic plate into position.

"But this whole Chinese thing," Josie went on. "There could be trouble, couldn't there?"

"Why no . . . no, of course not," Johnny said, crossing to her. He needed to get her mind off politics and back onto sex. But with a Jewish girl, he thought, there were no shortcuts. It had to unfold with their Talmudic logic.

"It's a political speech, darlin'," he said, "at the behest of some of the most influential men not just in the city but in the whole territory. These are the right fellas to get in with, darlin' . . . the kind that can assure a man's political future. I'm doin' it for us, darlin' Josie girl . . . so we can be married."

"It still scares me," Josie said. Her father had told her stories of European political rallies, and they were not pleasant; they were almost never good for the Jews.

"Oh, I know what you're thinkin'. . . . I start talkin' about a white Christian America and where does that leave you?"

"Where does that leave me, Johnny?" she said, her voice going suddenly flat.

"It leaves you right by my side," he said, putting his arm around her. "Mrs. Johnny Behan. Trust me, darlin', I'm doin' this for us. I love you, darlin' . . . only you . . . always you."

He kissed her and then went back to the camera. Even in the viewfinder, she was breathtaking.

"Why don't you open up that wee gown a little, darlin'," he said, hoping for some cleavage. "No one will ever see this picture but me. It's for me, darlin' . . . just for me."

She looked him square in the eye. Men were so simple, she thought. Here she was nineteen and he was forty, and she could control him, make him quiver with the looseness or tightness of her robe. "Is this what you want?" she said, her voice dropping low as she let the dressing gown fall and the tray of gunpowder exploded with a blinding light.

The sunset was beautiful and the cowboys were all drunk except for Mike Gray and Old Man Clanton. The two were off talking by themselves.

"I'm very pleased with the business we've done today, Mike," said Newman. "There's a real foundation for greatness here."

"Good . . ." said Mike in a measured tone. "I'm glad you feel that way, Newman. I think it would be a good idea, though, if my boy Dixie were to begin riding with you."

Old Man Clanton smiled. "You don't trust me," he said.

"Of course not, Newman," said Mike. And Old Man Clanton laughed.

"Finally," the outlaw patriarch bellowed, "a kindred spirit. I could weep with joy. Fine, Mike, Dixie Lee will be welcome with me. He can ride with me and report to you, and I'll treat him as if he were my own son."

Mike's hand reached out and took hold of the old man's still-muscular arm. "No. You won't," he said in a voice that promised murder.

"Pardon?" said Newman, his eyes narrowing.

"I saw how you treat your own son. You ever hit Dixie Lee with a log, and business or no . . . nothing you can do will prevent me from killing you. Understood?" There was no question that Mike Gray meant every word of it. But at the threat a certain look descended over Old Man Clanton. It was the same look that many men had seen just before their own untimely deaths at the elder Clanton's hand. He was, despite his age, a very dangerous character himself.

"I understand," he said.

"Good," said Mike, thinking that was the end of it.

But it was not. "I won't take a stick to your gimpy kid. But business or no . . . don't ever threaten me again."

Now neither of them had any doubts. Now the fireworks of this particular Fourth of July could begin.

Later that evening, with less than an hour to go before the promised fireworks display, Johnny Behan walked arm in arm with Josie down Fremont Street, past Fly's Photo Gallery, where he had just dropped off the camera. They continued down the street past the office of the *Tombstone Epitaph*. The newspaper's name was on the window, and under that were the words "John P. Clum, Editor."

John P. Clum, editor of the *Epitaph*, was a man of middle height and little hair that made him look older than his early thirties. There was as well about him a kind of solemnity, not as much as an undertaker but just enough to lend him the air of an Episcopal clergyman. He stood in the doorway of his newspaper office enjoying the evening air as Johnny passed with Josie on his arm.

"Evening, Johnny," he said.

"Evenin', Mister Clum," said Johnny. "Happy Fourth of July. You're a busy bee workin' on a holiday."

"Tomorrow's no holiday," Clum said. "Paper has to come out, someone has to prepare it."

Josie cleared her throat, and Behan said, "I'm forgetting my manners. John Clum, editor of the Republican rag the *Epitaph* . . . my fiancée, Miss Josephine Sarah Marcus of San Francisco."

"Pleasure, ma'am," said the editor.

"Thank you, Mister Clum," Josie said.

Clum took out his pipe and loaded it deliberately, looking Josie up and down. "I understand your fiancé is making a speech tonight."

"Yes," she said. "That is my understanding as well."

Clum turned to Behan. "I think from what I've heard you're going to say, it's a mistake, Johnny . . . a big mistake. The Chinese won't take it lying down."

Johnny Behan stuck his chin out like a little bantam cock. He really was a proud little rooster. "Oh, they'll take it lyin' down," he said. "Lyin' down, standin' up, any way I give it to 'em."

Clum looked him up and down, trying to figure the little Irishman out. "What's the angle?" he said. "Smart fella like you always has an angle."

"No angle," said Behan, puffing out his chest indignantly. "This is a white Christian town. I intend to see it stays that way. I think a lot of voters in this town see it the same way."

Clum looked over at Josie. "I see . . ." he said. "Marcus is a Jewish name, is it not, ma'am?"

"It is, and I am, if that was your next question," said Josie. There was no real defiance in the way that she said it, but there was no backing away, either.

"We have quite a few Hebrews in this town, Miss Marcus," said Clum as if he were extolling the virtues of the place in order to sell her a piece of real estate. "Dave Cohen, Jacob Meyers, the Solomons . . . fine, respected folks. That's one of the nice things about Tombstone. We've been remarkably free of racial and religious prejudice here." Then his tone changed. "It'd be a great pity," he went on, "if that were to change because some cheap politician thought racial hatred was a horse he could ride into public office."

"You go to hell," Behan said, whirling on him and planting his feet ready to throw a punch, as if the only thing that would stand between him and a fight would be Josie's imploring hand on his arm to keep him and his violent nature intact. But Josie put no such hand upon him. She simply looked at the two of them with a kind of detached interest that made Clum think there had been fights in front of this young woman before, aplenty. Seeing that Josie was not going to restrain him, Johnny decided to restrain himself. It put him in a foul mood, like a stage comedian who had delivered a punch line only to have it go flat. "Come on, Josie," he said, took her hand, and walked off.

"Pleasure meeting you, ma'am," Clum called after them.

As they were walking away, Behan turned to Josie and spoke in a furious whisper. "Can you believe the nerve of that son of a bitch tryin' to hang that Jew crap on me!?"

Josie said nothing, and Johnny mistakenly took her silence for acquiescence.

Had he looked at her more closely, or had the light perhaps been better, he would have seen, however, the hardness in her eyes. It was a look Mike Gray would have respected and of which he would have been wary.

For his part, John Clum reentered his office and turned to his fifteen-year-old apprentice.

"Wayne . . . I'll finish up with that," he said, indicating the typesetting at which the boy had been busying himself. "You go over to Hoptown. Find China Mary and tell her Mister Clum said it might be a good idea to keep her people indoors tonight. There might be trouble."

Wayne dashed down the block toward Hoptown. Once there, he saw a large middle-aged Chinese woman in the center of the street. She was handsome and heavyset and wore a brocade robe. Her name was China Mary, and she was the undisputed ruler of Hoptown and all its inhabitants, by means of her connections to the most powerful tongs in Shanghai. If a hotel wanted a cook, if a lunchroom wanted a dishwasher, if a saloon girl wanted opium, or a businessman wanted his shirts pressed, or if the railroad needed another hundred coolies . . . they all found their way to China Mary. Labor, laundry, or vice, it made no difference. If you had money, China Mary would supply your needs from the stock of human misery that swarmed the streets and alleyways of Shanghai.

But she was not merely a purveyor of hop and cheap labor. She was, for the Chinese who found themselves adrift in this strange land, not only their refuge and protector but the key to their immortality as well. For it was China Mary who guaranteed that at their deaths their bones would be shipped back to China to be buried alongside their ancestors and assure their life everlasting in the hereafter. Implicit in this arrangement was their certain understanding that, one way or the other, China Mary would outlive them all. She was the dowager empress upon the dragon's throne of Tombstone.

At this moment she had a young Chinese man by the pigtail and was screaming at him in Chinese and smacking him across the face. Wayne approached her timidly and said what Mr. Clum had told him to tell her.

She heard it and dismissed him with a look. There was no telling what she thought. As far as that went, there was no telling what any of the Chinese ever thought; at least that's the way it seemed to Wayne. But with China Mary, even if he could have, he didn't want to know.

Outside of town there was a flat part of land, desert really, where the Fourth of July fireworks were to be set off. People were pulled up in wagons. There were picnic blankets set out, and children running back and forth. Off to the side there was a bandstand bedecked with red, white, and blue bunting and a band playing patriotic tunes.

The Earps were there, the Earp women sitting on chairs around a little picnic table. Bessie and Allie and Mattie passed a bottle back and forth filling shot glasses. The Earp men, Morg, Virgil, and James, stood nearby. Morg and James passed their own small bottle back and forth between them as Johnny Behan, who had just come by with Josie, spoke in a neighborly way.

"Morgan and James Earp," he said grandly, "my fiancée . . . Josephine Sarah . . ." He was about to say "Marcus," but after the Jew crap with Clum he thought better of it. "Well," he said, "just plain Josie I guess is good enough, since pretty soon her last name will be Behan."

Virgil tipped his hat and said, "How do you do, ma'am," while Morgan smiled at the girl and looked at Behan, saying, "Care for a snort, Johnny?"

"Maybe just a taste," said the Irishman. Morg passed him the bottle, and he drank a deep swallow of the rye whiskey.

"Where's Wyatt?" Behan asked, bringing the bottle down from his lips. "Don't tell me he didn't come. He'll miss my speech."

As the band played on, in another part of the celebration area Wyatt walked and talked with Charlie Shibell, who wore a gold star on his coat. Shibell was in his early fifties, a pencil pusher and political hack more than a copper.

"I don't know, Charlie," said Wyatt, scratching his head. "I had a bellyful of workin' the law back in Kansas."

Shibell uncorked a flask but knew better than to offer it to Wyatt, whom he had never seen drink anything stronger than beer, so he imbibed a snort himself, shook with the kick of it, and said, "Look, Wyatt, this Pima County election against Bob Paul is gonna be a tough one. It'd be a real feather in my cap with the voters if you was my deputy."

But Wyatt shook his head. "That's not what I came out here for," he said. "There's no money in it."

Shibell gave a derisive laugh and patted Wyatt on the back like a boy about to be initiated into a secret society. "Says you. This is a county office. You get paid a sheriff's fee for processing every bit of paper there is. You could clear fifteen, maybe as much as twenty, thousand a year. Why, with the money you make you could buy half interest in a saloon. I know that's what you want to do, Wyatt, and any one of 'em would take you in as a silent partner just for the protection if you was a county deputy." To Charlie Shibell Wyatt Earp looked awfully interested, even there in the darkness.

Up on the bandstand Mayor Alder Randall stepped to the front, opened his arms out wide like Moses at the Red Sea, and said, "And now, my fellow citizens, will you join me in the singing of our National Anthem."

The band struck it up, and the more puckish children in the crowd changed the lyrics to suit their proximity to Mexico: "Jose can you see . . ." they sang and laughed.

Down along the periphery of the crowd, Mike Gray walked with Johnny Behan in the shadows.

"But I don't get it, Mike," Johnny complained. "You said I was supposed to get the deputy sheriff's job."

Mike put a hand on Behan's shoulder in much the same way as Charlie Shibell had laid his hand on Wyatt's. "Things changed, Johnny," he said. "Business is business, and that's what this is. I owed someone a favor, and the payoff is Wyatt Earp getting deputy sheriff of Pima County. But I'm going to take care of you. Because that's business too. Now, you just go up there and make the kind of speech I know you can make."

"All right, Mike," Behan said, none too sure of the shaky ground on which he now stood. "I'm taking you at your word."

"You won't regret it," Mike told him, flashing a smile. Behan walked off toward the bandstand, and Mike stepped back into the darker recesses of the shadows. It was then that a hand came down onto his shoulder. It was the hand of Curly Bill.

"Did I hear you right?" Curly Bill asked.

"Take your hand down, Bill," Mike said, softly.

Curly Bill's eyes bugged. "You just fixed it so Earp's deputy sheriff?"

"Of Pima County," Mike broke in. "Which means he will no longer be riding shotgun for Wells Fargo."

"No," said Curly Bill, trying to keep from hopping up and down like a tenderfooted chicken on a skillet. "He'll just be leading the posse after I rob the damned stage! I thought you was supposed to be smart. You're dumber than a stump!"

Mike had dealt with people of inferior intelligence most of his adult life. But practice did not make it any easier. It would be so nice, he thought, if he could just once be partnered with an intelligent crook. "Bill . . . Bill . . . Bill," he said in a tired voice. "Wyatt is now deputy sheriff of Pima County. Rob the damned stage after it passes the county line and it is out of his jurisdiction. That way he won't lead the posse and he won't be on the stage with his shotgun either."

"Oh . . ." said Curly Bill.

It could be so simple, but it never ended up that way with these rustler types. Ah well, Mike thought, and pulled out his watch and looked at it. "I think you have an appointment in town, if I'm not mistaken," he said.

Curly Bill was still marveling at the wonder of it all. "Right . . ." he said, "right." A few steps away was a wagon where his horse was tied and Johnny Ringo, the three Clanton boys, and assorted other cowboys waited. "Let's go," said Curly Bill. And they mounted up and rode off at a gallop. Mike Gray walked closer toward the bandstand. His face was flushed with patriotic fervor as the National Anthem reached its crescendo and Mike, who loved the tune, joined in with all the others singing. "O'er the land of the free, and the home of the brave."

On the road to Tombstone, Curly Bill and the others reached into their saddlebags as they rode in the moonlight. They pulled out masks made of flour sacks with cut-out eyes, while on the bandstand back at the celebration, Johnny Behan stood shouting out his speech.

"Every evening at sunset," Johnny shouted to the crowd, "the sweet sickly smell of opium rises up from out of Hoptown and permeates every corner of our fair city from the dens of iniquity of this yellow menace, which threatens the core and fiber of our beings. Well, I say to you on this Fourth of July, America should be for Americans and the Chinks should go back to China!"

A cheer rose up from the crowd, but Wyatt Earp's mind was not on Johnny's speech as he walked back toward his brothers. His mind was on his new job and the money it could pay.

"And I say to you," Behan shouted, pointing a stubby index finger at the crowd when he said "you," "that a method must be found, and found soon, to uproot this yellow peril," he mimed, pulling a weed up by its root, "which now occupies not through lawful means but through squatters' privilege almost one-third of our township and threatens to spill over into the rest!" Again a cheer went up, this time longer than the first and more sustained. Johnny bowed a little bow and bathed awhile in their adoration. And when he'd had all that they would give, he said, "Well, I want to thank you for your kind attention, and now without further ado . . . on with the fireworks!" This like a ringmaster introducing the pièce de résistance.

On the far side of the crowd, Wyatt approached his brothers and saw Josie in the shadows there with them.

"How'd it go, Wyatt?" Virgil asked.

"Fifteen thousand a year to be deputy sheriff of Pima County," Wyatt said, as if he couldn't believe it himself.

"Who do we have to kill?" asked James.

The brothers laughed. Even Wyatt smiled. "They haven't told me that part yet."

"Oh," said Morgan. "This here is Johnny Behan's girl."

Wyatt turned around and took in the eyes, long dark hair, and full lips. Wyatt looked again at Josie's eyes staring up and into his, unblinking. "I prefer not to think of myself as anybody's girl," she said. "My name's Josie. Josie Marcus."

Just then a skyrocket lit up the sky and illuminated her face for an instant. There was no tickle in Wyatt's throat, nor a sweet, clean smell of soap. He felt only desire. He wanted her as he'd never wanted any woman before.

"Wyatt Earp," he said, and their hands touched in the fading rocket's light.

As fireworks went off in the sky outside of Tombstone, the hooded men on horseback rode boldly into Hoptown and lassoed the corners of a Chinese-owned building. A dozen horses tugged at the ropes and pulled the building apart as the occupants came running out with children clinging to them and screamed as the cowboys' guns fired off into the air.

One elderly Chinese had his pigtail grabbed by a masked cowboy who dragged him along behind his horse. A Chinese woman ran up screaming, trying to rescue him, and was kicked to the ground.

"Go back to China, ya yella bastards!" Curly Bill yelled out through his mask, and as the fireworks continued to go off, the hooded men whooped and hollered, fired their pistols in the air, and rode off, running down as many Chinese as they could. The old man was lying in the street, with his daughter crying over his unconscious body. China Mary came out in the street with a rifle and fired after the retreating assailants as another rocket lit the sky.

Back on the edge of town, Wyatt looked at Josie as she watched the fireworks. Virgil stood next to them and, looking at the skyrockets, said out loud in awe and wonder, "I'd say that's about the prettiest thing I ever seen."

Wyatt looked at Josie, and she turned and looked up at him as more pyrotechnics went off. And from the shadows, Mattie saw in a glance the look that passed between the Jewess and her husband. Children oohed and aahed as Chinese gunpowder lit the darkened skies. It was then that Johnny Behan, congratulated and slapped upon the back as he stood there on the bandstand, saw Wyatt and Josie too, illuminated in the rocket's red glare, the bombs bursting in air, which lit occasionally the galloping retreat of hooded gunmen.

CHAPTER FOURTEEN

"You the sheriffs! Who else I go to? This America . . . Land of home . . . Land of free! Law and order."

A group of five Chinese children in pigtails crowded around the door eavesdropping on what was going on inside Sheriff Shibell's office on this day after the masked gunmen's attack on Hoptown.

"So you tell me law and order, huh!" boomed China Mary. Her breath reeked of garlic and her teeth were stained by litchi. She pointed a stubby finger first at Shibell and then at Wyatt, who wore now the star of a deputy sheriff above his heart.

"Calm down, Mary," Shibell said. "Just—"

"I plenty calm!" Mary bellowed, the veins in her neck bulging out, making her look more than ever like an exasperated Buddha. "I don't care about they pull down building." She ticked off one finger. "I don't care about they attack old man and woman." She ticked off the second. "But now they got company . . . Town Lot Company." She held up three fingers like a curse. "Man come from Town Lot Company. He say all Chinese got no right to land." The stubby fingers had clenched now into a fist. "He say all Chinese got to rebuy all deeds to get good title or they throw us off lots. They already throw three Chinese man off their lots! That against the law," she said to Shibell. And then, as if she knew that he was not the proper address for the missive she was about to send, she turned to Wyatt with dark eyes as cold as his were blue.

"You the law," she said low, in a growl that was almost seductive, and then in a whisper, a conspiracy between them both, she looked at Wyatt and said, "You go kill 'em!"

In many ways, though hardened by cattle towns and frontier life, Wyatt was still naive when it came to Chinese. He did not take them seriously.

"Now, Mary," he said, wiping a forelock out of his eyes as if talking to a chubby child instead of an opium dealer. "Nobody's killin' nobody here, so—"

"I should say not," said Shibell. He wagged a finger at her. "Now look, Mary . . . you know I got nothin' against you Celestials. I eat in your husband's restaurant and I send my shirts to your laundry—"

"We not talking about laundry," Mary said in a tone that tightened Sheriff Shibell's scrotum. He held up one hand, and the other involuntarily moved above his buttons.

"Now, maybe you got a beef . . ." Then Shibell noticed Wyatt looking at him and decided he could not lose face in front of his deputy. "You read-ie English on my window, it says 'Sheriff of Pima County,' " Shibell said, knowing he could always beat the Chinks down with words in English. "This is not a county problem. This is a *local* law-enforcement problem . . . if it's any kind of enforcement problem at all. I mean, from what you say this whole thing sounds like just some sort of real estate contract dispute to me," he said, and chuckled, glancing out of the corner of his eye at Wyatt to see just how much face he had saved.

But the saving of face was not a foreign notion to China Mary.

"Well," she said, "it sound to me like you more yellow than Chinaman. . . . I take care of problem China Mary way."

Mary stormed out of Shibell's office, scattering a group of Chinese children before her. They re-formed their attentive cluster in her wake and fell in behind her like ducklings.

* * *

Shortly thereafter, Mike Gray walked into the familiar warmth and safety of his house and, as was his habit, put his briefcase down on the credenza.

"Hello, Mista Gray."

He turned and saw China Mary sitting in his favorite chair with a long-barreled Navy Colt cocked and pointed at his chest.

"You're one crazy Chink, Mary," Mike said, smiling with everything but his eyes.

"Crazy Chink has gun pointed at your heart," China Mary said, knowing she did not need to smile. "Sit down."

Mike sat.

"We got business, you and me," she said, one eye trained along the sights at the place where she assumed his heart must beat.

"All right," Mike said evenly. He had not shown fear in front of Comanche chieftains even when their squaws were heating sharpened sticks and planning their points of entry. He would be damned if he blinked for this fat China-woman.

He had commanded troops of Texas Rangers when no other whites had dared be in the territories. Who did she think she was?

"Who you think I am," China Mary said in a voice that betrayed no fear. "Chinese laundry girl?" She leaned forward toward him, always keeping the gun pointed exactly at his heart. "I run Hoptown, every opium den, every restaurant, every laundry, every whorehouse. Every Chinese in Hoptown work for me! I *own* them!" she said, and her eyes bugged out like a bullfrog's. "I am tied to the Six Companies in San Francisco. And from them to the most powerful Tong in Shanghai. That," she said, "is who I am." She leaned back a bit in Mike's favorite chair. "I know Johnny Behan is just the tail and you the dog who wags him. You the Town Lot Company. Plenty smart . . ." she said, smiling for the first time. And as quickly as the smile came, so too it went. "Now you get smarter and leave Chinese out of it."

Mike Gray had had enough. He knew nothing of the Six Companies and less of the tongs of Shanghai.

"Or what?" he said disdainfully. "You think you can bluff

me? You think you can scare me?'' he said, rising. ''Or what?
Huh?''

Later in the night he would wake, sweating cold, bolting
upright, reaching for his gun as the hiss of her voice echoed
in his brain. And he would remember the look upon her, cold
as a statue, still as a snake, which told him she spoke not to
threaten, but intended to do exactly what she said.

''Or I kill your gimpy kid Dixie Lee,'' China Mary said.
''I slice off his ears and boil him alive like a nice duck dinner
. . . real crispy.'' And she smacked her lips as Mike felt sick
in the stomach. ''Yeah,'' she said. ''I know your weak spot
. . . Gimpy kid.''

Mike searched her eyes for weakness and found none there.

''Maybe you think China Mary hire Chinese killer . . . see
him coming a mile away. No. China Mary plenty smart too.
Got big *mucho dinero*. I hire plenty white man . . . you think
they no do it? I think they do it for plenty money. It good
business.''

Then she leaned forward, and her eyes seemed to burn and
grow colder still at the same time. ''Chinese been around
long time, got long memories . . . always get even.''

Despite himself, Mike Gray gulped . . . and then he
blinked.

That night in the saloon section of the Grand Hotel, Mike
Gray sat at a back table listening to Johnny Behan whine.

''But I don't get it, Mike,'' Johnny said.

''You don't need to get it, Johnny. It's off . . . that's all,''
Mike said, downing two fingers of rye whiskey both to hide
and shake the shudder that came over him. ''The anti-Chinese
thing served its purpose and now it's off.''

''But . . . but what about me?'' Johnny said. ''Where do
I come in?''

''I got plans for you, Johnny,'' said the Texan. ''Big plans.
Be patient . . . I'll take care of you.''

Then he put a thousand dollars under his hat on the table
in front of him and pushed it toward Johnny. Johnny tilted
up the hat, looked around, made sure no one was looking,
and then moved the hat toward him till the money dropped
off the table and into his lap.

''Sure, Mike,'' he said. ''Anything you say.''

"I say," said Mike, standing and extending his hand, "gimme my hat."

Behan gave it to him and Mike Gray said, "See you, kid," and was out the door before Johnny could pocket the money.

By the time Johnny got back to his place, Josie was there packing. And then he saw it. Saw it in her eyes and felt it in the edge in her voice.

"I want to talk to you, Johnny," she said, and he knew she was leaving him.

"Josie . . ." Johnny said, trying as fast as he could to think of a way to keep her from walking out the door. He knew with this one that once she was gone, she would not be back.

So like a hoofer in the footlights, Johnny Behan started dancing. "No . . ." he said. "First let me say something. I've been doing some thinking of my own. I know that I could ride this Chinese thing right into public office." He watched her eyes. "But I also know that it causes you distress, my dear. It offends you, and I can understand why." His voice grew softer. "I'm not an insensitive man, and I'd rather cut off my own right arm than risk losin' your love." He drew himself up and seemed to puff up in front of her with moral indignation.

"So, effective tonight, I told the powers that be that I'd have nothin' further to do with it."

"You did?" Josie said with detached interest.

"Oh, they put up a fuss," Johnny said with a wave of his hand, "but in the end I not only convinced 'em to let me out of it, I convinced 'em to drop the whole thing altogether." He stood there, looking, he hoped, like a saint. The pose was an attempt at heroic mixed with pride and humility.

But Josie looked him in the eye and said flatly, "What's the angle, Johnny? Smart fella like you always has an angle. . . . Isn't that what Mister Clum said?"

"Love, darlin' girl," said Behan, as if butter wouldn't melt in his mouth. "Love is the only angle here," he said, his brogue lilting as he pulled her to him.

Josie put her head on his shoulder, wishing she could believe him. But wishing, she knew, and believing were two different things.

At that moment, Wyatt was walking by and could not help

but look through the window at Josie being pulled toward Johnny. Her head was on Johnny's shoulder, and then her eyes flicked up to see Wyatt staring in at her from the street.

He stood there watching her look back at him, unable to take his eyes off of her. Johnny's arms went around her as he bent and kissed her neck, but Josie's eyes did not close in a swoon of passion . . . they stayed locked into Wyatt's gaze as Johnny backed her away from the window toward the bed.

The following day, a man named Hatch was putting up the frame for a house on a vacant lot on the outskirts of Tombstone. At least, that was his intent. But Curly Bill Brocious, Ike and Phinn Clanton, and Dixie Lee Gray were there with a piece of paper.

"But this is crazy," Hatch said. "I bought this land. I paid for it proper. . . . I got paper."

"You can use that paper next time you hit the outhouse," said Curly Bill. "The Town Lot Company has the deed to this land. You want clear title, you got to buy it from the Town Lot Company."

"I bought this land once," Hatch said, standing his ground. "That's enough. And if you say any different, you take me to court. You sue me."

"Sue you?" Ike laughed like a psychopath. "You're lucky we don't skin ya!" And then he searched for the word and found it. "You're trespassin'!"

He turned to the others. They threw lassos around the framing and pulled it down. Hatch tried to stop Dixie Lee, who kicked him in the mouth. And when Hatch fell to the ground, Ike picked up a brick and slammed it into the head of the fallen man, which split like a melon. Ike laughed and slapped his knee.

Wyatt sat in the Oriental Saloon, watching his Faro game like the prosperous burgher he had become. Everything Shibell had said about the benefits of law enforcement in Tombstone had come to pass. He and his brothers were a hairsbreadth away from making an offer for a saloon of their own. He was running the numbers in his head instead of paying attention to what John Clum and Fred White were saying. Fred White, the city marshal of Tombstone, was in his fifties, a former Army officer, an able man but one who was used to more civilized environs than Tombstone.

"Don't you see, Wyatt?" Clum said. "That whole anti-Chinese thing was all a fraud. Mike Gray's gotten Randall to deed the entire town of Tombstone over to a private company . . . *his* company, created and owned by Mike Gray," Clum said as if he could not believe the very words he uttered.

"And," said Fred White, "he's got Old Man Clanton's gang, the McLaurys, Curly Bill, and Johnny Ringo and at least a hundred of their men workin' for him to push folks off their lots."

They were a noisy pair, and this talk of lots, Clantons, and McLaurys was interfering with Wyatt's mental arithmetic.

"Now, Wyatt," Clum said. "I'm gonna run against Randall, and by God I'll not only win, I'll see him in jail for malfeasance. But that's for later. This right now is against the law, and I want both the City Marshal's Office under Fred here and the Pima County Sheriff Department out there doin' somethin' about it."

Wyatt scratched his head. "Well, I don't know," he said. "I'm under order from Charlie Shibell not to interfere. He said that this is a real estate matter and not a law-enforcement matter."

"Charlie Shibell?" shrieked Clum. "I thought you were supposed to be working for the people!"

That got Wyatt a little testy. He tended to steer clear of churches because he didn't care much for preaching. "Oh, come on, John," Wyatt said, getting up out of his chair. "I'm a *deputy* sheriff, and the people don't get shortchanged by the work I do for 'em. I got six drunks who were shootin' up the Benson–Tombstone road in my jail right now."

John Clum looked at him like a schoolmaster. "This is a little bit different than six drunken cowboys."

Wyatt didn't care much for schoolmasters, either. "You bet it is," he snapped. "That's part of the problem. I know what drunken cowboys are . . . but I'm not so sure about what this is. From the looks of it this is all just politics anyways." He threw the words out like an accusation, expecting Clum to deny it.

"Of course it's politics, Wyatt," Clum said as if speaking to a child.

Wyatt stared at him, thunderstruck. Then he regained his composure and drew an allegorical line in the sand, trying to delineate the border that he saw and believed separated him from Clum and those who would run for executive office.

"Well, I'm a policeman, not a politician, John," he said, certain of his ground. "You want the Town Lot Company to stop? File an injunction against 'em. You want me to enforce it? File it with a Pima County judge and I'll enforce it. But the law isn't politics."

And then John Clum spoke one of the few truths Wyatt had not heard first from his father.

"Everything is politics."

CHAPTER FIFTEEN

John Clum was calling his name when Wyatt strode in disgust out the Oriental Saloon and straight into into the path of the oncoming wagon hurtling down the street and hell-bent on running him down. The horses bore down on him at a gallop, and Wyatt dove, tucked, rolled, and pulled his gun. Surely this was an assassination attempt by some wretched desperadoes intent on eliminating the deputy sheriff of Pima County. Or had an old score followed him doggedly from Dodge or Wichita, an assassination meant to take place in broad daylight? Such an attempt was fit to be a scene out of one of Buntline's novellas.

"Startin' to look like New York, we got so much traffic, huh?" said Clum, stepping down gingerly from the wooden sidewalk, looking both ways before he crossed. Wyatt was still looking in the direction of the wagon loaded down with furniture, which the inexperienced driver had just halted at the end of the street. Wyatt brushed himself off and said, "Well . . . I never been to New York, so I wouldn't know."

"You wouldn't like it," Clum said, brushing the dust off the back of Wyatt's coat.

"Mebbe not."

"Oh, no maybe about it," said the mayoral candidate as they crossed the street together. "You wouldn't like what New York *is* and you may well not like what Tombstone is about to become."

"And what's that?" Wyatt said.

As they reached the opposite side of the street and mounted the steps that led to the wooden sidewalk that fronted emporiums and shops, lawyers offices and millinery stores, John Clum turned and gazed back over the dusty buildings.

"A city," he said, gesturing in a wide arc. "Not a town, not a mining camp, but a city. That's different than what you've been used to, isn't it?"

"And what exactly have I been used to, according to you, John?" he said. Wyatt didn't like people telling him about himself. He figured he pretty much had that one down pat. And if he didn't, it was nobody's business but his own.

"You've been used to knowing where the crime is."

"What's that supposed to mean?"

Clum looked him up and down like an experienced buyer sizing up a side of beef, knowing just where the steaks were and where the fat. "I would expect," he said, "that every town you've ever been in has had two sides to it—once they're big enough to be called towns, that is. Once they graduate from cow town or mining camp or railhead to actual town, they've got the respectable side where all the proper folks live and do their business." Here John indicated just such a side of Tombstone with a wave of his hand. "And they've got the other side of the Deadline, where the whores and the drunks are," John said, indicating Tombstone's very own such section just down the street. "And that's where the crime's supposed to be, isn't it?"

"You bet," said Wyatt.

"It's a drunken cowboy waving a gun or hiding it in the palm of his hand and blowing your brains out when you're not watching."

Wyatt looked at this man and wondered just how much about himself the other did know.

"And all you've got to do," Clum continued, "to deal with the crime is bat the cowboy over the head with that cannon of yours."

"Sounds about right," Wyatt said, and he thought for the first time in a long time of Ed Masterson.

Clum turned to Wyatt and said with the heaviness of a father who's finally got to tell a trusting son the awful truth, "That's not what a city is, Wyatt," he said, and fixed him with his eyes. "The stakes are higher and the crime doesn't do you the favor of staying on one side of some line. It comes at you from where you least expect it, and it wears a smile and a fancy suit and sometimes it uses a pen and ink instead of a Smith and Wesson, but it's just as deadly."

Wyatt smiled. "Sounds like a politician to me," he said, and chuckled at his own joke in the manner of men who make no jokes and are genuinely surprised when they come out despite their best intentions.

"That's what it sounds like to you?" Clum said incredulously.

"You bet."

That's when Clum realized just what it was that he found so infuriating about Wyatt Earp.

Clum had not just been talking, he had been philosophizing, for Chrissake! He had been pondering aloud the state of the ever-expanding frontier and the commercial pressures that would force an evolution from wilderness to urban existence, interwoven with a perspective on the very nature of good and evil in man himself. It was not only a meeting of minds but of the emotions behind them. He was sharing the intimate ruminations of his very soul. And to it all, the most he could get out of Wyatt Earp was, "You bet."

"Wyatt," Clum said, "my God, what does it take? I mean, let us then put subtlety aside. I have been talking to you about Mike Gray and the Clantons! And the threat they pose to every law-abiding citizen of this community!"

He waited for Wyatt's response, but Wyatt just looked at him.

Wyatt decided then and there that he didn't much care for conversations with John Clum. "I appreciate the civics lesson, John, but maybe that's just too complicated for a bumpkin skullcracker like myself."

"Sides are being drawn up, Wyatt," Clum said. "That badge you're wearing ought to tell you which side you're on if you can't figure it out already."

There was no way that Clum could have known Wyatt's feelings, for Wyatt was a stranger to them himself. They had not died with Urilla's death, but he had buried them just the same.

And now, as Wyatt felt them struggling up from the grave inside of him, he realized what had been sticking in his craw all this time. Not Clum, not the badge, not the wagonload of furniture that almost was his assassin. It was the girl.

"Well, let me tell you somethin', John," he said in a way that made Clum fear for his safety. "Maybe I don't want the badge. Maybe all I want's to own a saloon and to live my life. Maybe I got somethin' that's puttin' me in a real bad mood that you don't know nothin' about. Maybe you don't know me at all," he said, and suddenly Clum believed him, as Wyatt left without another word and Clum crossed over to the office of the *Epitaph*.

Wyatt continued across the street, thinking to himself, He wants to be mayor of this town . . . he's looking for an issue. Well, that's fine, but I'm not part of it. And he crossed over to the bank to see a man about a mortgage.

Wyatt sat in the leather chair that smelled of newly tanned hide and brass tacks and was across the desk from the bank manager, Mr. Owens, who pushed a set of forms across the highly polished desk, which forms came to rest near Wyatt's hand, waiting for his signature.

"Now, if you'll just sign there at the bottom, Mr. Earp," he said, smiling like a politician. "Why, then I can witness it. That's right . . ." he said as Wyatt signed, as if the signing itself were a singular achievement, an act of skill and daring that he, the bank manager, was privileged to have seen. "Wonderful," he said. "That's all there is to it."

Wyatt breathed out a sigh of relief. "It's an awful lot easier than it was the first time I asked for a mortgage."

Mr. Owens sat back in his own leather chair and smiled. "The first time you weren't drawing a deputy sheriff's pay," he said, pulling a cigar out of the wooden humidor on his desk and turning to Wyatt, saying, "Cigar?"

"Thanks," Wyatt said, genuinely surprised and pleased. He liked cigars, and he never figured a banker would give him one.

"You'll be using that money to buy more real estate?" the banker said, lighting the cigar for Wyatt.

Shoot, Wyatt thought, leaning back, feeling more comfortable, and allowing his mind to drift in an uncharacteristic way, now he's lightin' the damn cigar for me. Wyatt took a long puff off the cheroot, felt the fine old taste of well-aged filler and wrapper, and the trail of smoke he blew in the room looked like the stuff he always figured came out of Aladdin's lamp just before the Genie granted wishes.

He leaned back in the chair and took another puff, and for the first time in his life, felt rich. "Land speculation's too risky for the likes of me," he said in a voice that reminded him of nothing so much as the banker's own voice. "We're buying a piece of a saloon. And with any luck maybe a year from now I just won't need that deputy sheriff's pay either."

And when he said that, he wasn't thinking of the cigar or land or the saloon, or anything but Josie.

Wyatt walked down the street puffing his cigar, happy as a kid. The bank manager, for his part, stood at his office window smiling as he watched Wyatt leave.

A door behind the bank manager opened. It was a door that did not look like a door, rather like part of the paneling in the room. It had no handle to betray its function and it opened from the other side, from which side and through which door Mike Gray entered the room as if walking into a hotel full of well-wishers after winning an election. He put a friendly hand on the banker's back.

"And that, my friend," he said, "is how you turn a policeman into a conservative businessman. Give him something to conserve."

He crossed to the window and looked out at Wyatt. At that point, the banker saw a look cross Mike Gray's face, as if he had forgotten or overlooked something. When Mike spoke, it was not to the banker but to himself.

"Now," he said, "the only question is, is that *all* that Mister Earp wants."

And out in the street, Wyatt looked both ways as he crossed. There wasn't much to this traffic business once you got used to the idea.

CHAPTER SIXTEEN

That afternoon John Clum stood in shirtsleeves in the *Epitaph*'s office with his printer's cuffs on up to his elbows. Clum was busy setting type as Fred White entered.

"You got a second, John?" White asked.

Clum continued piecing the individual letters into the typesetting block. It was, surprisingly, an occupation he enjoyed as much as the writing of the text itself.

"Just a second," he said, setting in a period, then a slug, blocking in the rest of the line. "*Uno momento* . . . I just want to finish setting this down."

White came up behind him and peered over his shoulder.

"What is it?" White asked.

"The future," Clum said.

White looked at him quizzically.

"Tomorrow's lead story," the editor said with a smile. "Today's future, tomorrow's history."

"And the day after tomorrow's outhouse supplies."

Clum laughed, but Marshal White was not in a humorous mood. "So what about your friend Wyatt Earp, John?"

"What about him?"

"Is he with us or—"

"Are you familiar," said Clum, cutting the marshal off, "with the Zoroastrians, Fred?"

"They from around here?"

"The forces of light versus the forces of darkness," said Clum. He wiped his hands off on a rag soaked with turpentine and continued. "There's a struggle going on, Fred . . . for the soul of Wyatt Earp."

"A struggle."

"Um-hmm," said Clum. "An ancient one. A struggle with the devil for the soul of a man, if you will."

"I take it Mike Gray is playing the part of the devil?" said the town marshal, who now perched himself on a four-legged stool, knowing that he was in for the kind of long-winded philosophizing that the *Epitaph*'s editor and publisher liked to indulge in.

About the casting for the devil's part, Clum nodded with a smile and said, "Or a reasonable facsimile thereof."

"And that would leave you what, John? Playin' the part of God?"

Clum let that one go and neither answered nor laughed, which was fine with Marshal White. As an army man, he was comfortable with chitchat, but ultimately, any good field commander had to know how many and what troops were at his disposal and who was protecting his flank.

"Can I count on Earp or not, John? That's all I want to know. When push comes to shove, can I count on Wyatt Earp?"

"When push comes to shove," Clum said, "yes. I believe he'll be there, but it well may take push coming to shove."

"Fair enough," said White, sketching out the order of attack in his mind. "Then let's get started."

Marshal White left the *Epitaph* and stopped in at his office to pick up a shotgun. From there he went to the saloon of the Grand Hotel, where Dixie Lee Gray, Ike Clanton, and Billy Clanton were busying themselves drinking at the bar. Suddenly, Fred White stormed in with his shotgun pointed at the three of them.

"Dixie Lee Gray," he said. It was not a question.

"That's me," said the twenty-year-old, frail-looking youth.

"You're under arrest for assault."

* * *

In a black rig, dressed in black, pulled by black horses, Mike Gray came riding out to the Clanton ranch. He had been called away from business and his mood was dark. Mike drove hell-for-leather straight up to the main ranch house, where Old Man Clanton sat waiting at the heavy, green-painted Mexican table that dominated the main room of the house.

"What specifically is this all about, Newman?" Gray asked without any pleasantries as he walked in the door.

One of the few good things about Old Man Clanton, however, was the fact that he did not require pleasantries. "He's arrested your boy and mine specifically, Mike," he said. "He's pulled down all our 'no trespassing' signs."

Old Man Clanton watched the face of his business partner carefully, to see the effect of this news. "Now, Mike . . ." he said, holding up a hand as if to stave off an expected argument. "I know that your counsel against violence directed at the Earps was very wise . . . very wise indeed, but I'm just wondering if the same applies to Fred White."

Mike Gray's eyes flicked up and down, and you could damn near hear him calculating the number of guns that might be arrayed against their enterprise.

"He's not connected with the Earps or Doc Holliday."

Old Man Clanton pondered that a moment.

"You're sure about that, Mike?" asked Clanton.

The former Texas Ranger had made the calculations, figured out the connections, and had arrived at a decision in less time than it took Old Man Clanton to suck a tooth. "White is John Clum's man," Mike Gray said with great finality.

"And Earp isn't?" asked Old Man Clanton with some incredulity.

But Mike Gray revealed his insider's knowledge with no small amount of satisfaction. "He's got too much to lose and too much sense to lose it."

Newman Clanton seemed bolstered by his associate's confidence. "So Fred White's out there by his lonesome, huh?"

"That's right."

Clanton leaned in toward his business associate. "Then something's got to be done about the man."

Mike Gray reached inside his coat pocket and pulled out

one of Banker Owen's best cigars. He did not bite off the tip, which he considered a vulgar habit.

Rather, he pulled a little silver cigar clipper from his vest pocket. He wore it on a chain that looped around the third button of his vest. If one had read the inscription on the cutter they would have seen the words "For Dad, Your Loving Son, Dixie Lee." It gave Mike Gray a feeling of warmth and pride every time he touched it, so full of love was he for his only son. Indeed, in moments of reflection, he knew the world would be an infinitely better place if each and every person in it could know but once the kind of bond he shared with this boy who would continue his name. It was, in fact, in partial reflection on the love he had for this son and the hopes he held for the boy's future that he looked up at Old Man Clanton and said, regarding Marshal Fred White, "Kill him."

One week after the arrest of Dixie Lee Gray and the Clantons, Wyatt Earp was enjoying a particularly profitable evening at one of the gaming tables in which he and his brothers owned an interest. "We're lucky tonight, Mister Earp," the Faro dealer at the Oriental Saloon said to Wyatt, who sat behind him on a slightly raised platform, tilting back in his chair. The dealer raked in the winnings from a disgusted gambler.

"That's what I like to hear," Wyatt said, even allowing himself a smile.

"We have been," the dealer said, "ever since you bought into the saloon."

Wyatt said nothing but allowed himself a moment's reflection of his own. Never once, though, did he take his eyes off the gamblers' hands or where their guns might lie hidden.

Men whose hands went down to their boots during a game of cards were not often plucking out a pebble. But these looked like a calm enough bunch, and it allowed Wyatt the chance to daydream just a little about the money and about Josie. To his surprise, he found himself wishing for the latter more than the former. The sound of a gunshot in the distance snapped Wyatt out of his chair, and he was up and crossing to the saloon door with his hand brushing the long black coat back off the gun Ned Buntline had given him. From the sound of it, he thought the shot came from the sporting district.

He was met at the saloon door by Marshal Fred White. "Wyatt," the marshal said. "There's a bunch of drunken cowboys shootin' off their guns over by Tough Nut Street not far from Madame LeDeau's."

"How many of 'em?" Wyatt said.

"Ten or fifteen, from what they say," answered the city marhsal.

"Drunken cowboys, huh?" said Wyatt. "Finally a law-enforcement problem I can handle."

He and White laughed, and walked out into the street.

"My brothers are down the street," Wyatt said. "I think it'd be wise to get them too. If there are ten or fifteen drunks, we're gonna need some help."

"Well, I'll go on ahead," said Marshal White. "You catch up."

Wyatt caught ahold of his arm. "You'd be dumb to go out there till there's a few more of us, Fred."

White smiled at the younger man and gently disengaged his arm. "If they're over by Madame LeDeau's, more than likely they're just blowing off some steam. Maybe I can talk the situation down."

Wyatt looked at Fred White in much the same way his father looked at those who stood before his bench awaiting judgment. Fred White seemed like a nice man. "Don't be dumb," Wyatt said. "You wait for us and then go in swingin' . . . preferably from behind."

There was a gulch by Tough Nut Street down below a vacant lot across from the red-light district. That's where the drunk cowboys gathered to carouse, shooting their guns in the air. The rowdies in question included the Clanton brothers, the McLaury brothers, and Johnny Ringo. They were all firing into the air and passing a bottle back and forth.

It had taken Wyatt less than five minutes to find Morgan and Virgil, and now they were behind and to the sides of the cowboys, springing out without warning and knocking them over the head with their guns. It was at times like this that Wyatt especially appreciated the Buntline gun, which he knew full well was not something that the survivor of a thousand duels had commissioned be made to his specifications by Colt Firearms Company. More than likely, the old huckster had just bought a long-barreled revolver and had it engraved and put in a fancy case.

None of that, however, detracted one iota from the effectiveness of the extra-long barrel, either in terms of the extraordinary added range and accuracy or in terms of the damage you could quickly inflict by beating someone over the head with it. As Ike Clanton ran off, Wyatt and Virgil and Morgan quickly knocked out six cowboys. Wyatt looked down at the drunks who had been knocked into unconsciousness, saying, "You're under arrest."

Just then there was heard a shot ringing out from the vacant lot above, and the sound of City Marshal Fred White screaming in pain. Wyatt looked at his brothers and sprinted up and over the ridge of the gulch, where Curly Bill stood with his back to Wyatt. At Curly Bill's feet Wyatt saw Fred White. There was a bullet hole in the middle of Marshal White's stomach, and the clothes around the bullet hole were on fire, which told Wyatt that the gun had been fired point-blank. White's screams were subsiding now, and you could hear a rattle begin in the back of his throat as his body began to convulse. Wyatt came up behind Curly Bill at a run and hammered him over the head, splitting open his skull. Not yet unconscious, Bill turned to Wyatt, and Wyatt hit him backhanded with the long-barreled Colt across the side of Curly Bill's head, opening another huge gash and sending him crashing to the ground. Wyatt then bent over Fred, ripped off his own coat, and smothered the flames coming from White's stomach and clothes just at the moment Virgil and Morgan appeared on the scene.

The next day Wyatt and Virgil walked back from Doc McGraw's, past Fly's Photographic Studio and Boardinghouse. Virgil said, "Before he died, Fred told the Doc that he thought the shooting must have been an accident."

Wyatt looked coolly at his brother. Virgil went on. "He said he demanded Curly Bill's gun and Bill handed it to him barrel first, and he thought it just went off when Fred grabbed at it."

Wyatt shook his head. Even in death, Fred White was nice. Wyatt did not mean it as a compliment. He did not understand people who forgave their attackers. As far as he was concerned, they just made it that much more dangerous for the ones who were left alive.

"Gettin' killed didn't make Fred White any smarter," Wyatt said.

"What do you mean?" asked Virgil.

"It wasn't any accident," Wyatt said. "Curly Bill murdered him. It was a setup, neat as a whistle."

"How can you be so sure?" asked Wyatt's older brother. "The cowboys were supposed to be drunk, shootin' up the town?"

"Yeah?" said Virgil.

"Curly Bill didn't have any liquor on his breath at all," Wyatt said. "And there was only one shot fired from his gun."

"So?" Virgil said.

Wyatt looked at his brother. There was no doubt how much Wyatt loved him, how comfortable he felt in his big brother's presence, and it wasn't that Virgil was slow-witted, just not as fast as Wyatt. "So," Wyatt said, "he wasn't up there shootin' his gun off, was he? He was up there waitin'."

He could see by the look on Virgil that the latter was up to speed now. "An' I checked that gun," Wyatt said. "There's nothin' wrong with the action. It's a single-action Colt . . . means in order to fire it had to be cocked. And it was cocked—not because he was shootin' off rounds, but because he meant to use it on Fred White."

Charlie Shibell was at his table in the Grand Hotel eating breakfast when he looked up to see Wyatt standing, looking down at him.

"Wyatt," he said, swallowing a mouthful quickly. "Have a seat. . . . I just heard the news about poor Fred." He dabbed at his mouth with a napkin. "Terrible news, terrible news."

Wyatt, who did not avail himself of Shibell's offer to sit down, said in a flat voice, "It was the Town Lot Company who was behind it, Charlie."

Shibell shook his head and wagged a whole handful of fingers. "Now, Wyatt, I told you . . . that whole Town Lot

Company, that's none of Pima County's business. It's strictly a . . ."

He tried to remember the successful phrase he had used earlier, but since that phrase was "it's strictly a real estate matter" and this was now a case of murder, it seemed inappropriate. He searched for another phrase and found one, which he uttered decisively. "It's out of our jurisdiction and that's all there is to it."

Wyatt answered by lunging down and grabbing a terrified Shibell up out of his seat by his shirt.

"Damn you to hell, Charlie!" he said, shocking one and all within earshot, who could not recall Wyatt Earp as ever having raised his voice in this fashion to a friend. "I am being forced into . . . into a moral stand because of this thing!"

"Wyatt," sputtered Shibell. "I don't know what—"

"The man was murdered!" Wyatt bellowed as if against his will. "I know it and now you know it. And we both know who was behind it."

Shibell flushed purple. "I don't know anything of the kind, Wyatt, and—"

Wyatt suddenly seemed awfully tired. He set Shibell back in his seat. "Charlie," he said, and didn't finish the sentence. He realized suddenly that if he let this take him where it was heading, it would be war with Mike Gray. The fog that he had allowed to exist between him and his conscience, between him and what he at all costs had not wanted to see, was lifting.

Behind that fog, behind the banker's door, behind his sudden good fortune, behind the murder of Fred White and the woman he wanted as he had never wanted any other, behind it all was Mike Gray. Mike Gray owned half the town and controlled the rest. He had the power to make Wyatt rich or impoverished, and Wyatt could no more win in a fight against him than he could have against Wells Fargo or the railroads. There was the right thing to do, and in this case it wasn't the smart thing to do.

"Charlie," he said, "I wish you were either a stupid honest man or a smarter crooked one. I wish you could either hide the truth from me or give me a way out. I need this job, Charlie, I need the money it brings in. I got debts. I got things . . ."

And now it was Shibell's turn to grab hold of Wyatt. "Then ignore it, Wyatt," he said with sudden urgency, and thought to himself that any smart man ignores those things around him that cannot or will not be changed without costs so great as to outweigh the benefits change would bring. Ignore it like a horse with blinders who sees only straight ahead. Ignore it, for God's sake, because Charlie Shibell was too old to go up against men like Mike Gray and the Clantons.

He looked up into Wyatt's eyes and said again the words he prayed Wyatt would take to heart, words that would give them both the way out: "It's out of our jurisdiction."

Wyatt looked at him without seeing him. Nothing good would come of this. Nothing good ever again. He would lose. It was just a question of what. With a sharp intake of breath he had made his decision.

"I'm filing a warrant for the arrest of Curly Bill Brocious," Wyatt said.

"You goddamn fool," the older man said with great bitterness. Wyatt Earp might just have been forced into taking a stand, but Charlie Shibell would be damned if *he* was. "Not while you're working for me you're not," he said with no small amount of indignation.

"Okay," said Wyatt. "I quit." He took off the badge and tossed it on the table, where it bounced into Charlie Shibell's bacon.

John Clum was pulling out a proof sheet when Wyatt stormed into the *Epitaph* and said, "All right, you moral son of a bitch. You want me to choose sides? I just chose one. I just hope you know what you're doing, 'cause if you don't, people are gonna die."

Without waiting for a reply, Wyatt Earp banged out the door, sending a tray of type crashing to the ground.

Old Man Clanton sat chewing on a chicken bone with a plump and comely Mexican servant girl on his knee. He laughed and she giggled until they both looked up at Johnny Ringo when he barged into the room.

But Old Man Clanton, who was always in a good mood with a serving girl upon his knee, smiled and said, "Good evening, John, care for a leg?" He indicated the plate of chicken and then turned to the senorita's décolletage, "Or a breast?"

But Johnny Ringo was clearly not in the mood for either. "That cowboy-clubbin' cob-up-his-butt Earp filed a complaint and they just issued the warrant and arrested Curly Bill for murder!"

The chicken was savory and the young girl soft, but suddenly Old Man Clanton was unable to enjoy either one. "Does Mike Gray know about this?" he said.

"I don't give a fat rat's ass what he does or doesn't know," Ringo said, eyes darting with paranoia, his hand going down for his side arm. "Earp's gonna die, and that's all there is to it."

"Well," said Old Man Clanton, resigning himself to the way things seemed to be going and comforting himself at the same time by pulling the young girl a little closer to him. "If that's all there is to it, that's all there is to it, John. Earp's dead," he said.

CHAPTER SEVENTEEN

The following day, Johnny Ringo and Old Man Clanton sat with Mike Gray in Gray's office, where the former Texas Ranger worked at a ledger adding up figures with an abacus.

"You gonna stop playing with that thing and listen?" said Johnny Ringo.

"In a moment . . . in a moment," Mike said with equanimity. "Profit and loss, my boy. It's all profit and loss." He finished his computations and looked up, smiling pleasantly. "Yes . . ." he said.

Old Man Clanton cleared his throat. "Mike," he said, "Johnny here says Wyatt Earp has to die."

"Does he?" said Mike evenly.

"Yes," said the elder rustler, gravely serious now.

Johnny Ringo banged his fist for emphasis on the table. "Damn right," he said, glaring at the former Ranger. "Curly Bill wanted to kill him and you was too busy eatin' coffee and pie. And now Curly Bill's in jail, so I say this time we kill Earp and kill him good."

Mike nodded his head. "Because Curly Bill's in jail," he said.

"You got it," said Ringo.

Mike Gray sighed in distress. "And you condone this, Newman?" he said as if he could not believe his ears.

"Well," said the senior Clanton in embarrassment.

"Gentlemen . . ." Mike Gray said, rising for the occasion. "I'm shocked." He shook his head like a clergyman disgusted with the failings of his parishioners. "I'm distressed and shocked," he went on. "This is the United States of America. This is a democracy." He crossed over to Johnny Ringo and put a hand on the young man's shoulder. "We have a long and proud tradition of Anglo-Saxon jurisprudence that stretches from the Magna Carta down through the Founding Fathers and continues right up until this very day."

Ringo was about to say something, but Mike Gray was on a roll.

"This is a country where a man is innocent until proven guilty by a jury of his peers, and I will tell you right now that as long as there is breath in my body, money in my pocket, and a judge who can be bought off or a jury that can be intimidated, none of us have a thing to worry about from a two-bit pettifogger like Wyatt Earp or his would-be spiritual mentor, John Clum!"

A small stage had been erected in front of the offices of the *Tombstone Epitaph*. There was a banner hanging from one end of the roof to the other that read: "JOHN CLUM FOR MAYOR—SWEEP THE RASCALS OUT OF OFFICE!!" It featured a drawing of a broom sweeping a caricature of Alder Randall out of Tombstone. There was torchlight to light the stage and a crowd of people around it listening to Clum speak.

"I am here before you tonight," Clum told the crowd in stentorian tones, "to announce two things: First, I have this day filed on behalf of a group of Tombstone citizens an injunction with the district court against Mike Gray and the Town Lot Company and Mayor Alder Randall, designed to force them to cease and desist from issuing any further deeds in the city of Tombstone!"

Tremendous applause wafted up from the crowd of over a hundred who pushed in toward the stage.

"And second," Clum continued, holding his arms outstretched, "I have filed my candidacy today as the Republican candidate for the office of Mayor of the city of Tombstone, Arizona!''

Cheers all around from the good folk of Tombstone who had turned out this evening to witness the coming of this frontier messiah.

''And with your help we are going to sweep the rascals out of office come January, and the first step is going to be to elect Bob Paul sheriff of Pima County in November instead of the Town Lot Company stooge, Charlie Shibell!''

Clum held up a broom and mimed sweeping the rascals out as the crowd cheered louder.

Wyatt stood at the outer edge of the crowd, only half watching the speech. He saw Josie Marcus coming down the street toward him. She paused only a moment to look at the goings-on and continued on her way. It did not take long for Wyatt to catch up to her.

''Evening,'' Wyatt said, tipping his hat as he used to do in his Dodge City heyday.

''Good evening,'' she said, looking up into his eyes.

And again, Wyatt wanted her. ''Do you, uh . . . do you need someone to walk you home?'' was, however, all he could say.

''Why? Do I look lost?'' she said, the corners of her mouth turning up just slightly.

''Why no, ma'am,'' Wyatt said. ''No . . .''

Was she mocking him? He could not tell.

''Don't look so serious, Mister Earp. That was a joke,'' she said, and her voice washed over him hypnotic and low, mellifluous and silky. It made him feel all the more awkward.

''Oh . . . I see,'' he said. ''It's just that, well . . . a young woman walking alone at night . . . people could get the wrong impression.''

''What impression would that be?'' she asked. ''As far as I know, the red-light district is at the other end of town.''

Wyatt's head was spinning. This was not how he had felt with Urilla when he was an awkward boy. This was infinitely worse. ''Well, I . . . I certainly didn't mean to imply . . .''

''My fiancé is out of town on business,'' she said, looking not at him but straight ahead. ''I can either become a shut-in or walk alone on the streets of Tombstone.''

"If you'd rather walk alone, I certainly . . ." Involuntarily his hand reached up to his hat to tip it once again as if to say adieu. And then she looked at him.

"I didn't say that, Mister Earp."

He felt like a dog who had just run farther than his leash was long, jerked back in his place. Well, if she was going to toy with him, he'd get right to it. He was not a blushing schoolboy anymore either.

"No," he said. "What you said was, your fiancé is out of town."

Wyatt was now determined to see what, if anything, lay behind that face and that voice and the way her skin seemed to invite his touch.

"You're married, aren't you, Mister Earp?" she said.

"Yes."

"And I'm engaged to be married."

"So I'm told," said Wyatt.

"Mister Earp," she said, looking deep into his eyes, "you are a very handsome man, and if I wasn't engaged, I'd give you a lot of thought. But I am. So I won't. Good night, Mister Earp."

She turned and walked off, and all Wyatt could do was stand still and watch her, which of course was exactly what she wanted. And they both knew it.

Judge Wells Spicer looked up from the bench and asked, "Is the defendant represented by counsel?"

Curly Bill sat at the defendant's table. Next to him was a very slick and prosperous-looking shyster by the name of Haynes.

"He is, Your Honor," said the dude. "I am Judge Lucius P. Haynes of Tucson, and I have been retained to act on the defendant's behalf."

Wyatt and Clum sat side by side in the courtroom. Clum leaned in toward Wyatt and whispered, "You got to hand it to Gray. He buys the best."

"Your Honor," said the expensively purchased Judge Haynes, "since the unfortunate death of Marshal White was at worst an awful accident, we would respectfully request that bail be set immediately to enable the defendant to return to his livelihood. We should like to point out Mr. Brocious's many ties to the community and the indisputable fact that as a gainfully employed cattleman he does not pose a risk of flight.''

Outside the courtroom, Curly Bill enjoyed the friendly slaps on the back from Ringo and the Clanton boys and the McLaurys. Wyatt and Clum stood there and watched him go free.

"Five hundred dollars bail!" Clum said, shaking his head.

"Well," said Wyatt. "I knew justice was supposed to be blind, but I didn't think she was supposed to be stupid, too."

So the battle was joined, with John Clum and the Earps backing Bob Paul for sheriff of Pima County, and Mike Gray and the Clantons backing Charlie Shibell.

Depending on who won, the newly installed sheriff would either be someone who was working to put the outlaws in jail or someone who was on their payroll.

Doc Holliday stood out front of the Oriental Saloon banging on the closed door with his fist.

"Open up!" he shouted. "There's a man with a thirst out here. Open up, you lazy, slothful scoundrels. Where's your Christian work ethic?! Open this damned saloon, you sons a' bitches. . . .''

"Doc, take it easy," a voice said, and Doc turned to see Morgan Earp smiling as he approached.

"It's election day," Morgan said.

"Great!" proclaimed the Doc. "Let's get these sons of whores to open this saloon and we'll drink to democracy."

Morgan laughed good-naturedly as he always did when around the Doc. He thought of the man as his evil twin, and they loved each other. "All the saloons are closed, Doc. It's election day. That's what I was sayin'."

"They're actually gonna keep the saloons closed all day?" the Doc said in horror.

"Till the polls close," said Morgan.

"It's enough to turn a man into a monarchist."

A wagon pulled up in front of a ranch house in the San Simon district of Pima County. In the wagon were a half-dozen people, and behind that wagon another with the same load.

Therre were several outriders by the wagons: Curly Bill Brocious, Ike Clanton, Johnny Ringo, and Dixie Lee Gray. The newly freed Curly Bill was in the process of justifying his attorney's claims of the former's ties to the community by exercising his rights as a responsible citizen in a participatory democracy. To wit, Curly Bill presently dismounted and approached the ranch house, banging on the door. The door opened and an old man answered, "Yes."

"It's election day, old-timer," Curly Bill said presently. "See that fella over there? That's Johnny Ringo. He's your precinct judge, and that one over there's Ike Clanton, your voting inspector. We're here to help you go over and vote for Charlie Shibell for sheriff. So get your things and let's go."

"But," said the old man, "but I got a sick mule. I can't leave it."

"Well," said Curly Bill, "bring it along. Every other jackass in this county gets to vote for Charlie Shibell, so he can too."

San Simon Valley voted one hundred and three for Charlie Shibell and one for Bob Paul. Curly Bill and his boys voted all their horses and a dog or two and a stray cat to boot, and then just to make sure they voted them all again.

All this was pointed out to Wyatt Earp by his brother Virgil, who stood in the crowd of Bob Paul supporters waiting for the election results to come in. But as Virgil pointed out to his younger brother Wyatt, knowing it and proving it were two different things.

"No one'll testify against him," Virgil told Wyatt. "It's over."

But the look on Wyatt's face told Virgil it was definitely not over for him.

"Where's Curly Bill at now?" Wyatt asked in a cold fury.

"Over at the Grand," said Virgil.

Curly Bill and Johnny Ringo and the Clantons were at the bar at the Grand Hotel when Wyatt walked in alone. Curly Bill could sense something behind him. He turned, looked, saw Wyatt approaching. He smiled a nasty smile as he noted that Wyatt was not wearing a gun. Curly Bill pulled his own weapon on Wyatt, cocked it, and pointed it at Earp's head.

"You're stupider than I thought, comin' in here all alone without a gun, Earp," said Curly Bill.

Just then, however, he heard the voice of Virgil Earp call out, "Oh, I wouldn't say he was exactly alone." Virgil appeared at the back door with a shotgun in his arms pointed right at Curly Bill.

"And if I was you," said the voice of Doc Holliday, "I wouldn't call *anybody* stupid."

Doc stepped in through the low window on the opposite side of the room with his six-gun pointed directly at Curly Bill.

Just then Morgan stepped in through the front door and took a position to the right of Wyatt with a scattergun aimed directly at Brocious as well. "I don't have anything clever to say," he said.

"But he is a hell of a shot," said Doc. "Now drop the gun, Curly."

There was a moment of silence as Curly attempted to think his way through the situation.

"Drop it!" shouted Doc, not inclined to wait for Curly Bill to reach what for him was an all-too-obvious conclusion.

Curly Bill dropped his gun.

"Now what?" sneered Curly Bill.

And in reply, in the alley behind the hotel, Wyatt began to beat the daylight out of him.

At first Curly Bill charged like a bull as Wyatt jabbed and combination-punched like the boxer he was. Finally Bill charged him and lifted him off his feet. He slammed him into the wall of the hotel, knocking the air out of him. He did this again, again, and again until Wyatt pulled Bill's head back and then, in a move sometimes called an "Irish kiss," Wyatt head-butted him, once, twice, and three times until Curly Bill was crimson with blood and his nose was smeared across his face.

He let go of Wyatt, who then came in with three right upper cuts to Bill's solar plexus, each one knocking what little air was left out of him.

Then Wyatt bent way down so he was looking up at the doubled-over Bill, and from down in his toes he sailed upward with a crushing right that sent Bill back onto the wall of the hotel and then sinking slowly to the ground. Wyatt lifted Bill up and whispered into his ear so that only Bill could hear him, "Now, you son of a bitch," he said, breathing hard. "You're gonna admit that you rigged that vote or I'll testify that I saw you kill Fred White, and you'll hang for it, I promise you, or you'll be shot tryin' to escape."

When Mike Gray came to visit Curly Bill in jail, the latter could only whine, "I . . . I didn't know what else to do. I didn't have no choice, Mike, I didn't have no choice."

"Damn!" said Mike Gray. "Damn him to hell!"

A week later, Wyatt sat alone in the Oriental Saloon, empty of any patron but himself, drinking a cup of coffee and reading the newspaper. The front page of the newspaper proclaimed: "EXTRA! ELECTION RESULTS DECLARED INVALID!! Bob Paul Wins Sheriff's Race!" It brought a smile to Wyatt's face as he read the words.

"Savoring your victory, Mister Earp?" asked Mike Gray, who had appeared, silent as a snake, to stand opposite Wyatt's table. Wyatt put the paper down and looked at the corrupted former lawman.

"It's the voters' victory," he said. "Not mine."

Mike, responding to no invitation but his own, sat down, took off his hat, and put it on the table, saying, "Ahhh, yes . . . the simple code of the West: bare knuckles, man to man, a fair fight, and Bob Paul is sheriff of Pima County."

"Sounds good to me," said Wyatt.

"Grow up," said Mike disdainfully. "The voters don't run this territory. I do. As of next week the city of Tombstone will no longer *be* in Pima County. It will be part of a *new* entity—Cochise County." He watched Wyatt's eyes and took delight at the shocked look of betrayal he read there. "Catchy name, isn't it?" he said affably. Then his tone grew business-like. "Its sheriff will be appointed, not elected. There's ten thousand dollars under that hat, and more where it came from. It is not in my interest to fight you. Take the money," he said, "and get out of my way."

Wyatt could not believe what was happening. He stood up almost in a daze but managed to say, quietly, "I'd sooner meet you in hell."

He walked toward the exit, toward the sunlight, beyond the swinging doors, none too sure of anything anymore, with the sound of Mike Gray's laughter in his ears.

"You might just meet me in hell, but by then I'll own it! And the Devil will be payin' me rent!"

Wyatt pushed through the swinging doors and out into the sunlight. It enraged Mike Gray, who was not used to being ignored and who took offense at anyone who was not moved by cold, hard currency.

"I'll crush you flat if you're in my way!" he shouted after him. "Do you hear that, Earp!?"

Wyatt did not turn around, and this enraged Gray even further.

"I'm the one that's been trying to keep a lid on this!" he yelled. "I'm the one that's been tryin' to handle this like businessmen, and this is the gratitude I get?!"

He walked to the door and shouted out into the street, "You're nothing but a goddamned hypocrite. I was a lawman too before you were born! You think you're better than me."

There was no answer from Wyatt, who squared his shoulders and walked away.

"You're no better than me, Earp!" Mike shouted after him, and added the thing that had been gnawing at him the most. "I woulda treated you like a son, you stupid son of a bitch. YOU'RE NO BETTER THAN ME!"

CHAPTER EIGHTEEN

Within a week of Wyatt's last run-in with Mike Gray, as drunken cowboys caroused with the girls who worked on the line late that night, Wyatt sat near his Faro game in the Oriental Saloon watching the dealer and the bettors playing against each other. He sipped at a beer and smoked a cigar. To those who knew him, he seemed distracted. Over at the bar Johnny Behan, with his back to Wyatt, was talking to four or five locals. They were gathered around him and he talked loudly to them, so loudly that it drew Wyatt's attention from the game.

The bandy Irishman was regaling his fellow drinkers with a bawdy tale. "So she says to me, 'Oh Johnny, I'm scared,' so I says, 'Darlin' it's nothin' to be scared of, it's just a picture, you know?' So she takes her hair down a little . . . shakes it down, you know. . . . And I can see she's hot for it, so I says to her, 'Darlin' why don't you open up that little gown of yours . . . just a little' . . ."

Suddenly Wyatt sickened and realized that Johnny was talking about Josie. From the back it appeared that Johnny was showing a picture to the locals. Some whistled appreciatively. Wyatt hesitated and then started over toward Behan, but though he would not admit it even to himself, he was jealous and he too was hot to see the picture.

"Jeez will you look at that," said one of the locals.

"She just stood there and let you do it? Look at that . . ." said another.

Johnny took a pull of his drink and said, "I says, 'Don't worry, darlin' . . . nobody'll ever see it but me. Open up a little.' And what do you think . . ." He paused for dramatic effect and then continued. "She looks me right in the eye and says, 'Is this what you want?' and she dropped the whole filmy gown to the floor and just stood there buck naked. Look at that . . . ain't that somethin' an' they're just as good to . . ."

He suddenly became aware of Wyatt behind him.

"Hello, Earp . . ." Behan said with a leer. "You want to have a look too? You ever see a Jew girl naked? They're somethin', I'll tell ya."

Wyatt was dry-mouthed. Unable to take his eyes off the picture in front of him, he said, "You're a damned fool, Behan."

"Fool, am I?" said Johnny Behan, licking the whiskey off his lips and proffering the picture toward Wyatt. "Here, take a good look. I can see you droolin' for it."

Wyatt averted his eyes and said, "What's she see in you?" Then he turned to walk away.

"Ohhhhhh," Johnny said. "What's she see in me?" Then, shouting after Wyatt, "You want me to describe it for ya? Or shall I tell ya what she does with it?"

The locals laughed. Wyatt walked to his Faro dealer.

"I'm goin' out for some air," he said in a hoarse voice. "You need me, I'm outside."

"Sure, Wyatt," said the dealer. "You okay? You don't look so good."

"I'm goin' out for some air," was all he said.

That night, in his bed and staring up at the ceiling, Wyatt lay there listening to Mattie snore.

"You're snoring, Mattie," he said. "Turn over."

Mattie stirred in her sleep and said, "What? Wha . . . huh?"

"You're snoring."

Mattie turned over. She stopped snoring, but after a while she started again.

"There is, I believe, little satisfaction in life," said John Clum, "except in duty faithfully performed." He was addressing a group of dignitaries outside the county court offices from a stand decked with bunting. Next to it there was a platform on which Sheriff Bob Paul and Marshal Ben Sippy sat, next to Judge Wells Spicer. There was a sizable crowd gathered there to listen to John Clum's inaugural address that morning in late summer.

". . . And now that you have elected me your mayor," he said, "I intend to perform that duty. It is my pleasure to announce to you that former Mayor Alder Randall has been indicted and has already fled the territory."

There were cheers.

"But we are not going to stop with that. We are going to continue to go after the Town Lot faction, and I therefore intend to advocate to the territorial governor that he appoint Wyatt Earp for the newly created position of sheriff of Cochise County.

"And I will insist on vigorous law enforcement from our city marshal, Ben Sippy, even if it means drawing a line in the sand against those same rustlers who are bent on pursuing their plan of lawlessness and political domination."

Here the crowd burst into applause, with no man in the crowd clapping his hands more enthusiastically than Johnny Behan.

"Fine speech," he said. "As fine a speech as I've ever heard. The man makes a fine speech."

That night, Johnny Behan sat with Josie at a secluded table at the Maison D'Oree restaurant. She looked around the room appreciatively. Then she looked back straight into Johnny's eyes. A waitress poured champagne into their half-full glasses and left.

"What's the angle?" Josie said.

"The angle?" asked Behan, lifting his glass to his lips.

"It's been a while since you took me out to dinner, Johnny, and never to a place as expensive as this."

Behan put down his glass in a mock gesture of exasperation.

"You people always measure everything in terms of dollars and cents," he said plaintively. "Must a man be suspect for having a romantic dinner with his sweetheart?"

"You people?" said Josie, her eyes narrowing. "I'm the only one on this side of the table, Johnny. What other people are you talking about?"

Johnny did not even touch that one, simply danced away as if his comment had never existed. "You know I'm crazy in love with you, darlin'. Marryin' you is all I think of night and day," he said, "but I can't marry you if I'm a pauper, and it was because of you and for you that I dropped that whole anti-Chink thing.

"I coulda been elected to City Council on that, but I can see how, bein' of the Israelite persuasion, that could have upset you, as if I'd ever put you in the same category as a bunch of heathen Chinamen, which you know I wouldn't."

"That's mighty white of you, Johnny," said Josie.

"Look," he said, leaning in toward her. "All I'm sayin' is I deferred to your sensitivities at the expense of my career, which is after all the thing that's gonna bring home the bacon for both of us . . . you'll grant me that, I hope?"

When he saw there was no response, he continued. "So . . . seein' as how I've made a sacrifice for you and your love, I was thinkin' that you might want to help me out now in terms of my career."

Josie drank some champagne.

"Just so we could finally get married," said Behan.

Josie lowered the glass and said, "What do you want me to do?"

"I want you to talk to Wyatt Earp."

"Talk to him?" Josie said, watching Johnny very carefully now.

"He's crazy about you, you know," said Johnny, allowing himself a sip of the bubbly as well. "Cold and as highfalutin as he likes to make himself, I think he'd blab like a baby if ya'd just bat your eyes at him."

"Blab about what?"

Behan now spoke like a serious conspirator. There was no more brogue and no more "darlin'." It was business now, and there was an offer on the table. "I need to know how serious he is about this sheriff of Cochise County thing. Is it the money he wants or the badge? I need to know if there's a deal can be struck with him." He sat back in his chair, awaiting her response.

When it came, her response was softer than he'd expected.

"I don't think Mister Earp is the deal-making sort," was all that she said.

But Johnny was determined to get the conversation elevated to a higher and more businesslike tone.

"Look," he said, "the only reason he took Charlie Shibell's offer of deputy was for the money and because it gave him the chance to buy into the Oriental Saloon. Well, there's plenty of money to go around in that job, but I can't get my hands on it unless that badge is on me. It's a fair deal I'd be offerin' him."

Now it was Josie who had adopted the tone of businesswoman.

"Except you're asking *me* to offer it. Why?"

Johnny leaned back expansively. She had taken the bait. "Well, you can catch more flies with honey than you can with vinegar," he said graciously, alluding to his companion. "Besides . . . it's in your own interest too. The man who becomes sheriff of Cochise County will be able to support a wife. Right now, darlin', I'm just a pauper. You can see that clearly now, can't you?"

"Yes," said Josie, "I see it all clearly now, Johnny."

"You do?" said Johnny, surprised it was going so well. "Then you'll go talk to Earp?"

"Yes, I will," she said. "As you say, it's in *my* interest."

"Oh, God love you, darlin'; you *do* see. You know, sometimes I think I love you because you're a Jew and not in spite of it. If ever a people knew how to do business . . . Ahh, God love you."

He picked up his glass and clinked it with hers. "Happy days," said the Irishman.

"*L'chaim*, Johnny," Josie said, drier than the champagne.

The Oriental Saloon was abustle with activity even at this early hour of the afternoon. But the activity slowly died down as dance hall girls, drunken miners, and cowboys turned to stare at the very beautiful and proper young woman who had just come in through the swinging doors and looked, with her bustle, high-collared dress, and hat mightily out of place in this temple to the sins of the flesh.

With all eyes on her, Josie walked over to the bartender and said, "Good afternoon."

The bartender for his part stared at her and then slowly broke into a grin and forced himself to suppress a laugh. He was, simply, not used to being greeted with the words "Good afternoon."

"Good afternoon," he said. "Uhh . . . what'll you have?"

"Wyatt Earp," said Josie.

The bartender pointed down past the end of the bar to the door marked "Office."

Wyatt sat at his desk going over the books. There was a knock.

"It's open," he said, then looked up to see Josie. He stood up as she entered.

"Good afternoon, Mister Earp," she said.

"Good afternoon, Miss Marcus," he said. "What, uh . . . what brings you to . . ." And he remembered to offer her a chair. It was ridiculous, he was a grown man in his mid-thirties and yet awkward as a schoolboy with this woman.

"Johnny Behan sent me to talk with you," said Josie.

Wyatt's heart sank at hearing that this was Behan's idea.

"Oh," he said. "Well, as far as I remember Mister Behan had two good legs and was fluent in the English language . . . so if he wants to talk to me, I don't see why he sent you."

There was a bitter taste in Josie's mouth as she recalled Behan's remarks. "He said something about being able to catch more flies with honey than with vinegar. I assume by that he was referring to you as the fly and to me as the honey."

She said this with a kind of solemn dignity, to which Wyatt was not immune.

"I see," he said, completely missing the point. "And because of your affection for Mister Behan you agreed to be used in such a fashion."

"No, Mister Earp," said Josie. "It was not because of my affection for Mister Behan. And I don't intend to be 'used' by anyone.'' She said this looking square in his eyes, and then, "I've come to love the Arizona sunsets, Mister Earp. Could you take me out to see one right now, please? This office seems a bit close."

The sunset, spilt over the ridge overlooking Tombstone, was indeed magnificent. The buckboard was pulled up at the edge of the ridge, and Wyatt and Josie walked along the edge looking at the beauty of the desert with the town spread out down below them. Then Josie spoke her purpose plainly.

"Johnny will appoint you his deputy if you withdraw your name, and he'll split all the fees fifty-fifty with you and then support you for sheriff at the end of one year, if you'll agree to support him for the territorial legislature."

But Wyatt was not listening to the offer. There was only one thing he wanted to know.

"Why did he send you?" he asked quietly.

And Josie, as if not hearing, continued, ". . . He also said that you should realize that as a Republican you'll never get the appointment. It will go to a Democrat—either to Johnny or someone else. All you could do would be to spoil things for Johnny and yourself if you oppose him."

There was nothing further to say. She had said everything he had told her to say, and yet Wyatt still had only one question.

"Why did he send you?"

Josie took a breath and then let it out. "He said you were crazy about me. That you would 'blab like a baby' if I batted my eyes. I can only assume you gave him some reason to come to that conclusion."

The two of them stood there feeling trapped.

"He had a . . ." Wyatt said.

"What?"

And from Wyatt, finally, "A picture. . . . He was showing it in the saloon."

Josie felt sick and violated.

"I see," she said. "I see . . . and it was because of that picture." There were tears in her eyes as she looked away from Wyatt, feeling for the first time in her life like a whore.

"No," he said. "No, I expect he knew I was attracted to you before that. I expect that's why he brought that picture down there. He was showing that picture and I was jealous, like he knew I would be, before I even knew it. And that's why he sent you. Because he knew how I felt.''

Then Josie turned back to him. "He didn't send me, Wyatt. He couldn't have kept me away. Sooner or later, *that's* what he knew.''

The two of them looked at each other. Falling into each other's arms would be leaping into the abyss, and they both knew it.

"We'd be dancing on strings that Johnny Behan would be pulling,'' Wyatt said. "And there are other things, other people involved.''

"I don't give a damn about Johnny Behan,'' Josie said, as if throwing a yoke from off her shoulders. "He has no strings on me,'' she said, and then, "I don't give a damn who becomes sheriff of Cochise County, and I don't give a damn anymore about who you're married to. I'm nineteen years old. You're the one who's older and wiser. If this is a mistake, you tell me.''

They looked at each other, Wyatt looking deep into her eyes, wanting to pull back from the abyss and feeling nothing but the vertigo of one who knows he's going to jump. He pulled her to him, swept her up in his arms, and thought as he kissed her, Let the world burn around us.

CHAPTER NINETEEN

Two weeks later, Judge Spicer pinned the sheriff's badge on Johnny Behan. At about the same time John Clum was in the *Epitaph* office with Wyatt, demanding, "What could you have been thinking of?"

Wyatt didn't answer, but it should have been obvious to Clum that Wyatt would not appreciate Clum's scolding tone. John Clum, however, tended to overlook the obvious once he was on his high horse, and so he continued, "To make a deal like that with Behan?"

"I didn't know he was in Mike Gray's pocket," Wyatt said, sounding like a kid fumbling for an excuse despite himself.

"So what," said the mayor in that schoolmarm tone of voice of his. "You knew he was a cheap politician, didn't ya? And how could you not know he was in Gray's pocket? What could you have been thinking of?"

Wyatt liked that phrase even less the second time he heard it, but he said nothing.

"Do you know who Behan's appointed as his deputy?" Clum asked, and then exploded with the answer. "Harry Woods! The editor of the *Tombstone Nugget*. So now Mike

Gray's got his own sheriff and his own newspaper to back
him in the bargain, and with Judge Haynes in Tucson he's
got his own man on the territorial bench as well. What could
you *possibly* have been thinking of?!''

"I wasn't thinking, okay?" said Wyatt.

"Well, that's obvious," said Clum, having pushed just a
hair too far.

Wyatt's mood was now getting awfully dangerous. "I
wasn't thinking of Harry Woods or the *Tombstone Nugget* or
Mike Gray or *you* or Tombstone, if you want to know the
truth, John," he said. "And it's none of your damn business
what I *was* thinking of. 'Cause it has to do with *my* life and
what I'm gonna do with it."

They were both silent for a bit. Then Clum asked softly,
"What *are* you gonna do with it, Wyatt?"

Wyatt shook his head. He was plainly tired of thinking.
"I don't know," he said. "As God is my witness, I don't
know."

Then Clum pounced, and there was something in his manner reminiscent of Wyatt's father Nicholas. "Well, you better
know, Wyatt," he said. "This is a hard land and these are
hard times. And *no one*, if you haven't figured it out by now,
is going to let you just live your life!"

Wyatt looked down as if hearing his own father's words.

The mayor continued, "This whole territory is in transition, Wyatt," he said. "It's about to give birth to a state, and
it won't be an easy birth, it will be a bloody one. You and
your brothers are strong men. In any society when there's a
war or a rebellion or a time of transition, people look to strong
men like you. The weak people who just want to live their
lives look to strong men to protect them, to be their knights.

"And the lawless ones look to men like you and your
brothers and plot how to eliminate them. You have only two
choices, Wyatt," he said.

"Pick a side or leave. Because no one is going to let you
just live a life. You're too valuable to one side and too
dangerous to the other."

John Clum and Wyatt Earp were not the only two men who
had been strategizing. By the onset of winter Mike Gray and

Newman Clanton were having their own little powwow at the Clanton ranch.

"Clum's fired Ben Sippy and appointed Virgil Earp city marshal of Tombstone," Old Man Clanton said. "Not only that, now he's got the Federals to swear Wyatt in as deputy federal marshal for Southern Arizona. They're outflankin' us, Mike. I've looked to you to be smarter than them."

"Well," said Mike Gray, sighing, "maybe it's time to fight fire . . . with fire."

"What do you mean?" asked the old rustler.

"Just exactly what I said."

Christmas in Tombstone that year held little promise of rain. Just wind, cold hard biting whip-through-the-cracks-in-the-wall, chill-to-the-bone wind.

It was not the type of climate conducive to holiday cheer. But even if it had been a picture-perfect white yuletide season, there would have been precious little cheer in Wyatt's home. Boomtown or not, Tombstone was little more than a village, the kind that thrives on gossip that whips through town as fast as prairie fire. Mattie had heard the whisperings in the millinery shops and seen the sidelong glances at the Chinese herbalist where she bought her bottles of laudanum. She had heard it from shop girls behind her back and from her sisters-in-law straight to her face, and now it seemed as if the onset of Christmas added insult to injury. A present had been bought, a brooch by Mr. Earp. But not, it turned out, for Mrs. Earp.

Mattie slapped Wyatt hard across the face. "You think I haven't heard the gossip!" she screeched. "You think I haven't heard them laughing at me behind my back about Wyatt and his Hebie whore!? I saw the bill for the brooch you bought her! Where's my brooch, you son of a bitch?!"

Just then there was a banging on Wyatt's front door and Virgil's voice calling out. But Wyatt responded neither to the knocking nor his brother's voice. He looked at Mattie with much the same look as he got with drunken cowboys before he buffaloed them. He did not want to hit her.

"Keep your mouth off of her, Mattie," he said as he crossed to the door, more to get away from her than anything else, but she would have none of it.

"Keep my mouth off of her?!" she screamed. "What is she?! I'm your wife! Don't you walk away from me! You hear me!"

Wyatt opened the door to Virgil and said, "I can't talk now, Virg."

"There's no time for talk, Wyatt," said Virgil. "The whole damned town is on fire!"

Flames leapt from buildings as Wyatt and Virgil arrived with the fire department, and people screamed in terror as buildings collapsed in flame. Here and there amid the rubble, the charred remains of a Christmas tree could be seen burning.

As the stagecoach pulled into the city, its occupants, looking out, saw a war zone. Half the street had been burned out, with none of the buildings left standing. In many of the places there were tents that had been put up, and the tents were guarded by thugs from the rustler faction, among whom were seen Ike Clanton and the McLaury brothers.

McLaurys and Ike glowered at the stage as it drove through the town, and they paid particular attention to the stranger who stared back at them from the coach. He was a dapper gent with a mustache and a derby hat set at a rakish angle. He gave them the once-over as well, and though they may not have known that he was Bat Masterson they could tell that he was not to be taken any more lightly than the Earp brothers.

The stage continued down the road and pulled up in front of the depot office, where Wyatt stood waiting along with Doc Holliday.

"Bat! Hello, you old cob!" called the jovial dentist.

Bat stepped down from the coach and shook hands with Doc and then Wyatt.

"Hello, Doc," he said. "Happy New Year. You still with that vicious old whore?"

"Ah," said Doc, "then you remember my Kate. I'll give her your best."

"Hello, Wyatt," said Bat, greeting his old friend warmly.

"Bat," Wyatt said. "Not much of a New Year, is it? I can't thank you enough, though, for coming all the way from Dodge."

"What's going on here? The place looks like Atlanta after Sherman got through with it."

"Well," said Wyatt, "it's a war zone, that's for sure. And you and Luke Short, who's due in today too, are the reinforcements."

Doc pulled a flask from his coat pocket, took a long drink, and then said, "Some local yahoos burnt down some buildings and then sent out their hooligans to lay claim to the lots. They say that now that there are no buildings nobody can tell whose lot was whose and they're claiming squatters' rights."

"Since when did you become such a disciple of the law, Doc?" asked Bat.

"I don't give a putrid pile of puss about the law, Bat, and I don't care who knows it. I just like a good fight."

That night, the tents that had been put up by the squatters were silhouetted against the lights of the rest of the wide-open town. Ike Clanton sat out front of his tent drinking a bottle of whiskey.

The sound of horse hooves were heard nearby, but Ike paid it no mind. Then suddenly from out of nowhere a rope was thrown around him. Then another rope was thrown over the tent pole. Looking up, Ike could see that the ropes were in the hands of Wyatt and Virgil Earp, who tied off the ropes around their saddle horns and set their spurs into their horses' flanks, uprooting Ike and his tent alike.

Next to that, where another tent had been erected, Morgan and Doc rode their horses straight through the canvas, and the rustler and the girl he had bedded down ran off into the street. The two on horseback laughed, and Morgan called, "Lot jumpers, git!" and fired his gun into the air.

Bat Masterson and Luke Short drove a wagon through another tent and three others next to it down the line. The cowboys in them sprang out with guns drawn and ready to shoot, when Wyatt came riding up behind them and clubbed them over the head. All in all, Doc thought, it had been a long time since he had had such a good time.

The following day at the Clanton ranch, Ike fumbled with the bandage on his head as he whined to his father.

"I don't see why I can't come to this meeting," he said. "It's my head that got bashed in."

"A lumpy head ain't the ticket into this meeting, Isaac."

But Ike pushed his case even further. He was tired of being passed over by his father and the others. "I got ideas," he said. "I got plenty ideas."

"Problem is they're all stupid. Now if you don't want a lump on the other side of your head, get out of my way!" said Old Man Clanton as he pushed past. Ike made a face and mimed the words "get out of my way" like a snot-nosed kid, then grumbled to himself and walked off sullenly. A dog crossed over to him, wagging its tail. Ike paused long enough to kick the dog, which yelped and moved off, tail between its legs.

"You don't want me to do it again," Ike snarled after the dog, "get out of my way!"

Inside the Clanton house, sitting around the large parlor were Curly Bill, Johnny Ringo, Old Man Clanton, and Mike Gray.

"It's been two months since we hit a stagecoach," said Curly Bill, "and we still ain't seen a dime from this big land deal of yours. All we been doin' is riggin' elections."

"Curly Bill's right," Ringo said. "Our people who look to us for their incomes have expenses. They have obligations. If they're not makin' money, how long you think they'll stick with us? And while we're doin' nothin', the Earps are bringin' in firepower," he said. "Pretty soon half the Dodge City police force will be campin' out in Tombstone." He looked over to Curly Bill. "I say we not only rob a stage, I say we kill Masterson to boot!"

Mike Gray shook his head and pursed his lips. "Oh, that's really smart," he said. "Bat Masterson, who's only Wyatt's oldest friend. Then you'll have a real war on your hands."

Curly Bill could contain himself no longer. Knowing Mike Gray and being forced to think had been the two most frustrating experiences of his life. "So let's have a war!" he bellowed. "I want to kill *somebody*, damn it! Every time I want to kill somebody, you say no! Well, I had enough. Far as I'm concerned, it's killin' time!"

Old Man Clanton turned to his business associate. Perhaps now the man would understand the pressures under which he had been operating. "You see what I'm up against, Mike," he said.

"I know," said Mike appreciatively, "I know."

"Young men, hot tempers," said Old Man Clanton. "And I don't entirely disagree, either. I thought burning the town was an excellent idea. I supported that wholeheartedly. Didn't I?" he said reasonably.

"Yes, you did," Mike said, acknowledging the elder partner's cooperation.

Newman continued, "You said fight fire with fire, and I said give me a match. But now they've routed every one of our men. Maybe there are a few people who could do with a little killing right about now. It might relieve a lot of tensions. At least have an open mind about killing someone, Mike."

It was difficult to disagree with as affable a crook as Newman Clanton. "I have an open mind about it," Mike said. "Did I ever say a thing against killing someone?"

This was exactly the type of conversation Curly Bill hated. Next thing you knew, they'd be passing around pie and coffee.

"Well, every time *I've* suggested somebody to kill, *you* say no!" said Curly Bill.

"I'm just saying if we kill someone, let's make sure it's the right person and let's do it in an elegant fashion," said Mike Gray. "In a way that gets our message across but doesn't either start a war or get somebody in front of some hanging judge. Let's not just have killing for the sake of killing."

Curly Bill just looked at him as if he were a cretin. "What's wrong with killing for the sake of killing? It's what we're good at."

"It's *wasteful*, okay?" said the old Ranger who obviously hated waste. "Now you want to rob a stage and kill someone, and Johnny here is concerned about the men Wyatt's bringing in to Tombstone and Newman is concerned about our enterprise. *If* we're smart about who we kill and how, we can accomplish all of our goals."

Johnny turned to Curly Bill, much impressed, and said, "I'm willing to hear him out."

Mike, for his part, did not wait for Curly Bill's opinion. "Thank you," he said to Ringo. "There's a Chinese saying: 'Sometimes you kill the chicken to scare the monkey.'"

Curly Bill had clearly had enough. "I don't want to kill no

goddamn monkeys or chickens. I want to kill one of the Earps!''

Mike just threw him a look and went on. ''Bob Paul picks up a little spare change by riding shotgun for Wells Fargo when they have a big shipment going out, doesn't he?''

That got Curly Bill's attention. ''Oh, I'd *love* to kill that son of a bitch.''

''You'd love to kill anybody,'' said Johnny Ringo good-naturedly.

When Johnny quieted down, Mike continued. ''*And*,'' he said, ''that would send a loud and clear message to Masterson and Short and anyone else that was to come here that Tombstone wasn't the most hospitable place in the world, wouldn't it?''

''It would,'' said Ringo.

''I'll do it personal,'' said Curly Bill, chomping at the bit.

''No, you won't,'' Mike Gray said.

Curly turned to Johnny. ''There he goes again, tellin' me who I can kill and can't.''

Mike ignored him and continued. ''Isn't Billy Leonard a friend of Doc Holliday's?''

''So what?'' said Curly Bill, fighting a yawn.

''Maybe we give this thing to Leonard and his bunch,'' he said. ''Then if anybody recognizes 'em or they get caught, we say Holliday was in on it with them. We got a newspaper now, we could get that story out.''

''Who cares about Holliday?'' asked Ringo.

Mike turned to him. ''Holliday is Wyatt Earp's Achilles' heel. Holliday's a carouser and a mean-spirited drunk. People don't like him, but Wyatt won't ditch him. Now, then, you tar Holliday and you tar the Earps with the same brush.''

Appreciative looks passed from one to the other.

''To me,'' said Mike, ''that's a killing that makes sense. An Ides of March kind of killing. That's a killing I could support with a clear conscience.''

''Well, thank you, O Lord,'' said Curly Bill reverently, ''it's about time.''

And Newman Clanton said, ''Amen.''

CHAPTER TWENTY

It was March 15 when the Benson stage rode along with Bob Paul riding shotgun and an old geezer named Bud Philpot as the driver. Inside the coach was a single passenger, a salesman. Up on top Bob Paul looked over at Bud Philpot and noticed that the older man was leaning to his left and was obviously in some discomfort.

"What's wrong, Bud?" he asked solicitously.

"Piles," was what the old man said.

"What?"

"Piles!" said Philpot, who did not like having to discuss the subject at all, let alone shout it out for one and all to hear. "Piles," he said again. "Got the damned piles! Got 'em so bad I can't sit right. Oh, Lordy . . ."

Bob Paul was a compassionate man, but he had a sense of humor as well, and so he laughed.

"What you laughin' at?" declared the wretched Philpot. "You live as long as me, you'll get the piles too. Shaved ice . . . 'at's the onliest thing that helps 'em. . . . You wouldn't mind tradin' places, would ya?" he asked plaintively. "I can't drive this team with these damned piles."

"Okay," Bob said. "Okay . . . let's trade places." It

133

seemed the least he could do, and since he felt bad about laughing at the older man's infirmity and knew in his heart of hearts that the old man's words were true, and that if he lived long enough, piles were just around the next bend, Bob traded places. He could not have known that that act of kindness would save his life and cure Bud Philpot's piles forever.

Marsh Williams, the Wells Fargo agent, was sitting at his office desk doing paperwork while the telegraph operator, Wilbur Higgins, sat dozing in his chair. Suddenly the telegraph started clicking out a message, waking Wilbur with a start.

"Oh, my God," said Wilbur to himself as he scribbled the message down.

In the Oriental Saloon Wyatt was swapping stories with Bat Masterson, who was busy dealing a hand of Faro at that very moment.

"You remember," Bat asked Wyatt, "when Clay Allison came into Dodge buck naked except for his gun belt and a bottle of rye?"

But the saga of Clay Allison's butt-naked ride and his demise at the Long Branch was cut short by Wilbur's fevered entry into the saloon. He held a telegram in his hand and waved it as he said, "Marshal Earp. This just come for you. From Bob Paul. They held up the Benson stage. Poor old Bud Philpot was killed."

Wyatt glanced at the telegram, looked up, and called out, "Faro bank's closed, folks." Then he turned to Bat. "Bat, you're deputized. I'll go get Virg and Morg and Doc."

"Doc left for Contention this morning," Bat said. "Told me he wouldn't be back till tomorrow."

"Well," said Wyatt, "he'll miss all the fun." Then he turned to Wilbur and told him, "You tell Mister Williams over at the office I'm forming a posse. I assume he'll join us."

"Yes, sir," said Wilbur.

Over at the Wells Fargo office Wyatt and Virgil and Morgan were with Bat and Marsh Williams, saddling up their horses and loading their firearms, making ready to leave, when Johnny Behan came running over with Harry Woods.

"What's going on here, Wyatt?"

Wyatt turned to Johnny Behan. There was no question that he did not like the man, nor did he wish him well, but this was a professional matter and he would conduct himself in that fashion.

"Benson stage got robbed," he said. "I'm leadin' out a posse. You want to come, you're welcome to."

Behan puffed himself up like a bullfrog and said, "You got a hell of a nerve. *You're* leadin' out a posse. If that stage was robbed it's outside of Virgil's jurisdiction," he said, looking at Virgil, then continuing with a good deal of self-importance. "It's a county matter, and I'm sheriff of Cochise County in case you forgot."

Wyatt just looked at him, his ice-blue eyes going dead as if there were an inner eyelid that slipped down over them, filtered out all life, all emotion, all compassion. It was a look that prudent men feared, the kind of look that preceded sudden death. "I ain't forgot, Johnny," he aid softly, "I ain't forgot nothin' about you."

There was a deadly silence as those gathered around wondered if the two lawmen might not fight it out then and there.

But this was a professional matter, and Wyatt was determined to hold his personal views in check and, more important, provide no opportunity for idle tongues to wag about the real reason for his enmity with Johnny Behan.

"You want to lead this posse," he said, "fine with me. . . . Only, let's stop talkin' and let's get goin'."

Behan seemed to sense Wyatt's reluctance to push their personal matters into the light of public scrutiny, and he perceived this as a weakness that he could exploit. "I'll lead it, all right," said Behan, "and I don't need you or your brothers." He made a derisive gesture with his hand in the direction of the Earps. "Harry and me can handle things just fine. You all can go about your business."

Wyatt stepped close enough to Johnny so that Johnny could see the blood pumping through the vein on Wyatt's temple. "That stage was carrying a mail sack. That makes it a Federal offense. These men are part of a Federal posse, and if you don't like that you can blow it out your keester. Let's ride!"

he said, and swung up into the saddle and led his men off into the night.

"Boy, he rubs me the wrong way," said Behan, eating the dust of the Federal posse that had just galloped out of town.

At the Drew Station, the posse found the stagecoach shot full of holes. Bob Paul was there with Wyatt, Bat, Virgil, Morg, and Marsh. There were two corpses on the ground with blankets over them. Wyatt pulled one blanket back, revealing the late Bud Philpot.

"Poor old Bud," Wyatt said.

Bob Paul shook his head, acknowledging the tragedy. "I feel terrible about it, Wyatt," he said. "I traded places with him 'cause his piles was botherin' him."

"Well," Morgan said, suppressing a laugh, "they ain't botherin' him no more."

"Morgan," Wyatt said sharply.

"Just havin' some fun, Wyatt," said his younger brother.

Virgil shook his head and turned to Wyatt. "I swear him and Doc has the same sense of humor."

That was a subject Wyatt wished not to go into. He was well aware of the influence of his friend upon his brother, so he turned his attention to another corpse instead. Wyatt pulled back the blanket off the other body and said, "Who's this?"

"He was a salesman," said Bob Paul, "on his way to Benson. Just caught a slug, that's all. They fired their shots. I whipped up the team and we got out of there, but not before Bud and the drummer here got hit."

Wyatt put the blanket back over the dead body. "So they didn't get away with anything, neither the shipment nor the mail?"

"Not a thing," Bob said. "It's almost like it was second-ary, you know?"

Wyatt and Virg exchanged looks. Then Wyatt turned back to Bob. "Philpot got hit with the first shots?"

"Yeah," said Bob Paul. "I think I recognized two of the fellas. Billy Leonard, and I think I saw Luther King holdin' their horses."

Wyatt put a hand on Bob's shoulder. "They could have been after you, Bob," he said.

"I expect they was after whoever was ridin' shotgun," replied Bob Paul.

"Could be," said Wyatt. "Could be not. Anyways it'll be daylight in a couple hours, then we can pick up their trail."

Back in Tombstone at the office of the sheriff of Cochise County, Johnny Behan was there with his patron, Mike Gray, who was in a purple rage at the former's incompetence.

"But I tried, Mike," whined Behan.

"I tried, Mike," the ex-Ranger mimicked. "You sound like my kid, except he wouldn't even whine like that. Now you get out of here, Behan, and if they catch anybody by God you make sure he winds up in your jail! Got it!?"

At dawn Wyatt and his posse were saddling up their horses at the Drew Station, when Johnny Behan and Harry Woods came riding up.

"Shoot," said Virgil, spilling out what remained of the coffee in his cup. It was a wretched concoction that the local stationmaster brewed by simply dumping grounds in tepid water.

Virg figured he would've been better off eating the grounds and washing it down with the water. But he turned his attention back to Behan. "You're just in time, Johnny. We're goin' out to pick up these desperadoes' trail. Make a real colorful story for the *Nugget*."

"The trail?" Behan said incredulously. "The trail's cold by now, Virg. There's no point in it."

Wyatt, who had had some of the same coffee, was in a foul mood too. He swung up into his saddle. "Then don't come, Johnny," he said, and wheeled his horse and started off with his men following.

The enlarged posse rode through the countryside, with Bat and Wyatt reading trail signs. By midafternoon they were on a hill above the Redfield ranch, looking down at it. Wyatt and Bat dismounted from their horses. Johnny crossed over to them. The rest of the posse stayed mounted.

"Trail looks like it leads down to that ranch," Bat said.

"That's the Redfield place," said Wyatt.

"Is this Redfield one of the rustlers?" asked Bat.

"No," Wyatt said. "But most of the ranchers around here are friendly to the Clanton gang. Some of 'em even keep a pot of beans on for 'em so they can drop in day or night."

"I don't get it," said Bat. "Since when do ranchers like rustlers?"

"The rustlers don't steal from them," Wyatt told him. "They steal from the Mexicans and then drive the beef across the border and sell it cheap to the local ranchers. Then the ranchers blend 'em in with their herds and sell 'em to the Army."

"That's a vicious rumor, Wyatt," Behan said, sticking up for his electorate.

Wyatt looked at him and, in an offhand way, said, "Shut up."

The posse, minus Wyatt and Marsh Williams, rode down into the ranch. Rancher Redfield came out to talk with them. Johnny Behan elected himself not only unofficial spokesperson but town crier as well.

"Mister Redfield," he said in a very loud voice that echoed off the mountains, "my posse and I are tracking the alleged robbers of the Benson stage. There is a possibility that those tracks may have led to your ranch."

"Why don't you talk a little louder, Johnny," said Virgil. "There still might be one person in the territory of Arizona who didn't hear ya."

Shortly thereafter, a scraggly cowboy, Luther King, was stealthily leading his horse off on foot through the mesquite and scrub brushes, trying to sneak away from the ranch. He walked straight into Wyatt and Marsh Williams's drawn Colts.

"Hi, Luther," Wyatt said.

And Luther screamed, "Ahh!"

"Little jumpy, huh?" inquired Wyatt.

"You scared me, Wyatt," Luther complained.

"Sorry, Luther," Wyatt said almost sweetly. "You know Marsh Williams, don't ya . . . the Wells Fargo agent."

"Why you got those guns out, Wyatt?" said Luther. "What you all want with me?"

"You got no idea?" asked the Wells Fargo man.

"No, sir," Luther said.

Wyatt put his mouth close to Luther's ear in a gossipy fashion. "Benson stage got robbed last night," he said, "At least they tried to. What happened was they wound up killin' a couple people. We followed the tracks right to this ranch. One of the horses threw a shoe. . . . Looks like your horse threw a shoe, Luther."

"I don't know nothin' about it," Luther said, stealing a look back at his horse.

"You sure?" asked Wyatt, as if he had just offered someone a cup of coffee and they said, no, thanks.

But Luther was indignant nonetheless. "My horse threw a shoe," he said. "But that ain't a crime."

The conversational tone now vanished from Wyatt's voice. "Maybe not. Maybe I can think one up by the time we get back to Tombstone. Drop your gun there, Luther. . . . You're under arrest. You want to tell me who else was with you?"

"I don't know what you're talkin' about," Luther said, dropping his gun belt. "Go ahead and arrest me. . . . I ain't worried about no trial."

Wyatt looked at the man. He could beat it out of him, that was certainly true, and it was equally true that Wyatt had enjoyed a good deal of success as a lawman by cracking people's skulls. But in this instance he thought trickery might be more productive. And so he feigned an innocent air and said, "A trial's gonna be the least of your worries. If I were you I'd be worried about Doc Holliday."

"Doc Holliday," said Luther, looking up in fear at the mention of the killer's name. "What's he got to do with anything?"

Wyatt put a friendly arm around Luther's shoulder. "Why," he said, "Big Nosed Kate was on that stage . . . didn't you know? One of the bullets hit her, killed her deader than a tin of corned beef. You know how Doc felt about Kate, don't you, Luther?"

Luther gulped. "I know they was together."

"Together?" Wyatt said incredulously. "Why, the man was devoted to her. Positively devoted."

Luther was growing edgier every second.

"You know," said Wyatt, "Doc is really the only guy I ever seen who would actually just step out into the street with somebody just to shoot with them. You know, not 'cause he was angry . . . I seen him sittin' at a table once and a fella said something about Kate. Just a word, Luther . . . I believe it was about her nose. But it doesn't really matter.''

He spoke like a Dutch uncle explaining the dangers of life to a favored nephew.

"Doc just sat there sippin' his whiskey, cool as can be, and he says, you go along now, go out into the street and I'm just gonna finish my drink and then I'll come along and kill you.''

Wyatt looked at Luther. Luther looked at his boot.

"You got somethin' on your boot there, Luther? You keep on looking at it.''

"Did he do it, Wyatt?'' Luther asked quietly.

"What . . . oh, kill the guy?'' said Wyatt, enjoying law enforcement for the first time in a very long while. "Sure. Just like he said he would. And all that fella did was insult Kate's nose . . . let her rest in peace,'' he added respectfully.

Wyatt looked to see the effect this tale had on its audience. "Yeah,'' he said, stretching luxuriously as if *he* hadn't a care in the world. "If I was you I'd sure as hell rather be in a nice safe jail than out on the street with Doc Holliday lookin' for me.''

Luther clutched at Wyatt's arm like a drowning man for a float.

"I didn't fire a shot,'' he said. "You got to believe that, Wyatt. Doc's your friend . . . you got to make him believe it.''

"Now, now,'' said Wyatt, trying to reassure the frightened wretch. "You tell me who did fire those shots and I'll make sure he knows it wasn't you.''

Luther looked relieved for the tiniest second, until Wyatt added, "Provided, of course, that I can find some way to penetrate the poor man's veil of grief.''

Wyatt walked Luther, all tied up, over to an empty horse and lashed his hands to the saddle horn. Johnny Behan was busy arguing jurisdiction, but Wyatt would have none of it.

"We already had this conversation back in Tombstone, Johnny. He's my prisoner and it's my arrest.''

"Okay, look, Wyatt,'' said Behan in a conciliatory fashion. "Maybe I was a little out of line back in town. I was afraid you were steppin' into my jurisdiction. You already stepped into my jurisdiction in a personal way, so—''

Wyatt cut him off ice cold. "You might not want to go where this conversation's headed, Johnny."

"But this is different, Wyatt," Johnny said quickly. "Hell, I was fond of old Bud, and there coulda been women and kids on that stage. My own mother's comin' out to visit in a few weeks and she coulda . . . Anyways, what I'm saying is if you make the arrest, what's he gonna get? All you got on him is *attempted* mail robbery. That's the only Federal law he broke. If I make the arrest, I got him on accessory to murder."

Wyatt thought that one over. There was no doubt that Behan was right. "Marsh!" Wyatt called.

Marsh Williams looked up.

"Sheriff Behan's taking Luther back to Tombstone," Wyatt said. "Why don't you ride along with him, make sure he actually gets there."

Behan turned to Wyatt with an expression of shocked disappointment upon his countenance. "Are you casting aspersions on my integrity, sir?"

Wyatt looked him up and down. "Yup," he said. "And your sense of direction, too. Let's ride!"

CHAPTER TWENTY-ONE

Marsh Williams, Johnny Behan, and Harry Woods rode with their forlorn prisoner, Luther King, whose hands were shackled behind him on the horse back toward Tombstone. When they reached the town, Williams, Behan, and Woods led Luther's horse with Luther on it, hands still tied behind his back, through nighttime Tombstone and on to the Cochise County sheriff's office and jail facility. They dismounted, helping Luther down.

Behan said, "All right, Luther m'lad, down you go."

Marsh Williams stood there watching the proceedings as Behan turned to him, all Irish charm.

"Well, Mr. Williams," he said, "I've enjoyed your company and companionship on the trail. It's been a true slice of heaven havin' ya at me side." So saying, he pushed Luther over toward Harry Woods. "Deputy Woods," said Sheriff Behan, feeling the full weight of his badge upon his breast, "escort the prisoner to the hoosegow, if you please, and incarcerate him therein."

Williams did not seem to be buying this charade and continued to keep an eagle eye on Johnny Behan.

"You're welcome to come and tuck the prisoner in if it'd

make you feel any better, Mister Williams. He is *my* prisoner now, and he's in *my* jail.''

''And if I were you,'' said Marsh Williams, ''I'd make sure he stayed there.''

''Oh, Mister Williams,'' Behan said, feigning fatigue. ''If you were me you'd have a much more interesting love life, too, I'd expect. Nighty-night.''

So saying, Behan followed Woods and Luther into the jail building as Williams walked off. Shortly thereafter Johnny Behan moved stealthily out the back door of his jail, through the alley, and down the street, making sure that no one saw him, and then entered the office, where a light still burned. Once inside, Behan sat with Mike Gray over a glass of sipping whiskey.

''Okay,'' he said, ''I've got Luther safe, locked up in my jail, and the brothers Earp are still out prancin' around in the boonies. What do I do now?''

Mike Gray sat back expansively, took a languorous puff off his cigar and a long sip off his Kentucky whiskey, and sighed. ''Now, Johnny boy, you pay a call on a lady.''

Fly's Boardinghouse was the abode of Big Nosed Kate, and it was there that Johnny Behan appeared with a bottle in his hand, a smile upon his face, hope in his heart . . . and knuckles knocking on her door.

''All right, all right,'' said Kate from within, in her peculiar accent. ''Hold up your pants.'' She opened the door.

''Good evening, Miss Harony,'' said Johnny Behan.

''Evening, my arse,'' came the reply. ''It's the middle of the night.''

''Where's Doc?'' said the sheriff of Cochise County, getting down to business.

''Why?'' asked Kate. ''Got a toothache?''

''No . . .''

''Then get lost,'' said Doc's paramour, stepping back into the lantern light of their love nest.

''Miss Harony,'' Johnny said, ''I'd like to come in if I might.''

''I'm the madam, not one of the girls anymore. . . . Doc's the only one who comes in here at this hour.''

''Please, Miss Harony,'' said Behan, exercising all the charm at his disposal. "We'll leave the door open so as not to sully your reputation. I have a few questions I'd like to ask."

"Not interested," said Kate, starting to close the door in his face.

Being a former salesman, Johnny moved his foot forward to act as doorjamb as he all but cooed, "It's about Doc and that little tart from Madame LeDeau's." Suddenly Big Nosed Kate was interested as Johnny continued. "Lizette the Flying Nymph, I believe is her name. You did know about them, didn't you?"

He could see the blood rise in Kate's eyes.

"My Doc and that slut?"

Behan placed a hand over his heart in sympathy for her predicament. "In the words of the bard," he said, " 'tis true 'tis pity and 'tis pity 'tis true. Doc's been dipping his wick in a different batch of oil."

"I'll kill him."

"I can help."

"Come on in," said Big Nosed Kate, and he did.

At about the same time, a horse was tied up outside the back of the Cochise County sheriff's office and jail.

The back door opened and Harry Woods poked his head out, making sure that no one was around. Then he looked back into the jail.

"It's clear," he said, "come on."

Out stepped Luther King, who looked around cautiously and then mounted up. Harry Woods grabbed hold of the reins and said, "You don't stop till you get to Old Man Clanton's, you hear?"

"Brother, you don't need to tell me twice," said Luther, who spurred the horse and galloped out of town.

At sunrise, Doc Holliday, who was drunk, drove a buckboard up the road toward Tombstone. He drank from the bottle that sat at his side as he sang a little ditty to the tune of "Jeannie With the Light Brown Hair."

"I dream of Jeannie with a big brown bear . . .
Jean-nie liked haa-iir so she married the bear . . .
Oh I dream of Jeannie with a big broo-wwnn——"

Just then he heard Johnny Behan's voice call out: "Throw your hands up, Doc. And don't give me an excuse to kill you!"

Behan and Woods stepped out into the road with their weapons pointed at Doc.

"If you need an excuse," Doc said with disdain, "you haven't got the guts." Thus, paying Behan no mind, Doc continued driving the buckboard. But the sheriff of Cochise County fired off a load at the horse and dropped the poor animal in its tracks, thus effectively halting Doc's progress.

"Well," said Doc, "you're hell on wheels against horses, I'll grant you that."

"John Holliday," the sheriff of Cochise County shouted out, "you are under arrest for murder."

CHAPTER
TWENTY-TWO

The following night, Mike Gray's black-on-black horse and rig rode out through the desert countryside between Tombstone and Old Man Clanton's ranch. Once at the ranch, Gray pulled up his rig, dismounted, and entered the house, bellowing out, "Newman! Newman! Where are you, you ancient degenerate."

Old Man Clanton entered the living room from his bedroom, hurriedly fastening his pants, somewhat out of breath and just a little flushed. He had his long johns on with the tops showing.

"I don't like being called a degenerate in my own home, Mike."

Mike Gray ignored the comment and asked, "Where is he? Where's Luther?"

"I have him hidden out with friends," said Clanton.

"I have a job for him."

"He's going to want to lay low, Mike," Clanton said.

But Mike Gray had other plans. "He can lay low in Kansas. Let's go."

* * *

A week later in Dodge City, Kansas, not far from the Alamo Saloon, six cowboys gathered together in a tight semi-circle in a little alleyway. Chief among them was Luther King. He spoke with another cowboy named Wesley, who pointed at several figures crossing the street, coming toward the Alamo Saloon.

"See those three over there?" he said.

"Yeah," said Luther. "Which one's Bat Masterson's brother?"

"That one on the end," Wesley said. "On the right side. That's him . . . Jim Masterson. He's had a fight goin' on with his partner, A. J. Peacock. Everybody knows about it. They been threatening to kill each other for weeks."

"Sounds good to me," said Luther. "Long as they can't tie it to me or my boss."

Jim Masterson and two companions neared the Alamo Saloon. Suddenly from out of the shadows a horse and wagon came careening directly in front of them. The three men all jumped back as the tarp over the back of the wagon was thrown off, revealing five gunmen with Luther King driving the rig. The gunmen opened fire, hitting Masterson and his companions. Jim Masterson was torn with bullets and fell to the ground writhing in pain. Luther shouted out to him, "Hey, Jim, your pal A. J. Peacock says hello." Then the wagon sped down the street out of sight.

The news got back to Tombstone, and within short order, Bat Masterson and Luke Short, who was, after all, Jim Masterson's best friend, departed with apologies to the Earps for Dodge City, Kansas. In one stroke, Mike Gray had depleted the Earps' forces by two of their most formidable soldiers.

Wyatt, Virgil, and Morgan Earp went, meanwhile, to make sure Doc was still alive in Johnny Behan's jail, and second of all, to hear from him what the hell had happened.

"Well," said Doc, none the worse for wear and even somewhat sober, "Behan put Luther in his jail and left Harry Woods in charge of him, and wouldn't you know it, why, somehow, Lord only knows how, Luther managed to escape. Then that weasel Woods writes in his paper, the *Nugget*, that he must have had help on the outside, and implicates me!

Well, of course Luther had help . . . but not on the outside, on the inside. Harry Woods! He's the one who let him get away."

Wyatt let out a sigh. "And what about this affidavit that Kate swore out against you?"

"Oh, well," said Doc. "That's nothin', Wyatt. You know Kate."

"Nothin'?!" Virgil exploded. "From what I heard it's an affidavit that says you confessed to her that you were in on the holdup and helped kill Bud Philpot."

Doc chuckled. "Yeah," he said, "but Kate was drunk when she wrote it. Behan took her out and tells her I was sneakin' around with that French tart who works over at Madame LeDeau's, and Kate has conniptions and then Behan gets her drunk, which of course in Kate's case isn't exactly the most difficult thing in the world, and she goes and signs this damn fool letter saying I'm guilty of murder. But it's nothin'. You know Kate. She was only jokin'. She'll cool down and tell 'em it's nothin'."

"It's more than nothin', Doc," said Wyatt, shaking his head.

"Ohhh . . ." Doc said. "Who's gonna believe a drunken whore?"

"Who's gonna believe *you*?" said Virgil.

Doc looked over at Virg knowing that what Virgil said was true, but he pushed on sheepishly nonetheless. "Well . . . she'll take it back."

The brothers exchanged dubious looks.

"I *know* she will," Doc continued. "She'll swear to everybody that it wasn't true."

"But by then," said Virgil, "half the people in this town will believe it *is* true."

"Well, by then half the people in this town can line up single file and kiss my skinny tubercular ass."

Morgan laughed, but Virgil said, "Doc! It's not just you! They implicate you and there's rumors goin' around now about us bein' involved, because Wyatt's your friend and no matter what you do he always covers for you! And your attitude isn't helpin' us any here."

Wyatt put a hand out to Virgil. "I'm his friend because he saved my life, Virg."

"My attitude?" Doc shouted, not believing his ears. "I don't have an attitude! And just let some syphilitic pimp son of a whore say something against Wyatt in front of me and I'll kill him."

"Good thing old Doc doesn't have an attitude," Morgan said and laughed, and after a second they all joined in.

Harry Woods sat in his chair with his feet on the desk and jumped up as the door to the cells opened and Wyatt, Virgil, Morgan, and Doc Holliday walked into the sheriff's office. Wyatt hung the keys up on the peg.

"Here's your keys," Wyatt said politely.

But Woods, looking at Doc Holliday, sputtered and stammered, "What's he doin' . . . what you doin'? You can't take him . . . he's a prisoner. He's a— Just a second there. He's an accused felon."

Morgan looked in shock at Doc. "Is that true, Doc?"

"I'm afraid it is, Morgan," Doc said.

"You *can't* take him," Deputy Woods said to Wyatt.

"If you need him," Wyatt said, "he'll be in *my* custody. I just want to make sure he doesn't get shot trying to escape. People *do* have a habit of escaping from this jail, from what I hear."

Outside, Wyatt, Doc, Virgil, and Morgan walked down the street. A storekeeper with a self-righteous air who was reading a copy of the *Nugget* that carried a headling proclaiming: "Earps Implicated in Holdup Murder," called out to the brothers and Doc as they passed, "It's a black day when we have to fear our own law enforcement in this town, *Marshal*."

Morgan turned to answer him. "Hey, why don't you—"

"Forget it," said Wyatt to his hot-tempered younger brother.

At Virgil's house, Wyatt, Morgan, Virgil, and Doc sat in the parlor passing a bucket of beer from one to the other.

Wyatt said, "We need somebody from inside the Clanton gang to give up Leonard and Head and Crane. They're the three that Luther King said were in on the holdup, and they work for the Clantons."

He passed the bucket to Virgil. "What about Ike Clanton?" said Virgil. "From what I hear, there's no love lost between him and his pa. And he's jealous of Curly Bill and Johnny Ringo 'cause they're higher up than he is.''

"Him and the McLaury brothers might help," said Morgan. "Wells Fargo is offerin' thirty-six hundred dollars' reward. You could buy those three for a lot cheaper than that.''

Wyatt thought it over for a moment. "Might be worth a shot, at that,'' he said.

The bucket of beer had now come to Doc. He took a sip and then looked at all three of the brothers. "Might . . .'' he said. "Course, you know sooner or later we're gonna have to kill them.''

Wyatt looked at Doc for a long time before he spoke. "No I don't, Doc. I don't know anything of the kind.''

Springtime signals the onset of numerous activities, from young love to melting snows that give way to carpets of wildflowers. For the cattleman it is time for the roundup. Rustlers, on the other hand, must be patient. Their time comes only once the cattle have been brought down from winter quarters and fattened on the new grass that springs up as if by magic seemingly overnight, turning dirt-brown hillsides to the color of money. Thus, late May and early June become the time of the rustler.

There were campfires outside on the Clanton ranch land with cowboys grabbing a last cup of coffee, a last biscuit or bite of beans, something warm to take the early-morning chill out of the air. Preparations were under way for a trip. Cowboys were tying on bedrolls, sticking last bits of food into oilcloths and putting them in their saddlebags. All this was supervised by Old Man Clanton. Off to the side, Mike Gray walked with his son Dixie Lee, who limped along next to Papa. There was something tender about this scene, a powerful and proud father explaining the family business to his son, obviously in the hopes that the boy would someday be able to run it as efficiently as his dad.

Mike had his arm around the boy as he walked and said, "Now we've gotten Bat Masterson and Luke Short out of the picture, so the Earps are a little bit weaker. We've gotten Doc Holliday implicated in a murder . . . now they're a little weaker still. And because Doc is implicated, they're implicated. The hoi polloi don't trust them so much anymore. Isolate them, you see, son?"

"I guess so," said his boy.

"Cut their power base," Mike continued, trying to illustrate his point. "That's what I'm talking about. Nothing happens in a vacuum. Everything has its context. Remove them from their power base, isolate them from their allies, and they're defeated—"

Mike was about to complete his sentence when his son Dixie Lee spoke up, delighted at understanding his father's logarithm. ". . . without a battle!" he said. "We defeat them without ever having to fight them!"

Mike fairly burst with pride.

"That's my bright boy," he said, hugging his son. "You're smarter than all these hyenas put together," he said, indicating the Clantons.

"Then why can't I stay with you, Pa," Dixie Lee asked his father, and it was clear how much the boy loved him. "Why do I have to ride with Old Man Clanton?"

"Because I need you to, son," said Mike. "You're my eyes and ears. You're the only one I can trust. See, that's the power the Earps have, and I respect them for it. They have a real sense of family . . . not like these hyenas. They'd sell their own grandmothers for a ha'penny *and* deliver."

The following day, in a vacant lot behind some buildings in Tombstone, Wyatt walked with Ike Clanton and Frank and Tom McLaury. Wyatt had just put an offer on the table, and Ike was obviously interested.

"Thirty-six hundred dollars? You sure?" said Ike. He was definitely the stupidest and possibly the greediest of Old Man Clanton's sons.

"I'm sure, Ike," said Wyatt. "I saw the wire from Wells Fargo's San Francisco office offering the reward."

"How do we know we can trust you?" asked Tom McLaury, who had never trusted anyone.

"I want the glory of catching those three," Wyatt explained, "because I want to run against Johnny Behan in the next election. This will put me over the top."

Ike scratched his head. The effort of thought made him

itch. "Is that reward good dead or alive? 'Cause I want 'em
dead. They're in Mexico with my old man now, but if we
trick 'em into comin' down so you can arrest them, I don't
want them being able to tell Curly Bill or my ol' man that we
was the ones what gave 'em up."

"The reward's good dead or alive," said Wyatt. "Now
. . . are you sure you can deliver those three?"

"Of course we can," Ike said. "They trust us. We're their
friends."

A large herd of cattle was being driven across the Mexican
border to the U.S. side by Old Man Clanton and his band of
men.

"I never breathe easy on these things until we cross back
into the good old U.S. of A.," said Clanton, who felt particularly patriotic after every cross-border raid.

He and his men drove the herd up through a canyon. On a
mountain, looking down into the canyon through which Clanton and his men drove their herd of cattle, were a hundred
and seventeen Mexicans, with sombreros at their sides or on
their backs as they looked down through rifle sights at the
American rustlers whom they were about to slaughter.

Outriders pushed strays toward the center of the canyon,
while somewhere up ahead a scout came racing back along
the flank of the herd at full gallop toward Old Man Clanton.
The scout's name was Billy Leonard.

"Newman . . . Newman," he called out.

"Settle down, you lunatic. You're scarin' the cows."

"We got a little trouble up ahead," Leonard said.

"What?"

"Blockin' party," said the scout. "I seen them, they didn't
see me. Ten, maybe twenty men waitin' up at the mouth of
the canyon."

"They wasn't Apaches, was they?" said Clanton, momentarily afraid.

"Oh no, hell no. Mexicans," Leonard said.

"Mexicans!" Old Man Clanton laughed.

"Ten or twenty Mexicans."

"Mexicans . . ." Clanton laughed again. "Well, that's
different. You had me goin' for a second. Thought it was

Apaches. Felt my bunghole pucker. But Mexicans . . . hell, we'll go through them like pellets through a goat.''

Newman laughed again, a wheezy laugh that was punctuated by the hole that exploded in his upper right chest. The blood spurted out and Newman Clanton looked down, confused until he heard, finally, the crack of the rifle from which the bullet had just been fired.

He put his hand over the hole in his chest, looking down at it and then all around as, suddenly, three more new holes exploded in his torso and one tore through his leg as the sound of gunfire echoed around him.

''Whoa,'' he tried to say, reining in his horse and coughing up blood. He was a dead man whose body had not yet dropped and continued to function on sheer meanness. He pulled out his gun and clumsily dismounted, looking around for someone to shoot.

''Where are ya, ya yella Mexican bastards?'' he said, falling to one knee, then trying to stand, his eyes rolled back in their sockets. ''Oh Lord,'' he said. ''Oh Lord, forgive me.'' And he pitched forward onto his face and died sucking dust and his own blood.

From the mountain overlooking the canyon, a whole line of Mexicans exploded with continuous gunfire, raining down upon the rustlers there below. The cattle, panicked by the gunfire, scattered in all directions as the cowboys, realizing they were in a death trap, pursued their various visions of salvation.

Billy Leonard spurred his horse forward, trying to get out of the gunfire.

Head and Crane wheeled their horses toward the canyon walls to try to make it to the beckoning safety of several scrub bushes and rocks. Head's horse was shot and went down. Crane's horse tripped over Head's, sending Crane up and over and landing with the sickening crunch of bones that broke in his neck and killed him instantly. The bullets that slammed into his body were redundant.

And Dixie Lee dismounted, like a frightened child. He was unable to hold the reins, and his horse bolted away from him. He stood there like a little boy who had just lost his mother's hand in a crowd. He looked about as men and animals coughed and snorted and groaned in death agonies all around him. As the dust swirled up, choking Mike Gray's gimpy kid, his gun came out, was there in his hand as he looked around and saw no one to shoot at, only muzzle flashes in the distance. He said nothing, only made little whimpering noises. He tried running for the rocks and was shot in the leg, in his poor, crippled leg.

"Oh God oh God oh God oh God oh God . . ." he said as he fell and ripped open his pants leg to see the wound, exposing the brace that was on this leg. As bullets splattered around him in the dust, he tried to move again. Two more bullets slammed into him, one in his shoulder, one in his other leg, and he called out again more like a terrified child, screaming, "Stop it!"

Leonard raced for the mouth of the canyon, whipping and spurring his horse mercilessly. Up in front of him he saw the blocking party of which he earlier spoke.

He saw the muzzle flashes and little puffs of smoke and heard the whiz of bullets. He reined his horse in and whirled it about.

Mexicans came down off their mountain, into the canyon, slaughtering whatever cowboys were left alive. There was no way out, and he knew it. He looked around, panicked, and suddenly his horse reared and bucked and he was thrown.

The horse raced off and he pulled himself up, grabbed his handgun, and yelled out, "All right . . . come and get me. Come on, come and get me!"

Dixie Lee crawled toward the rocks. Blood poured from his wounds, seventeen in all. Dixie crawled another step and then another until he came to a pair of torn Mexican boots that stood in front of him. His eyes followed the boots up to the face of the bandito, who looked down at him with a gun in his hand pointed straight at Dixie Lee's head. Dixie looked at him, knowing this was the end. He bowed his head a little and said, "Oh, Daddy."

He shut his eyes tight against the sound he knew was coming. But it did not come. He could take it no longer, and so opened his eyes, stared up at the bandito, and screamed, "Shoot me!"

* * *

A dusty patrol of light horse cavalry entered the mouth of the canyon with no sense of foreboding or mission, only the boredom of soldiers on duty on a hot dusty day, a hundred miles from nowhere.

All of them had that same glazed look except for the one middle-aged grizzled sergeant who saw the buzzards. "Lieutenant . . ." he said, and pointed.

The cavalry patrol rode up through the street in Tombstone. There was a wagon drawn by a team of horses driven by the sergeant. In the back of the wagon, corpses. Wyatt saw them and approached the wagon.

Mike Gray was sitting at his desk going over some papers when Wyatt walked in. Mike looked up in surprise. "God, you look glum, Earp," he said. "Been accused of another crime lately?"

"No," said Wyatt quietly.

"Well . . . you got something to say? Say it," said Mike. "I'm a busy man."

"A platoon of cavalry just rode into town," Wyatt said. "They came across a group of Americans who had been ambushed by Mexicans. The Americans evidently stole some cattle south of the border. The Mexicans pursued them and set an ambush in Skeleton Canyon. The three outlaws who were suspected of robbing the Benson stage were among those killed. So was Old Man Clanton . . . and so was your son."

Mike sat there unable to believe his ears. "This is . . . this is some kind of . . . this is a trick, isn't it, Earp?" he said, almost begging that it be so. "To get me to . . . to get me to . . . It's a trick. It's smart, I'll give you credit, but . . . but . . ."

"It's no trick, Mike," Wyatt said softly. "The only child I ever had died with my first wife. He never even got born, and she was just nineteen. I know what family means. I know how you felt about your boy. . . . I'm sorry."

Mike suddenly seemed very, very old to him. His eyes brimmed but no tears came down his face. His head, almost imperceptibly at first, started to bow.

Wyatt spoke. "I had them put your son's body over at the doctor's. I thought you might want to . . . I'm very sorry."

Mike just sat there, and then almost inaudibly, said, "Thank you."

The shingle out front identified the office of Doctor Thaddeus McGraw. Slowly, shakily, Mike Gray crossed the dirt street toward the office. He paused ever so slightly before opening the door.

Dixie Lee's body lay on the examining table under a bloodstained sheet. The only sounds in the room were Mike's breathing and somewhere a fly buzzing on his boy's body. Mike swatted out at the fly. Then as he pulled the sheet back he gasped. His head shook back and forth as he looked down at the ruined body of his only child.

Lying next to his son was the bloodstained leg brace Dixie Lee had hated so because it made him different from the other children. Mike remembered it, remembered holding the frail child crying in his arms, remembered telling him that he was different, that he was special, that he was the "specialest" boy in the whole world to his daddy. Mike remembered the little boy's arms around his neck and the child's tears against his cheek, remembered rocking him until the tears subsided, until everything was all right once again. There was a time when Mike Gray could make everything for his son all right once again. Mike looked at the brace, picked it up, rocked back and forth, held it to his chest, and made the same little whimpering sounds that his son had made in the face of death.

On the sidewalk in front of the doctor's office, two little girls played jacks, a dog sat sleeping in the sun, and a man was tying his horse to the hitching rail on which a large crow perched.

The explosion of the gunshot from within the doctor's office made the little girls and the sleeping dog, the horse, and the fat bird jump.

CHAPTER
TWENTY-THREE

Hours later, a buckboard was silhouetted on a mesa outside of Tombstone at sunset. There was a blanket near it on the ground on which Josie sat looking up at Wyatt, who stood, his back to her, looking off into the distance.

"I feel so . . ." He left the sentence uncompleted and shook his head, unable to find the words, but it was obvious that he needed to talk, and so Josie would listen and pull the words out of him if they would not come of their own accord.

"What?" she said. "What is it?"

"I don't know," said Wyatt. "He told me I was no different than him."

"That's not true," she said.

"Isn't it?"

"No!" And she was on her feet next to him, not yet touching but close enough so he could feel her next to him.

"He had a moral line somewhere that he wouldn't cross," Wyatt said. "Mine is just in a different place. A little closer in maybe, but . . ." He was quiet, and then, "He loved his son."

"That doesn't excuse anything," said Josie, who was not about to excuse anything.

157

"I wasn't looking to excuse him," Wyatt said, taken aback by the ferocity of her tone. "He loved his son, that's all. And I expect his boy loved him. It makes you wonder . . . what it's all for. What's the point?"

Josie took Wyatt by the arm and turned him to her. When she spoke, it reminded him of his father, unyielding, unforgiving, as if her words were to be written into stone. "I'll tell you something," she said, "and I won't apologize for it either. He wanted you dead, and so I'm glad he's dead. Period. That's the end of it."

Wyatt shook his head and almost smiled at her. "Is it?" he said.

"Old Man Clanton is dead. Gray, Leonard, Head, Crane. Half their gang, and most important, the leaders. It's got to be over now," she said, moving closer to him and linking her arm through his.

"Maybe," Wyatt said, "but I don't think so. He once told me he was the one who was keeping a lid on things. I think that was true."

"You don't know that," she said, and huddled closer to him as the wind kicked up from the shallow canyon and blew cold across the mesa.

"Don't I?" he said, putting his arm around her and then turning to her again. "Imagine what Doc and Morg would do if Virgil or I weren't around to . . . keep a lid on things."

The following day Ike Clanton rode up to his father's ranch, got off his horse, and walked into his father's house. He had heard nothing about the massacre in Skeleton Canyon.

And, since he saw nothing amiss, he went about the business of betraying his comrades. He walked into the ranch house looking for his father.

"Hey," he shouted in a surly fashion. "Anybody home?"

"Your pa's dead," came the voice of Curly Bill Brocious.

Ike turned and saw Curly Bill and Johnny Ringo sitting, splitting a bottle with their feet up on the dining-room table. A killer named Pony Deal was passed out drunk in the corner.

"Huh?" Ike said.

"Don't huh me, stupid!" said Curly Bill, and as if to add emphasis, he pulled out his gun and shot at Ike, narrowly missing his head. Ike ducked, raised his arms, rolled his eyes, and waved his hands in panic. "Wh-what are ya . . ." he stammered. "Don't shoot at me, Bill. Please."

"Your pa's dead, you understand?" Bill said, still tracking him in his sights.

"Sure . . . sure," said Ike. "It's okay with me. You say he's dead, he's dead."

"Mike Gray's dead," said Curly Bill, leaning forward across the table. "His gimpy kid Dixie's dead. Leonard, Head, and Crane are dead . . . and as far as I'm concerned, you're next."

Ike began talking fast to save his hide. "Me?" he protested. "Me? Why me? You don't need to kill me, Bill. Far as I'm concerned, if they're dead you're the boss . . . you and Johnny, I guess, huh? Well, that's fine with me . . . I guess you're takin' over the house and the ranch now too," he said, looking around the room in which he had been raised. "Well, okay . . . that's okay. so you got no reason to kill me."

"Sure we do," said Johnny Ringo, sneering over the bottle at Ike. "A little bird tells us that you were over in Contention drinkin' in a saloon braggin' about how you and the McLaurys were gonna split thirty-six hundred dollars 'cause you made a deal with the Earps to give up Billy Leonard and the others."

Ike took off his hat and threw it on the ground, the gesture of an honest man whose honor was being impugned. "Well, that's a lie, Johnny. . . . Bill, that's a lie. . . . That's a filthy, stinkin' lie," he said, and tried to think of what could be worse than a filthy, stinking lie. But filthy and stinkin' were as far as his imagination would carry him, so he simply said, "That's what that is. I wouldn't have done that. Who said somethin' like that . . . I'll bet it was one of the Earps just spreadin' stories or . . . or Doc Holliday maybe. He woulda said somethin' like that. He's a liar . . . yeah, that's it. They're all liars, Bill . . . you know that."

"We're through with strategy and plans," Curly Bill said. "You know? It's time to kill the Earps . . . once and for all."

"Well, I'm for that, Bill . . . sure, that's a great idea."

"Good," said Curly Bill, " 'cause you're gonna do it . . . you and the McLaurys. You go into Tombstone . . . talk it up, fair fight, all that crap," he said, rising. He walked over to the now even more terrified Ike Clanton. "Get 'em out in the open . . . we'll be there to back you up and we'll kill 'em.''

"Well," said Ike, thinking about the odds of living through a confrontation with Wyatt, Virgil, and Morgan Earp and Doc Holliday. He concluded that the odds of besting them in a gunfight were only slightly less than the odds that Curly Bill would keep his word and be there to back him up. "I don't know, Bill," he said, and then offered what he thought simple logic would dictate. "Why don't we just bushwhack 'em from behind—you know, one at a time. Kill 'em that way . . ."

" 'Cause I don't want to kill 'em one at a time. I want to kill 'em all at once . . . an' if you don't like that idea then I'll kill you. 'Cause I'm through thinkin' and I'm through talkin'. . . . It's killin' time."

Johnny Ringo had, however, prevailed upon Curly Bill to bide his time just a bit in order to consolidate their forces. The killings in Skeleton Canyon had weakened them by lessening their manpower. "Take some time," Ringo had said. "The Earps'll still be there to kill tomorrow and the next day. Let's just make sure we have enough men to kill 'em good."

By fall, they were ready. The Occidental Saloon had undergone new renovations, with a low guardrail to section off part of the establishment for a lunchroom. Eating lunch at a table were Morgan and Wyatt Earp. On the other side of the guardrail in the saloon section, Doc Holliday was sitting in on a game of cards, while standing at the bar off to the side was Ike Clanton.

Ike was drunk, and Doc kept an eye on him as he played. Ike was at that stage of drunkenness that most mean drunks aspire to; it is the point at which they feel an awful lot braver than they actually are. Doc coughed violently, prompting Ike to speak.

"Hey, Doc," he called.

Doc coughed again and threw down half a water glass of whiskey, holding up his hand in a gesture that implored Ike to wait just a moment.

"I got a cure for that cough," Ike said, feeling braver still. An evil gleam came into Doc's eye. He knew exactly where

Ike was going in this converstaion, and it was his destination of first choice as well. "Do you, Isaac?" he said soft as a cobra.

"Yeah, I got a cure for that cough."

"Well," said Doc, barely above a whisper, "we're all atwitter with expectation."

Ike was drunk enough either not to have heard or not to be able to focus his attention on what had been said, and so he simply pushed on.

"Yeah, tomorrow I'm gonna cure it for ya. Permanent."

Doc put down his water glass, scooted back his chair, and turned to face Ike. "Well, Mother always said never put off till tomorrow the people you can kill today."

Ike said nothing.

When Doc spoke again, it was very affably. It was always a great curiosity to those who knew him, the affection Doc seemed to feel for the people he killed. "You run along into the street now, my scabby little friend," he said. "And as soon as I finish this hand I'll be pleased to get a gun and come out and shoot you."

Ike tried to dismiss him with a drunken wave of his hand, but fear was eating through his stupor. "Not now," he said, "but it's comin'."

"Don't be a tease, Isaac," Doc said, and threw down the last of his drink. He folded his cards and turned to his companions, saying, "I'll sit this hand out."

Then he turned to Ike and spoke the two most frightening words Newman Clanton's eldest son had ever heard.

"Let's go."

As Ike's father would have said, he felt his bunghole pucker. "I . . . I . . . I ain't fixed right," he said. "I ain't got a gun."

"He ain't," Doc said, enunciating every word, "got a gun." Doc turned to the assembled, stretched his arms out wide, and cried, "Someone, please dear God, give this walking puss-ridden sty a weapon!"

Wyatt was just tucking his napkin under his chin, about to dig into the lunchroom's juicy fried chicken. He turned and spoke quietly to Morgan. "Morgan, you're a peace officer now. You ought to go over and break that up."

Morgan put his napkin on the table and stepped over the railing separating lunchroom from saloon, crossing over to Doc.

"Hey, Doc, come on. He's just drunk."

"There's no law against killing drunks, Morgan."

"There is if he's unarmed, Doc."

Doc looked Morgan in the eye and implored him as a friend. "Loan him your gun, Morg, please."

Morgan leaned in toward Doc and said in a voice low enough that he hoped his elder brother would not hear, "Doc, I'd do it in a second if Wyatt wasn't around, but he is, so . . ."

"All right," said Doc, disgusted once again at the petty injustices that it seemed to be his lot in life to suffer. "All right." He turned to the card table and said in a resigned voice, "I'm back in."

"Did you see him back down from me?" Ike Clanton whooped. "He's ascared of me. Oh, I love it." He started walking toward the door of the saloon and then turned back to Doc. "It's comin', Doc, and I won't be alone, either. I got brothers and friends too, and you're gonna be dead, Doc. You and the Earps with ya. Do ya hear me?"

Ike walked out into the street as Morg tried to soothe Doc's temper. "He's just a drunk," he said.

"He's drunk," Doc said thoughtfully. "But he's right. It's comin'. You know it, and I do too."

Within a week, when the sounds of nighttime Tombstone cut through the air, there occurred a beating whose outcome would seal the fate of Wyatt, his brothers, and all the men who were plotting to kill them. Rinky-tink piano music, boisterous shouts of cowboys and miners, harness and horses and wagon wheels cutting ruts deeper in the dirt streets formed the background to the sound of a woman screaming half in Spanish, half in English as she was being beaten by her husband.

The noise emanated from the Spence house. There were the sounds of furniture crashing and knuckles hitting flesh, punctuated by the same woman's heartrending screams. Suddenly the door was thrown open and Pete Spence, drunk, pock-marked, and mean-eyed, hurled a woman out into the street.

"Go on," he slurred, then shouted, "Go on, and don't come back until you're ready to apologize, ya Mexican slut." He slammed the door and crossed back to his bottle, sinking down into a chair.

The woman, whose name was Marietta, was still very much in the shadows. She got to her feet, wobbly, and mumbled to herself, "Okay, I fix you." When she said it, murder was in her voice. "*Hijo de puta!* I fix you good."

A short while later Josie, in her house in bed, alone, heard a pounding at her door. She got up frightened, lit her lamp, and moved to the door. "Who is it?" she said. "Who's out there?"

"It's Marietta Spence."

"Who?" said Josie.

She knew, however, that the voice belonged to a woman, and she was less afraid to open the door, especially seeing as how the woman's voice was Mexican-accented and therefore could not possibly be an Earp wife. She opened the door and now saw Marietta's ruined face.

"Oh my God," said Josie.

"*Mi esposo . . .*" Marietta said. "My husband, he rides with the Clantons and Curly Bill. You're Wyatt Earp's girl, yes?"

"How did you—"

"Yes or no?" said the Mexican woman, having no time for niceties.

"Yes," said Josie.

"So you better let me in if you want Wyatt Earp to live."

Wyatt's house was dark. The figure of a woman came walking quickly up the street. She approached the door and knocked. Wyatt was in bed next to the snoring Mattie. He heard the knock, got out of bed in his long johns, threw on a pair of pants, and opened the door to Josie.

"We have to talk," she said.

Wyatt turned and looked back into the room where Mattie slept. Then he walked down the street a little ways with Josie.

"Men are coming to kill you," she said. "They're coming to kill you and your brothers and Doc."

Wyatt looked at her closely. There was nothing hysterical about the way she said it. She just laid it out there like Wyatt would have done himself.

"How do you know this?"

"This woman, Marietta Spence, her husband rides with Curly Bill. Her husband beat her up, so now she wants to get even by telling me their plans."

She looked up at Wyatt. His pale eyes were dead serious, all business. "Go on," he said.

"Curly Bill and Ringo will send the Clantons and the McLaury brothers and Billy Claiborne into town to pick a fight with you. Then the rest of the gang will come in and they'll murder you and your brothers and Doc."

Wyatt said nothing.

"It's just what you said would happen," said Josie, watching to see his reaction. "We could leave, Wyatt," she said. "We could leave tonight . . . you and me."

Wyatt looked as if he had not heard her right. "Leave?" he said. Such a thing was incomprehensible to him. "I'm not gonna leave . . . my brothers and I are not gonna leave, Josie."

"Wyatt," said Josie, "you don't owe this town a thing. I don't care what John Clum says, half the people don't even *want* you here, Wyatt. The ranchers are in with the rustlers, and half the townspeople don't want to be caught in the middle of a war. *Ich hob dem in drerd arein*, Wyatt. The Clantons and the McLaurys and Tombstone . . . all of them. Let's leave."

How could she not understand? he thought in amazement. How could she not see what was the most important thing in his life? "It's not because of John Clum," he said, "or because we owe anything to anyone, or—"

"Then because of the badge. Is that it? Because if it is . . ."

"It's our home!" Wyatt said, and Josie just looked at him, truly surprised.

"It's our *home*," he said again fiercely, and then pointed with his finger. "That place is Virgil's . . . that place is Morgan's. That house over there is James's . . . that one's mine. We *live* here, Josie. My brothers and me. This is our home."

"Wyatt," she said, "it's nothing." What was he talking about, she thought to herself, understanding as little about him as he had understood about her. She looked around at the town. "It's a mining camp with . . . with bigger brothels and a few decent restaurants, but . . ."

"When I was a kid," Wyatt said quietly, "and the war had just ended and it ruined James, Josie, it turned him into . . . a drunk and a pimp. Our father packed us all up and put us in a wagon train and took us to California. And you know what that did to us? It ended us as a family, Josie. We picked up roots and we never put them down again. Instead of making it work in one place, we tried running away. My pa was running away from James's drunkenness and nightmares, but it didn't work."

Josie looked at him as if seeing the man for the first time.

"When my pa figured out that you couldn't run out on your troubles, he moved us back to Missouri. You know why?" he said. "We had family there. We could *be* a family there. It's where I wanted to start *my* family."

"What happened in Missouri, Wyatt?" Josie said very quietly.

"And then all those years bummin' around," Wyatt continued. "The buffalo hunts and cow towns where you got two dollars and fifty cents for every skull you cracked open . . ."

"What happened in Missouri, Wyatt?"

Wyatt looked at her, about to open a wound he had not touched in many years. He looked straight into her eyes.

"I loved a girl," he said. "I loved her more than I'll ever love anyone else as long as I live." Wyatt's pale eyes stared straight into Josie's, and she did not flinch.

"I married her and I felt our child move inside of her and she died and our child died and I wanted to. I burnt everything we owned . . . I poured kerosene over all of it and set a match to it and watched it burn." He stopped for what seemed like a long time, and then when he spoke again, his voice was cold-steel hard. "This is our home . . . my brothers and me . . . our family. We've staked it all on this place. It's the only home we're ever gonna have. No one's making me leave, Josie—not the Clantons, or the McLaurys, not Curly Bill . . . and not even you."

He let it sink in. Josie was quiet, then she made up her

mind. "Then give me a gun," she said. "Give me a gun and let me stand with you."

Now it was Wyatt's turn to look at her in surprise, as if seeing her for the first time.

"I'll kill anyone who tries to hurt you," she said, and held out her hand. "Give me a gun!"

"Go home, Josie," Wyatt said, and slowly smiled. "Thinking about you could get me killed."

Josie bristled at being sent home like a child. "Wyatt—" she started, but he cut her off.

"Chances are if Ike Clanton's involved this is all hot air. If not, we'll handle it. Go home."

Josie looked at him. "I love you, Wyatt." She watched him carefully to see the effect of her words as she spoke as honestly with him as he had done with her. "I love you more than I will ever love anyone else as long as *I* live. And I want to marry *you*. And I want you to feel *our* child move inside of me. And I will give you a family . . . me and *our* children. And I will be your home, Wyatt. . . . And I *won't* die on you. I swear that to you. I swear to God."

He had never met a woman like her. He had not known such a woman could exist.

"I'll go home now," she said, and added when she was far enough down the street so that he could not hear, *"Gottinu."*

The sun rose quick that morning, like God or fate saying, Let's go.

At his home, Wyatt was finishing breakfast. Mattie stood over him, haranguing.

"If you don't break it off with her I don't know what I'll do," she said, sobbing. "I swear to you, Wyatt . . . I don't know what I'll do. I'm not . . . strong enough to stand this, Wyatt."

Wyatt got up from the table and wiped his mouth.

"If you leave me, I'll kill myself, Wyatt . . . I'll commit suicide! I swear, swear before God almighty I'll kill myself if you leave me! You hear me!"

Wyatt said nothing.

"Talk to me, you coldhearted son of a bitch!"

Wyatt looked at her and spoke very calmly, as if talking

to a crazy person. "I have no time for this today, Mattie. There are men I may have to kill today. So I'm not in the mood."

He walked past her.

"You're never in the mood to talk to me!"

At Fly's Boardinghouse Doc was in bed, bottle in hand. In walked Kate. She pulled the bottle out of the unconscious dentist's hand and took a swig and then poked him awake.

"Doc," she said. "Doc . . . wake up."

Doc awakened. "What . . ." he said. "Oh, Kate dear. . . . Is that my bottle or yours?"

"Ike Clanton's in town," replied Big Nosed Kate. "He's armed and he's drunk and he's tellin' everyone he meets that he's gonna kill you if he finds you."

Doc got that old gleam in his eye. "Is he, now," he said, smiling despite his hangover and the early hour. "Well . . . if God lets me live long enough, he *will* find me."

Wyatt walked into the city marshal's office. Virgil and Morgan were already there. "Any word?" Wyatt asked.

"Supposedly Ike's got a Winchester and a pistol on him," Virgil said. "He's been up all night drinking and trying to screw up his courage to kill us, from what he says. Tom McLaury's somewhere in town too, and they're waiting for Billy Clanton, maybe Phinn and Frank McLaury, Billy Claiborne . . . and then the rest of the gang sometime later in the day." Virgil looked at his younger brother. "How do you want to handle this, Wyatt?"

"You're the city marshal, Virg."

Virgil just looked at him, and there was a silent understanding that though this was his jurisdiction and he was the older brother, Wyatt was the boss. "How do you want to handle this, Wyatt?" he said again.

"Okay," said Wyatt. "Let's find Ike, disarm him, take the wind out of his sails . . . see if we can't do the same thing with Tom before the others get here. These guys'll only have the guts to do something if they're together in a bunch. . . . Maybe we can intimidate 'em and send 'em packing."

"And if not?" asked Morgan.

Wyatt turned to him. "Frank McLaury's the best with a gun," he said. "Then his brother. Those are the first ones we have to kill if it comes to that."

"Well, wait a second, Wyatt," said Virgil, holding up a hand. "Come on. . . . We're not in the fight *yet*."

Wyatt looked at Virgil cold as can be. "Sure we are," he said.

Virgil pondered that, then reached resignedly into his desk and pulled out two stars.

"Here, put these on. . . . You're both deputized city policemen now and have a legal right to disarm anybody in the city limits."

Morgan and Wyatt put on the badges. Wyatt took off his gun belt and put the gun in his overcoat pocket.

"What are you doing?" Virgil asked.

"Puttin' my gun out of sight. No sense provokin' anybody to thinkin' I want a fight."

Wyatt walked up Allen Street looking for Ike, ready for action.

Virg and Morg headed up Fremont Street. As they turned the corner onto Fourth Street they saw Ike with his Winchester and six-shooter. He had his back to them. They started quickly toward him. Just then Wyatt appeared, turning up onto Fourth Street.

"I hear you're hunting for some of us, Ike," he said.

Ike was intent upon Wyatt and did not realize until too late that Virg and Morgan were behind him. Morgan grabbed the barrel of the Winchester and Virgil hit Ike over the head with his pistol, knocking him out. Virgil and Morgan collected Ike's guns and dragged him off to the courthouse for rapid arraignment.

In the courtroom, Ike stood before Judge Wallace, holding his sore head. Wyatt and Morgan were in the court sitting on a bench behind him.

"They hit me over the head, Judge," Ike complained. "I didn't even see them. I never did nothin'. They just hit me for nothin'."

"Mister Clanton," said the Judge, "it is illegal to carry firearms within the city limits. Your weapons are confiscated and you are hereby fined twenty-five dollars."

In the vestibule of the courtroom, Ike paid the bailiff and walked out to where Wyatt and Morgan stood.

"You'd be real smart to get out of town now, Ike," said Wyatt.

"You just wait," Ike said like a smack-faced brat. "You're not gonna live through the day. None of you are! I got friends on the way . . . I got brothers too!"

"You talk too much to be a fightin' man, Ike," said Wyatt. "But if you want to shoot with me, let's do it now!"

Ike was plenty scared but tried his own bluff. "You talk big now that you took my gun away," he said.

Morgan smiled, recognizing his cue. "You can borrow mine," he said helpfully, holding his gun out toward Ike.

"Oh, sure," Ike said. "When you got me outnumbered two to one . . . I'm not leavin' this courtroom! You want to murder me, you got to do it in front of the judge!"

"You goddamned coward," said Wyatt. "You make me sick. If you're smart you'll get out of town now while you still can." Wyatt pushed him aside and walked out.

Outside on the steps of the courthouse, Wyatt bumped into Tom McLaury.

"You want to fight too, McLaury?" he said.

Tom started to go for his gun when Wyatt slapped him across the mouth with his left hand, then pulled his gun out of his long coat's pocket and whacked McLaury over the head. McLaury crumpled to the ground, and Wyatt walked past him. His mood had soured some.

Wyatt headed for Hafford's Corner Saloon and Cigar Store. "I'll take one of these," he said, picking out a cheroot.

The clerk looked at him and said, "Talk is, someone's gonna get killed today, Wyatt, and that someone could be you and your brothers."

"Could be," said Wyatt. "That was ten cents for the cigar, right?"

"I can just put it on your tab, Marshal," said the clerk.

"Well . . . I don't know. All things considered, might be a good idea to get the cash," said Wyatt, putting ten cents on the counter.

And at the far end of the street, Frank McLaury, Billy Clanton, and Billy Claiborne rode slowly into town.

CHAPTER
TWENTY-FOUR

Wyatt stood outside the cigar store about to light up his smoke. Just then, Wilbur the telegraph operator from Wells Fargo came running up to him.

"Wyatt," he said breathlessly, "I just seen Billy Clanton, Billy Claiborne, and Frank McLaury ride in. They met up with Ike Clanton and Tom McLaury, and Ike told 'em how you took his gun away."

"And what'd they do?" Wyatt asked.

"Well, they just headed over to Spangenburg's Gun Shop to buy Ike a *new* gun, I guess."

Wyatt sighed. "I was hoping," he said, "for a little different reaction."

Through the window of Spangenburg's Gun Shop, Wyatt could see Frank and Tom McLaury, Ike and Billy Clanton, and Billy Claiborne. Frank McLaury's horse was not securely tied, and the animal walked up onto the wooden sidewalk and poked his head inside the door just as Wyatt pushed past the horse and entered the gun shop.

"What are you lookin' at, Earp?" said Frank McLaury. "It's not against the law to carry a gun if you're in a gun shop."

"No," said Wyatt, "It isn't."

"Not against the law to buy bullets, either," said Frank, putting a dollar on the counter. Spangenburg looked over at Wyatt.

"Better make that *two* boxes of cartridges there, storekeeper," said Frank. "I got some *more* friends who are comin' to town." He smiled pointedly at Wyatt and then turned back to the storekeeper. "Might as well buy them some bullets too."

"It's legal to have a firearm in a gun shop," Wyatt said, "And it's legal to have a gun at a livery stable when you're either comin' into town or leavin'. And that's just what you better do."

Wyatt started out of the store. The horse was standing on the sidewalk blocking his path. It was the kind of little irritation that could set a fella off, and Wyatt hauled off and busted the horse in the mouth and pushed it off the sidewalk.

"And keep your horse off the boardwalk," he said. "That's against the law too."

Wyatt walked back over to the cigar store, where Virgil and Morgan were approaching with Doc. Virgil carried a sawed-off shotgun with him. Doc was limping and carrying a cane and coughing so hard that Wyatt thought he would fall over. Doc offered Wyatt a cigar in between coughs.

"Care for a cigar, Wyatt?" he said. "I'm tryin' to cut down."

"That may not be a problem after today," said Morgan.

At about the same time, Frank and Tom and Ike and the two Billys entered the Dexter Corral.

"When's Curly Bill and Johnny supposed to be here with the others?" asked Ike.

"They'll be here, don't worry," said Frank. "They'll be here when they get here."

"Anybody got a bottle?" asked Ike. "I think I could use a snort."

Ike's brother Billy pulled a bottle out of his saddlebag and tossed it to Ike, who took a long swig.

At Hafford's, the three Earps and Doc Holliday stood in front of the store, smoking cigars and watching the street.

At the Dexter Corral the Clantons and the McLaurys and

Claiborne passed the bottle back and forth and what had started out as a pretty full bottle was now pretty near empty.

"What corral they comin' to?" Ike said.

"What?" said Frank.

"Curly Bill and Ringo and the rest," said Ike. "They comin' here?"

"I don't know," Frank said.

"Maybe they're coming over to the O.K. Corral. Maybe they're there right now, looking for us. I say we go over there. Maybe they're there," said Ike.

"Maybe," Tom McLaury said.

"So," said Ike, "let's go. . . . We can drink over there as good as we can drink over here."

The others shrugged their shoulders and left.

Back at Hafford's, the Earps and Holliday were still on the corner. The cigars in their mouths had burnt down to stubs.

Wilbur came over to Virgil. "Marshal," he said, "they left the Dexter Corral a while ago and then went over to the O.K. Corral. . . . Looks like they're waitin' for somebody."

"I say we go get 'em right now before the others get here," Morgan said.

"Well," said Virgil, "as long as they stay inside the O.K. Corral they haven't broken any law."

"Oh," said Wilbur, "they're not *inside* the corral, Marshal. . . . They're out in Fremont Street the other side of the vacant lot over by Fly's. They're talkin' about killin' you all, Marshal."

Wyatt turned to Virgil. "There's nothin' left to think about, Virgil," he said. "Let's go."

Virgil faced Doc and took his cane from him and gave Doc the shotgun. "Here," he said, "gimme that cane and you take this . . . put it under your coat so nobody sees it." He looked at Wyatt. "No use provokin' anybody," he reasoned.

"Provoke, my ass," said Morgan, "I've had enough of hittin' people over the heads, Virg, and enough of being threatened. I say they make a move against us this time, we *kill* 'em."

Doc smiled. "You know," he said, "I saved your life, Wyatt, but I swear I *love* Morgan."

"Well, I say we still might be able to arrest them, and if

we can, that's what I intend to do," said Virgil, brandishing Doc's cane.

Virgil and Wyatt walked in front and Doc and Morgan behind them down Fourth Street up to Fremont.

The Earps turned to the left on Fremont Street, walking up past the Epitaph Building toward the vacant lot between Fly's Photograph Gallery and the Harwood House out behind the O.K. Corral. Wyatt pulled his gun out of his overcoat pocket and held it at his side, ready for action and possible ambush as they walked down the street.

Down the street by Fly's, Johnny Behan was talking to the Clantons and the McLaurys and Claiborne. He turned and started back toward the Earp party.

Halfway down the street, Behan met them. "Now look," he said, "don't go down there or there'll be trouble."

"You're a policeman, Johnny," Virgil said. "You help us arrest them, then."

"There's no need for that. I've disarmed them," said the sheriff of Cochise County.

"Then there won't be any trouble, Johnny," Wyatt said in a deadly tone.

Wyatt and the others pushed past the sheriff. Having heard that the cowboys were not armed any longer, Wyatt placed his gun in his coat pocket, though he kept his hand in that pocket as well just to be on the safe side. Doc and Morgan came out from behind the two older Earp brothers and fanned out as they approached the Clantons and McLaurys. Tom McLaury stood next to his horse and his hand slowly went up to a Winchester in a sheath on the saddle. Ike stood off to the side a bit, and Claiborne moved next to him as the Earp party approached.

"All right, boys," said Virgil. "Throw up your arms!"

With that, almost simultaneously it was as if everyone understood what Virg said . . . or perhaps not. At any rate, Doc unfurled the coat and brought up the shotgun, though he didn't fire. Billy Clanton and Frank McLaury went for their guns.

"Hold on," said Virgil, "I didn't mean that!"

Virg shifted his cane from right to left hand and Wyatt, seeing Billy Clanton's gun come up, ignored it and drew on

Frank. Throughout, Wyatt's shots were rapid and on their marks. He moved neither left nor right, and he made no attempt to seek cover. He simply picked targets and shot. His brothers and Doc reacted in a more prudent fashion, crouching and trying to turn themselves into the smallest targets possible, but not Wyatt. He was not ducking. He was killing.

Billy's first shot went wild. Wyatt's first shot hit Frank in his belly, sending him down. Wyatt then turned and fired at Billy, hitting his arm and spinning him around into the dirt. Virgil, meanwhile, drew down on Billy Claiborne, who panicked.

"Oh God, don't shoot me!" he cried.

He ran, and Virgil kept his gun on him until he had run off the scene and into Fly's. Tom McLaury, meanwhile, got behind his horse and unsheathed the Winchester. He fired over the saddle, using the horse as a shield.

Ike threw open his coat, revealing he was unarmed. "Don't shoot me, Wyatt. I'm unarmed, I swear . . . please don't shoot!"

Wyatt, who had his gun on Ike now, didn't know whether to believe him or not, nor whether Claiborne had run off or was somewhere aiming at him or his brothers. "This fight's commenced!" Wyatt shouted. "Shoot or get out!"

Ike ran off just as Tom got off a shot with the rifle, hitting Morgan in the shoulder blade and neck. Morgan went down. Wyatt whirled and shot at Tom and the shot grazed the horse, who bolted. Doc let go with both barrels of his shotgun, hitting Tom; then Tom, holding his torn open stomach, fired again and hit Doc in the hip, sending him down. At the same moment Wyatt yelled at Morgan, "Get behind me, Morgan!"

Wyatt turned with his gun on Tom, who was still alive and trying to get off another shot. Wyatt shot him and Tom fell. Billy Clanton, meanwhile, rose up to shoot Wyatt, and Morgan and Virgil both put bullets into him as Virgil was struck by a bullet from the still-living Frank McLaury. Virgil went down as Doc and Wyatt fired at Frank McLaury and killed him.

It was over less than a minute after it began. Tom and Frank McLaury were dead. Billy Clanton was dead. Morgan and Virgil Earp were severely wounded. Doc Holliday was slightly wounded in the hip. Wyatt was unscratched.

He bent over Morgan after holding his aim on the downed combatants to make sure they were no longer a threat. He then started to tend to his younger brother.

"Morgan," he said, "we're going to get you to a doctor. . . . Don't die on me. Don't you die on me."

You could hear in Wyatt's voice the fear that his worst nightmare was about to come true with his younger brother. Just then a gun cocked very loudly. Wyatt looked up into a pistol being held on him, pointed right at his head. It was Johnny Behan.

"You're under arrest, Wyatt," he said. "You and Doc and your brothers if they live . . . you're under arrest for murder."

PART THREE

Wilderness

CHAPTER TWENTY-FIVE

"Get up slow, Wyatt," Behan said.

Wyatt ignored Behan, even though the latter had a gun pointed right at his head.

"Somebody get those wagons, damn it!" Wyatt called out.

By now the street was filling with passersby and curiosity seekers as well as partisans of both the Earps and the Clantons. Several men grabbed two wagons and pulled them out of the O.K. Corral stable. They didn't even bother hitching horses to them, just grabbed the shafts and pulled them over toward the fallen Earps and Doc Holliday, who helped Wyatt with Morgan.

"All right," said Wyatt. "Let's put 'em in nice and easy. Morg first. He's hurt the worst."

Several men helped as Wyatt lifted his wounded brother into the wagon. Doc, though he was injured, helped pull the wagon as well.

"Get him over to Virgil's house and tell the doctor to get over there and hurry," Wyatt shouted.

He next bent down to Virgil. "How's Morg?" Virgil asked weakly.

"He's hit. You don't talk now," Wyatt said.

Several men helped Wyatt lift Virgil into the wagon.

"All right," Wyatt said. "Go!"

The men who helped him with Virgil grabbed the wagon's shafts and pulled it down the street in the direction of Virgil's house.

Just then Behan put his hand on Wyatt. Wyatt was in no mood for this. "Take your hand off."

Behan backed off, removing his hand, but still tried to play his card.

"Now look, Wyatt . . . I told you—" he said.

"I'm not gonna be arrested today, Johnny," Wyatt said. He still held his six-gun, and his shirtfront was soaked with blood. "Not by you," he said, looking around the crowd of onlookers to see if there were any more potential enemies or dangers there, "and not by anyone else."

He backed away from the crowd, gun still out, as John Clum came running up with a rifle in his hand.

"Wyatt . . . My God," Clum said.

Just then a woman called out in panic. "Wyatt!" It was Josie. She ran to Wyatt from across the street, ran straight into his arms as Behan looked on. She saw the blood covering his shirtfront. "Wyatt, are you . . ."

"I'm okay," he said.

"Are you sure?"

"I'm okay, Josie," Wyatt said. "You go home now . . . you hear?"

"No. I want to be with you now. . . . I—"

"You go *home* now," Wyatt said. "It might not be over. They might send in more men to get us tonight. I don't want you in the way . . . and I don't want you near Mattie. There's been enough bloodshed today. God, I've got a headache."

He pressed his temples and turned to Clum. "John . . . see her home."

"Miss Marcus . . ." Clum fumbled. "Wyatt's right . . . please . . ."

Behind him a fight had begun in the street between an Earp supporter and a Clanton supporter.

"They murdered 'em," cried one. "Them Earps killed 'em in cold blood! Murdered 'em!"

"Ike Clanton's been in here threatening to kill 'em all morning," countered the other. "It was a fair fight!"

The two men threw punches and wrestled each other to the ground. Behan stepped between them.

"Here now! Here now!" he shouted.

As Clum led Josie off, Wyatt backed down the street in the direction of Virgil's house, when Allie came running up from the cross street. She was wearing a sun bonnet.

"I'm huntin' Virg," Allie said to a passerby. "Where is he?"

Just then she looked up and saw the wagon as it was being pulled in front of her, and she screamed.

"Virg! Virg!" Allie cried. "That's my Virgil! Let me through, damn you!" She pushed past the crowd to the wagon.

One of the men pulling the wagon parted the crowd for her. "Let the poor man's mother through," he said.

Allie stopped dead.

"His mother!?" she said indignantly. "I'm his wife!"

"Allie," Virgil said weakly. "Don't argue about it. . . . Let 'em get me to the doc."

Virgil and Morgan were brought in and laid out on two beds in Virgil's house that were brought by friends from the bedroom. The doctor came in, escorted by Wyatt with Allie behind him. Lou had thrown herself over Morgan.

"Oh, Morg honey," Lou cried. "Look what they did to you. . . . Oh please, dear God, don't let him die."

She looked up at Wyatt as he entered with the doctor.

"It's your fault," she said bitterly. "I wanted to get him away from here, but he wouldn't leave you or the damn brothers! Well, damn you to hell, Wyatt Earp."

She stood up and slapped him hard across the mouth.

"You're not the only one who loves him, Lou," Wyatt said quietly. "Let the doctor tend to him now."

Wyatt still had his gun out and was still looking around for potential enemies as he crossed the street back over to his house. Several hangers-on followed behind him. He turned to them at his front steps.

"Wait here."

Then he entered the house, looking for Mattie.

"Mattie . . . Mattie," he called.

He crossed into the bedroom. There she sat on a chair by the bed, her head lying on the table in front of her. There on the table was a half-empty bottle of laudanum, the opiate Mattie bought in Hoptown.

Wyatt bent down to the almost unconscious woman.

"How much did you take, Mattie? How much of the laudanum did you take?"

A very lethargic Mattie looked up at him. " 'Nuff to ease my pain, sugar," she said, " 'nuff to ease the pain."

Wyatt carried her in his arms across the street as behind him several of the hangers-on carried two more mattresses to Virgil's house.

Wyatt squeezed by the Earp supporters, who now crowded the living room. "Everybody who isn't family but the doctor, get out," he said. Allie looked up and saw Wyatt carrying Mattie.

"Allie, get me a chair for her," he said.

"Don't you tell me what to do in *my* house, you tinhorn."

Wyatt spoke softly at first and then bellowed. "Allie, I know I'm not your favorite brother-in-law, but men may be coming into town to kill us all before this day is through, and we have to make certain preparations and cooperate with one another, so GET ME A DAMNED CHAIR!"

Allie stood and brought over a chair, and Wyatt propped Mattie up in it.

"What happened to her?" Lou asked.

"She took laudanum," Wyatt said. "A lot of it."

Allie turned to Lou. "Can you blame her?" she said. "If I was married to him I'd get it by the gallon."

Wyatt stepped outside and came back in carrying the two mattresses that the hangers-on had brought over. "Lou, help me get these mattresses in front of the windows, please."

Lou started to cry. "I can't believe this is happening. This is our *home*," she cried. "This is our home."

CHAPTER
TWENTY-SIX

An hour after the gunfight, Curly Bill and Johnny Ringo had almost fifty mounted cowboys ready to ride. Whether they would or not was very much dependent on the outcome of the parlay going on between the two stalwarts and Johnny Behan, who huddled with them in the now tumbled-down barbecue area where once Newman Clanton and Mike Gray had held their lofty councils of war and that now showed the wear and tear of too many violent binges. Carcasses of dead animals and people, broken bottles, chicken bones, and other assorted garbage were everywhere. The charm had gone out of the place.

"You boys leave the Earps to me," Behan said.

"Leave 'em to you, huh?" Curly Bill laughed.

"That's right," said Behan. "The town's ready to throw them all out. Half of 'em really believe they were behind that stage holdup. The other half just don't want to be caught in the middle of a war."

"Yeah?" said Johnny Ringo. "So what are you gonna do? You couldn't even keep Earp away from your woman," he said and laughed, and Curly Bill joined in.

This public derision of his manhood offended Johnny Behan to the quick. But even if he had been brave enough to go up against a psychopath like Curly Bill, it would not have been sound tactics. It would not have been what Mike Gray would have done, and Gray was Behan's mentor, even in death.

Now the sheriff of Cochise County saw perhaps an opportunity to supplant the former Texas Ranger. He could be the brains and Curly Bill, Johnny Ringo, and the other jackals would be his muscle.

"I can see to it," said Johnny Behan, striking what he hoped was a Mike Gray pose, "I can see to it Earp and the others hang for murder. That's what I can do."

"I say we just go in and finish the job now," Johnny Ringo replied.

"They're waitin' for you now," said Behan. "Let me try. You got nothin' to lose. . . . If it doesn't work you can always pick 'em off one at a time when they're *not* ready for it. I can be as good a friend to you fellas as Mike Gray was if you let me."

"Mike Gray wasn't no friend of mine," said Curly Bill, sneering his upper lip off teeth that looked more like fangs than anything else.

"A better friend," Behan put in hastily. "I can be a better friend . . . a much better friend."

That night at Virgil's house all the windows were covered from behind. No light shined through. Virgil and Morgan lay on blankets on the floor, their wounds oozing through the dressings and both of them fitfully asleep. There was the sound of a fly buzzing in the room, lighting on blood seeping through the gauze. Mattie was sitting staring forlornly out into space.

Wyatt and the wounded Doc stood by the windows, which had mattresses propped up against them. There were Winchesters propped up near the windows, and Allie, Lou, and Kate were busy loading weapons and gun belts. Allie leaned forward and shooed the fly viciously off of Virgil's wounds. Wyatt and Doc peered out through the cracks into the darkness, and James sat on the floor drinking.

He fell asleep holding his bottle. Bessie took it out of his hand and took a swig, looking around in disgust. "Well," she said, "here we are. One big happy family."

"Shut up," Allie said, and as if in reply, Bessie belched.

By the time the sun came up, Allie and Lou were dozing on the floor next to their sleeping, wounded husbands. Bessie and James leaned against each other, passed out, as was Kate. Doc slept in a chair by one window and Wyatt stood alone at his window-keeping vigil. Then he saw something.

Three black hearses pulled slowly by teams of black horses proceeded up the street. The undertaker rode in the lead hearse. Wyatt opened the door and stepped out onto Virgil's porch, watching the hearses pull by. The undertaker looked over at him proudly. "It's gonna be," he called to Wyatt, "the grandest funeral you ever see'd. . . . Watt and Tarbell Undertaking thank you for the business, Mister Earp. And we stand ready to serve your needs as well."

The undertaker, dressed in black and looking like Death himself, smiled a ghastly smile at Wyatt as his hearses rolled by. Wyatt shuddered.

Down the street, propped up in the window of Ogilvey's Hardware Store, were three ornate coffins with the top halves open. They revealed the bodies of the two McLaurys and Billy Clanton. Above them was a hand-painted sign in the window that proclaimed: "Murdered in the Streets of Tombstone." There was a huge crowd out front of the hardware store.

Up the length of Allen Street, past brothels whose balconies were lined with weepy-eyed whores throwing flowers down onto the funeral procession, through the business district and through Hoptown and the implacable faces of the town's Oriental community and the stern and unreadable face of China Mary, the funeral procession made its way toward Boot Hill. It was led by a band playing a dirge for drunks. Ike Clanton and Johnny Ringo and Curly Bill, followed by their men and ordinary folks enjoying the pageantry, all made their way down the street to lay the martyrs to their final rest.

The sky was gunmetal gray and a cold wind kicked up off the desert, blowing sand across the hill from the freshly dug graves, into the eyes of the mourners, who wiped away the grit and tears. The polished wooden coffins creaked against the ropes that lowered them down, banging against the sides of the graves, till they touched bottom and the onlookers, all dressed in black, stood like statues against the howling wind.

Later that afternoon, Judge Wells Spicer sat behind his desk. In front of him were Ike Clanton, Johnny Behan, and Harry Woods. "Have you filled out the necessary complaint forms, Mister Clanton?" Judge Spicer asked.

"I have," said Ike with newfound dignity. He handed the forms over to the judge, who examined them.

"These appear to be in order," Spicer said. He dipped his pen in ink and filled out an arrest warrant, signed it, then another and another and another. "Sheriff Behan . . ." said the judge.

"Yes, Your Honor."

"These are warrants for the arrest of Wyatt S., Virgil W., and Morgan Earp and for the arrest of Doctor John H. Holliday for the crime of murder. Because the medical condition of Morgan and Virgil Earp is, I believe, still grave and prevents their incarceration, you will serve warrants only on the persons of Wyatt S. Earp and John H. Holliday. Is that clear, Sheriff Behan?"

"Yes it is, Your Honor," said the sheriff.

Spicer handed the warrants to Johnny Behan, and Ike Clanton burst out in patriotic fervor.

"God bless America!"

Outside the courtroom, as Ike and Behan and Woods stepped into the street, Behan stopped Woods and handed him the warrants. "There you go," he said.

"What do you mean, there you go?" said the frightened Deputy Woods.

"I mean," said Behan, "there you go."

"Well . . ." stammered Woods, "what are you givin' these things to me for?"

" 'Cause you're gonna serve the warrants and take the prisoners in."

"I got to take in Wyatt Earp and Doc Holliday?!" cried Woods.

"Well, sure, Harry," said Behan, miffed at having to explain the obvious. "You don't expect me to do it, do you? There's bad blood between Wyatt and me."

* * *

The mattresses were by now pulled away from the windows, but there was still an air of siege about the place. Wyatt was feeding soup to Virgil. Morgan was asleep and Doc was playing cards with James, when there was a knock at the door. The women, who were in the kitchen, poked their heads out at Wyatt. He cocked his gun and crossed over to the window, saw who was outside, and put the gun down, opening the door to John Clum and Harry Woods.

"Hello, John," Wyatt said evenly.

"How're Morg and Virg, Wyatt?"

Wyatt didn't answer, just looked at Woods. "Is he here as Behan's deputy sheriff or Clanton's newspaper man?"

"I'm here with warrants for your arrest, Earp," said Deputy Woods.

Clum spoke quickly to head off trouble. "He came to me," he said, "because he was afraid to come here alone. I told him that he was a fool. That you believe in law and justice and that any trial will vindicate you."

"Law and justice aren't necessarily the same things in this part of the country, John, despite what you may think."

"You have friends, Wyatt," said Clum. "We'll make your bail and get you the best attorney, but . . . but the warrants *are* legal."

"As legal as can be," said Woods, and then added, "I advise you to come along peaceably, Earp."

"Or what?" said Wyatt, ready for the first killing of the day.

John Clum turned to the deputy. "I advise you to shut up, Harry," he said, then looked over at Wyatt. "We have to . . . go by the rules of the law, Wyatt."

"I won't let them use the law to kill me and my family, John. I will not allow that."

Wyatt and Doc came out, both of them blinking in the sunlight. Woods stood behind them with his gun out and pointed at their backs as they walked down the street toward the jail. And as they walked down the street, passersby stopped to stare, people looked out of windows. Wyatt Earp was going to jail.

Wyatt lay on his bunk in the cell, staring at the ceiling.

Doc had his deck of cards and was trying to flip cards into a crack in the wall and make them stick.

"Good Lord, Wyatt," he said, "don't be so glum. You're taking this far too seriously."

"I don't take it lightly," said Wyatt.

"Don't be a cob. I know it's your first time on this side of the bars, but . . ."

"It's not my first time," said Wyatt.

Doc sat up. "Come again?"

"It's not my first time," Wyatt said.

"Where?"

"Arkansas . . . a long time ago."

"For what . . . breaking the Sabbath, perhaps?" queried the dentist.

"Horse theft."

"Horse theft!?" he exclaimed. "Wyatt, I'm shocked. . . . Did you serve time?"

"No," said Wyatt, "I ran."

"I *am* shocked," said Holliday. "*And* impressed."

Just then, the two heard Woods say, "You're free to go . . . both of you."

Wyatt and Doc looked up and there with Woods was John Clum and a lawyer called Tom Fitch, who was known in those days as "The Silver-Tongued Orator of the Pacific Slope."

"Spicer set bail at ten thousand dollars apiece," said Clum. "We raised that much in less than an hour. This is the gentleman who's going to be your attorney. . . . Tom Fitch."

"Pleased to meet you, Mister Earp," said Fitch. "Doctor Holliday."

"Mister Fitch," said Wyatt, extending his hand.

Then when the two newly liberated jailbirds started out of the cell, Doc turned to Woods, "Oh, I left a little something, loose, for you in the bucket, Harry."

The trial began on Halloween. The courtroom was packed. Josie was there. Mattie was not, nor were any of the other Earp wives. Doc and Wyatt sat at the defense table with Fitch. The prosecutor was a man named Goodrich. Judge Spicer was at the bench and in the audience were the likes of Ike Clanton, Johnny Behan, Woods, and Clum.

Fitch leaned over and whispered to Wyatt. "It doesn't look good that your wife isn't here, Mister Earp."

Wyatt looked over at Josie, who threw him a secret smile. "Trust me," he said to Fitch. "It would look a lot worse if she were."

The clerk rose up. "In Justice Court," he said, "Township Number One, County of Cochise, Territory of Arizona, before Wells Spicer, Justice of the Peace, the Territory of Arizona versus Wyatt Earp et al., defendants for the crime of premeditated murder."

"How do you plead?" asked the judge.

Fitch stood. "The defendants plead innocent, Your Honor."

"Is the prosecution ready?" Spicer asked.

"We are, Your Honor," said Prosecutor Goodrich.

"Call your first witness."

"The prosecution," said Goodrich, "calls Sheriff John H. Behan."

Behan was sworn in and led through his version of events.

"When I arrived within a few feet of the Clantons and the McLaurys," he said, "I heard one of the Earp party, I believe it was Wyatt Earp, say, 'You sons of bitches have been looking for a fight and now you can have it.' And then I heard another voice say, 'Throw up your hands.' The Earps already had their pistols out and in their hands."

"And then what happened?" asked the prosecutor.

"When the order was given to 'throw up your hands' I heard Billy Clanton say, 'Don't shoot me. I don't want to fight.' Tom McLaury at the same time threw open his coat and said 'I am not armed,' or something like that. And he caught hold of his coat at both sides and threw open his coat to show he was not armed."

"He was not armed," repeated Goodrich.

"No, sir," said Behan solemnly. "He was not, and he showed that to the Earp party as well."

"So," continued the prosecutor, "the Earps command them to throw up their arms and they appear to comply and show they are not armed, and say they do not want to fight. . . . And then what happened."

"Two shots were fired almost instantly from the Earp party," said the sheriff. "I can't swear by whom the shots immediately after that were fired. My impression is that the next three shots came from the Earp party as well."

Wyatt looked up and said, "Objection, Your Honor. . . . The witness is giving impressions."

Spicer turned to look at Wyatt. "Are you acting as your own counsel, Mister Earp?"

"Uhhh . . ." said Wyatt, who had simply been caught up in the legal proceedings. It was strange how he enjoyed courtrooms, always had since seeing his grandfather and father in them. And he thought to himself how different it all might have been had he read for the law, had Urilla not wanted a ranch, had Urilla not died.

Then he heard Fitch say, "It's a good objection, Your Honor. . . . I'll make it myself."

"Overruled," said Spicer.

And Behan continued piously, "That *was* my impression."

"Go on, Sheriff," said Prosecutor Goodrich.

"I suppose there were as many as eight or ten shots before I saw *any* arms in the hands of any of the McLaury or Clanton party."

"So," Goodrich said, "you are saying that the Earps opened fire without any provocation whatsoever, and that eight or ten shots were fired by them before you saw any of the Clantons or McLaurys with a weapon in their hands."

"That is my impression," Behan said.

"Your witness," said the prosecutor.

Fitch was a tall, sinewy man who didn't so much stand as uncoil his lanky frame. But when he spoke, it was quick and to the point.

"As the Earp party was approaching the site of the shooting," he said, "did you not say to them regarding the Clantons, 'I have disarmed them' or words to that effect?"

"No, sir," said Behan with a straight face.

"Did the Earp party, after that remark or one like it from you, not put their guns farther back in their pants and did not Holliday put his coat over his gun?"

"No, sir, they did not."

"Were you not aware," asked Fitch, "of threats having been made by the Clantons against the lives of the Earps and Doc Holliday?"

"I am aware of no such threats."

"Never heard of such a threat?" Fitch asked again.

"No, sir, I did not. Not at any time."

"Were you aware of no difficulties between them?" asked Fitch, taking another tack.

"No, sir."

"Well, then," asked Fitch in an exasperated tone, "why, pray tell, did all this happen?! Did the Earps just up and decide to shoot these poor unarmed people that day?"

"I don't know," said the sheriff of Cochise County. "But I believe . . . it is my impression, that there may have been dealings between the Earps and Isaac Clanton which may have soured . . . but I don't know," he said, looking at Wyatt. "That's just an impression."

It was clear from the look on Behan's face that he could imagine a heavenly Mike Gray smiling down on him.

For his part, Wyatt looked up at Fitch and pulled at his sleeve. Fitch bent down to him.

"Don't ask him any more questions," Wyatt said.

"But," said Fitch, "he's killing you, Wyatt."

"It'll just be his word against ours. . . . Wait till Ike Clanton gets on the stand. I know where they're going with this thing and I know how to beat 'em."

During the recess, Fitch and Wyatt and Doc stood to one side while Clanton, Goodrich, and Behan were off to the opposite side. Both groups eyed each other.

"All right, Wyatt," said Fitch, "how do we beat Ike Clanton?"

Before Wyatt could answer, Doc broke in. "With a club or your fist . . . Or why don't we just forget the beatin' and shoot the little son of a—"

"We let him talk," said Wyatt, putting a hand on Doc's arm to quiet him down. "It's the one thing his father never let him do. Every time he opened his mouth the old man would hit him."

"That's because," said Doc, "everything he said was stupid."

Wyatt turned to Doc. "That's just my point, Doc. When you have someone as stupid as Ike, it's almost a wonder of nature. Why shut it off?"

Once Ike Clanton was on the stand Goodrich led him through his recollections of the events, which were remarkably similar to those of Johnny Behan. He was a victim, a poor, unarmed victim of the murderous Earp clan who grieved now for his fallen brother and comrades.

"One final question, Mister Clanton," said Goodrich, properly respectful of the trauma that his witness appeared to have suffered. "Have you ever threatened the Earps or Doc Holliday?"

"No, sir," said Ike with heightened solemnity, which had been augmented by his newly acquired status as martyred brother and son. "I never threatened the Earps or Doc Holliday, so help me God."

Goodrich patted Ike's shoulder in a manly gesture and then said in what was really a lovely basso profundo, "Your witness."

Before Fitch could rise to question Clanton, Wyatt leaned in toward him and said quietly, "Just ask him why. And no matter what he says, just keep asking him why."

Fitch looked at Wyatt, neither understanding the tactic nor appreciating advice from an amateur. "Wyatt," he said, "I know my business."

"I'm sure you do, but I know Ike Clanton. Just ask him why."

Fitch shrugged his shoulders as if to say, "Your funeral," which he suspected it just might be. He crossed to Ike Clanton and said, "Mister Clanton, you have stated that you believe the Earps initiated this gun battle because they wished to kill you."

You could tell by Ike's expression that he liked this question. It gave him a chance to be cute. "Isn't that the reason somebody always initiates a gun battle? 'Cause they're tryin' to kill somebody?"

Fitch looked over to Wyatt, blocking Ike's view of the accused. Wyatt mouthed one word to Fitch: *Why?*

Fitch then sighed and turned back to Ike. "Why?" he dutifully asked.

"Why what?" said Ike.

"Why you?" asked Fitch.

Ike looked around. He relished being on the stand, he relished the chance to talk and have all these people want and have to listen. Wyatt's lawyer had just opened the door, and Ike was about to step through.

"Well," he said, "because . . . well, because I knew certain things. Because . . ." Ike scratched at his head, a sure sign that he was trying to think. "Yeah . . ." he said, suddenly catching what he had been fishing for—a thought. "Yeah . . . Wyatt Earp approached me. Yeah, that's right."

Fitch looked to Wyatt, and Wyatt smiled.

"Why?" asked Fitch.

"He told me he wanted me to help put up a job to kill three men. Crane, Leonard, and Head. He said there was between four and five thousand dollars' reward for 'em and he said he would make the balance of six thousand dollars' reward up out of his own pocket."

"Why?"

"Yeah, that's what I asked him. Why? So he says that his business was such that he could not afford to capture them. He would have to kill them or else leave the country."

"Why?"

"Because he and his brother, uh . . . Morgan, yeah, it was Morgan . . . had piped off to Doc Holliday and William Leonard the money that was going on the Benson stage."

"By piped off," asked Fitch, "you mean—?"

"Stole it," Ike was quick to say. "Yeah, they stole it and then they were gonna pull a fake robbery of the stage with Leonard, Head, and Crane to cover up the fact that they already stole the money. And that's why they wanted to kill Leonard, Head, and Crane, because *they* knew the truth."

Ike had never enjoyed himself so much in his life. He looked around the courtroom, grinning at everyone. He smiled at Johnny Ringo and Johnny Behan, and he smiled at Curly Bill. Fitch stood there in amazement.

"Wyatt Earp," he said incredulously, "told you all this?"

"Yeah," Ike said, adding, "And Morgan. He told me too . . . and . . . and . . . and Doc, that's right."

"Why?" asked Fitch in astonishment. "Why would they all tell you this?"

"Because they wanted my help, see? To kill Leonard, Head, and Crane. And Doc told me he killed Bud Philpot."

Ike looked over at the stenographer. He was really rolling now.

"No, scratch that out," he said. "Put it down just the way Doc told me. He said, 'I shot and I saw Bud Philpot, the damn son of a bitch, tumble off the cart.' They piped off fourteen hundred dollars, *that's* what they told me.

"And *that's* why they staged the robbery and *that's* why they wanted Leonard, Head, and Crane dead because they knew it all, see? And *that's* why they shot us all up . . . because they were trying to get me, see?"

"Fascinating," said Fitch. "Why?"

"Because I . . . well, because I know it. I know everything I just told ya."

"You do?"

"So help me God, again," Ike said with renewed reverence.

"Remarkable," said Fitch. He turned to Wyatt and whispered, "You were right. I didn't think anybody could be that stupid." Then he turned back to Ike, smiling. "Mister Clanton, are you aware that the robbers of the Benson stage never got away with any money? Never got the strongbox?"

"Well," said Ike, marveling that someone supposedly as smart as an attorney could so easily fall into his trap. "They didn't need to. Because the Earps had already stolen the money. The robbery was just for show."

"Are you aware, Mister Clanton," said Fitch, "that *all* of the money arrived at the Wells Fargo office in Benson? That no money was ever reported stolen by Wells Fargo?"

Ike didn't get it. "So?" he said.

"So are you suggesting that Wells Fargo was involved in this conspiracy as well? To steal their own money?"

"Well . . ." said Ike, starting to scramble. "Well . . . well, maybe they put it back. Yeah, maybe they put it back."

"The Earps," said Fitch, looking from Ike up to the judge, "the Earps put it back? When? After Bud Philpot was shot . . . while the horses were galloping to Benson? The Earps somehow managed to board the stage and replace the money?"

Ike said nothing. He was beginning to feel that perhaps there was a flaw he had overlooked in his story.

"Are you saying," Fitch continued, "that the Earps stole the money from the Benson stage, then enacted a fake robbery to cover the fact that they had stolen the money, then *replaced* the money to cover the fact that their holdup was a fake? Can that *possibly* be what you are suggesting, Mr. Clanton? Is that in fact what you are saying?''

People were laughing openly at Ike now, and he was confused. He tried to think what his father's advice would be in such a situation. He conjured up the image of Old Man Clanton in his mind and the image hit him upside the head with a stick and said, ''Shut up, stupid.''

''I'm not saying anything,'' Ike said. ''I said what I said and that's what I have to say. And you can't twist it anymore, either.''

Wyatt wrote something on a piece of paper and handed it to Fitch. Fitch looked at it and nodded his head, then turned back to Ike.

''Mr. Clanton,'' he said, ''you say the purpose of the gun battle at the O.K. Corral was to assassinate you.''

''That's what I said,'' Ike said, stepping very carefully now. He would not be tripped up again.

''Then,'' said Fitch, ''why aren't you dead, sir? I take it you *are* alive. Why?''

''Why what?''

''Why,'' Fitch said, ''if the purpose was to assassinate you . . . and Wyatt Earp, the supposed leader of this conspiracy, stood no more than a few feet from you, and seeing as how he had no problem shooting anyone else that day, why did he not shoot and kill you?''

Ike looked around the room for help, but there was none.

''Well . . .'' he said. ''Well . . . uhhh . . . uhhhhh . . . because I was unarmed! Yeah, I was unarmed and it wouldn't have been fair.''

Johnny Behan just shook his head as he watched Ike Clanton destroy his chances to supplant Mike Gray.

No testimony given during the rest of the trial got any better than that of Isaac Clanton.

On November 30, Judge Spicer faced those assembled in the court after duly deliberating the proceedings and said, ''This case has now been on hearing for the past thirty days, during which time a volume of testimony has been taken and eminent legal talent employed on both sides. The great importance of the case demands that I should be full and explicit in my findings and conclusions. Isaac Clanton is the prosecuting witness in this case. It is therefore only proper that his testimony be given extra weight." Spicer looked over at Ike and Ike actually smiled, glad to have this reassurance that the judge, at least, believed him.

"The testimony of Isaac Clanton," said the judge, "that this tragedy was the result of a scheme on the part of the Earps to assassinate him and thereby bury in oblivion the confessions the Earps had made to him about stealing a shipment of coin from Wells Fargo and Company, falls, I must say, short of being a sound theory. On account of the great fact, most prominent in this matter, to wit, that Isaac Clanton was not injured at all and could have been killed first and easiest if it was the object of the attack to kill him. Instead, the would-be assassin, Wyatt Earp, told Mister Clanton upon seeing that he was unarmed to go away, which, I might add, Mister Clanton did and thus was not harmed."

Ike looked up, confused. Curly Bill, who sat in the audience behind Ike, leaned across the bench and slapped him upside the head. "See, stupid?" he said.

Spicer continued. "I cannot but believe that the Earps acted wisely in defending their own lives. They saw at once the dire necessity of giving the first shots to save themselves from certain death. Their shots were effective, and this alone saved the Earp party from being slain. I cannot resist the conclusion that the defendants' act was a necessary one done in the discharge of an official duty. There being no sufficient cause to believe the defendants guilty of the offense mentioned within, I order them to be released. This hearing is adjourned."

The courtroom erupted into pandemonium. Wyatt and Doc warmly shook hands with Fitch. Josie, from her vantage point, spied the photographer at the back of the courtroom and rather than embarrass Wyatt with a public display, mouthed the words *I love you*, to him, which he caught from the corner of his eye. Flash powder exploded and pictures were taken, and John Clum proclaimed, "It's a great day, Wyatt. Not just for you, but for Tombstone. Law and justice *do* walk hand in hand in our city."

"Sounds like an editorial, John," Wyatt said in a dry tone.

"That's because it is," said Clum, smiling. "But no less true because of it."

Four weeks later Virgil Earp walked out of the Oriental Saloon, crossing the corner of Allen and Fifth streets. Winter had set in now and the winds that whipped off the desert floor and up from the canyons into Tombstone rattled the doors and shutters and tore loose shingles from the roofs. Lightning flashed and thunder crashed and rolled, booming like a cannon roar and making Virgil jump with the sound and sending his hand down a time or two toward his gun belt. He was limping still, but otherwise seemed to have recovered from his wounds. On the southwest corner there was a building site. Virgil did not see the three men standing there in the building site hidden behind plank boards and peering out at him as he crossed the street lit now and then by lightning flashing in the dark.

One of the men was Curly Bill. The second was Ike Clanton. And the third was a gentleman by the name of Stillwell. Virgil approached the center of the street, shuddering in the cold. As he walked, the light glinted off his marshal's badge and the first assailant stepped out of the shadow, leveled his shotgun, and presently the air exploded with the blast that ripped into Virgil's left shoulder and arm.

He moaned aloud as he was hit and spun to the ground. He reached for his gun and the two other assailants stepped out of the shadows, and one after another four more shotgun blasts were fired, one hitting Virgil in his left side, another, as he rolled over, hitting him in the back. Virgil managed somehow to stand again and fire off a round from his revolver. The final two shotgun blasts were then fired, one hitting his leg and one missing, shattering the window of the Eagle Brewery Saloon on the northeast corner. Virgil fell, firing his weapon wildly, and the assassins fled off into the darkness, racing down the embankment toward Tough Nut Street with Ike Clanton's hat blowing off in the wind as he ran. Virgil, blood flowing from his many wounds, arose and walked through force of will across the street where he collapsed into his brother Wyatt's arms, the latter having just come running out of the Oriental.

Wyatt cradled Virgil in his arms as others, including Doc

Holliday, poured out of the saloon and gathered around them.
Virgil looked up at Wyatt and said, weakly, "Do you believe
this?"

Wyatt rocked his brother in his arms. There was nothing
he could say to succor him but "Shhhh, Virgil . . .
Shhhhh . . ."

"Do you believe this, Wyatt?"

CHAPTER
TWENTY-SEVEN

Tough Nut Street sloped down from one embankment to another, leading off to the outskirts of the town and desert country that opened out past the miners' shacks. Flitting from shadow to shadow, the assassins ran toward the open land where horses awaited them. Voices rang out in the night.

"There they go! Get 'em!" were the cries. Shots were fired at the fleeing figures without effect.

Josie in her nightgown, lamp in hand, crossed to the window as she heard the commotion off in the distance and the gunshots that were fired. She heard a voice call out, "They shot one of the Earps over at the Oriental!" And she felt her heart sink. "Oh, my God," she cried aloud; it was happening again.

Wyatt led almost a dozen men. Four of whom carried the wounded Virgil up the stairs of the Cosmopolitan Hotel. Wyatt's gun was out, and Doc strode right next to him with his out too. They reached the top landing of the hotel and set to kicking in the doors, breaking in upon a potbellied traveling salesman who was enjoying the favors of one of Tombstone's ladies of the evening, a plump middle-aged Chinese woman with truly terrible teeth. The salesman was terrified at the sight of Wyatt and Doc and their guns and the men behind them, carrying what looked to be a bloody corpse.

"What the . . ." sputtered the salesman. "I got money, you want money . . . Don't shoot. Just take the money."

"We're not takin' any money," said Wyatt. "We're just taking your room. Get out."

"But," said the salesman, "I paid two nights in advance."

"For the woman or the room?" Doc inquired.

The Chinese woman, meanwhile, said many things in rapid-fire Chinese, none of which mattered to the salesman, who said indignantly, "Now see here, this is my room and—"

"My name's Holliday," said the Doc. "I assume you'll accept my marker for the room, sir?"

"Doc Holliday? Oh, my God! Listen, you can have the room," the salesman said. "And the woman."

So saying, he grabbed his pants and shoes, stuck his hat on his head, suitcase in hand, opened the window, and beat a hasty retreat out onto the balcony as Wyatt and the others lay Virgil down onto the bed.

A stream of irate guests of the hotel in nightshirts and various states of disarray made their way down the hallway and down the stairs under the none-too-gentle prodding of Wyatt and Doc, as Doctor McGraw pushed his way in the opposite direction up the stairs.

"Wyatt!?" he said. "I thought it was you that was hit."

"It's Virgil" was the reply. Then Wyatt turned to Doc Holliday. "Doc, take him to Virgil's room and post guards around the hotel. Nobody gets in here tonight that doesn't know you personal."

Wyatt then led a dozen men down Fremont Street, all with six-guns or rifles in their hands, all of them checking the street for any trouble.

The men stood in the center of the thoroughfare as Wyatt went up the steps to Virgil's house and knocked on the door. Allie appeared at the door. Wyatt said something to her the men could not hear, and then they heard Allie cry, "NO!"

Wyatt put his arm around her. She threw it off and raced down the street. Wyatt turned to several of his men. "Go with her," he ordered, "and don't let her out of your sight till you're in the hotel." He then crossed the street to James's house, knocked on the door, and presently out came James and Bessie. Wyatt's men formed a circle around them as Wyatt went next into his own house and got Mattie, who complained through the numbing effects of narcotics, "But I don't want to go to no hotel, Wyatt."

"It doesn't matter what you want, Mattie," he said. "We're all going."

"Where's my medicine?" she said, looking around. "Did you take my medicine?"

Josie was in the final stages of hurriedly getting dressed when there was a loud pounding at the door. She moved to her dresser and pulled out a huge Colt .45, which she cocked and pointed at the door. "Who is it?" she said, and her voice did not tremble.

"Wyatt."

She uncocked the revolver and raced to the door, threw it open, and leapt into his arms. "Oh, thank God you're all right," she said, kissing him.

"We have to go now, Josie."

"Go?"

"They've made a move on us . . . they got Virgil. I don't know if he'll live the night. We're all moving into the Cosmopolitan. They're not gonna get any more of us."

Inside the knot of armed men were all the Earps but Allie and Virgil. Morgan was propped up between two men, with Lou at his side and Bessie lending a helping hand to the very woozy Mattie, who looked up to see her husband bringing his mistress into the confines of their family circle. She let out an anguished wailing cry that reverberated throughout the street, rushing straight at Josie with her claws out. Before she could gouge her rival's eyes out, Wyatt intercepted her and held her back.

"You son of a bitch!" Mattie screamed at Wyatt, flailing at him. "You're not bringing your whore!"

"Forget it," Josie said, drawing back a fist with which to defend herself, "I'm not going to be under the same roof with that—"

Her sentence was cut short by Wyatt firing a shot into the air. "ENOUGH!" he roared, and they both were quiet.

The strange band of armed men, wives, and mistresses all in nightshirts arrived at the entrance of the hotel, which was guarded by what appeared to be a dozen more armed men with shotguns. More men were visible on the roof and balconies, busy transforming the hotel into an armed fortress. Mattie cried hysterically on Bessie's shoulder. "He's a bastard. . . . He's such a bastard!"

"They all are, dearie," Bessie said. "Give it a rest."

As Wyatt herded his group into the hotel, two more armed men came from the adjacent street with Kate. She took one look at the parties assembled and exclaimed, "Ohhh no, you're not coopin' me up in a hotel with all of them. I'll take my chances with the Clantons." Whereupon she turned on her heel and scampered off into the night.

Inside the hotel on the upper floors the doors to the various rooms were opened. A large knot of people stood around Virgil's room. Wyatt marched his family up onto the landing, assigning quarters: "James, you and Bessie take that room over there. Morg, that's for you and Lou. Make sure you move those dressers in front of those windows."

Just then he heard Virgil cry out in pain, "No! No, damn your eyes . . . no!"

Wyatt pushed his way into Virgil's crowded room. Doc stood rifle in hand at the window, looking out into the street. Allie was at Virgil's side as Doctor McGraw ministered to her husband.

"How's he doing?" Wyatt asked, ashen-faced.

"Get out of here," Allie shouted. "Get out!"

"Shut up, Allie," Wyatt said, ready to hit her if need be.

"Hey, Wyatt," he heard Virgil say. "Don't talk to her like that. She's a little upset, is all."

Wyatt's eyes teared up, and at the same time he all but chuckled. "She's a little upset, huh, Virg?"

"Don't let 'em take my arm off, Wyatt. He wants to cut my arm off," Virgil said, looking at the doc. "Don't let him do it."

The doctor looked at Wyatt beseechingly. "Wyatt . . ." he implored.

"You heard him, Doc," Wyatt said.

"Either way," said the doctor, "he's gonna be a cripple, Wyatt. If he lives. If he doesn't bleed to death, which is very much in doubt."

"Then," Virgil said, trying to raise himself up, "I'll be a two-armed corpse instead of a one-armed one."

Allie broke down in tears, sobbing. "Oh, my God . . ."

"Oh, now," said Virgil gently, "don't take on. . . . I'll still have one arm left to hug you with."

Wyatt bit his lip to keep from crying himself, and turned and walked away.

A dozen armed men surrounded Wyatt and Doc as they examined the site of the assassination attempt. Wyatt pointed over to the building site. "That's where they must've been hiding," he said. He and Doc, surrounded by their body-guards looking every which way for a sign of trouble, crossed over to the building site.

Wyatt saw something on the ground. Embossed on the leather sweatband inside the hat he picked up were the initials "I.C."

"Ike Clanton," Wyatt said. "I want to form a posse, Doc. I want as many men as—"

"Wyatt," Doc said, cutting him off.

"Is there some reason we're talkin' instead of getting our horses?"

"Wyatt," said Doc. "You can't ride out there lookin' for anybody. We've got to lay low for a while."

"What are you *talking* about?"

Doc spoke softly and, for the first time anyone could recall, reasonably. "Morg's out of commission and now Virgil. . . . Somebody's got to stay back here and protect them. So who does that leave you with to go out looking for Ike? Just you and me? Against all of them?"

Wyatt just looked at him.

"I'm dead anyway," Doc said. "So if you want to go out in a blaze of glory, I'm with you. You know me, Wyatt, I can't pass up a party. . . . But if you want to live, you gotta lay low for a while."

"Lay low," said Wyatt. And in his mouth was the taste of bile.

Curly Bill, Stillwell, Ike Clanton, the one they called Pony Deal, and several others were asleep under blankets arrayed on a hillside that night when they were awoken by the sound of a horse galloping up. They all reached for their firearms and then saw it was Johnny Ringo. "He's alive," Ringo said. "The son of a bitch is alive!"

"What the hell does it take to kill those people?" Curly Bill cried out in frustration.

"They pulled out four inches of bone off his left arm," Johnny said. "He's a gimp for life. It's better than dead. Now they gotta take care of him."

"Where are they?" asked Ike.

Johnny said, "Wyatt's pulled 'em all into the Cosmopolitan. There's no way to get at 'em. The place is like a fort. Every lawman friend the Earps have is over there with a shotgun."

"They are, huh?" said Curly.

"So," Johnny continued, "we're not gonna get another shot at any of the Earps for awhile, if that's what you're thinking."

But that was not what Curly Bill was thinking. "I'm thinkin' that maybe while they're all holed up like a bunch of rabbits, we go back into business. Like you said, all the lawmen are at the Cosmopolitan Hotel."

One month later, the following article appeared in the *Tombstone Epitaph*:

A period of unparalleled lawlessness has descended upon Cochise County following in the wake of the shoot-out between the Earp faction and the rustlers and the attempted murder of City Marshal Virgil Earp which has left Marshal Earp maimed for life and left the city of Tombstone without its chief law-enforcement officer. Since then, there has been a mailed death threat against Judge Wells Spicer advising him to leave the county or get a bullet in the brain. This was followed in close order by the attempted assassination of Mayor John Clum. With the entire Earp clan taking refuge in the Cosmopolitan Hotel, the lawless factions have unleashed a reign of terror, robbing first the Bisbee stage of sixty-five hundred dollars and the very next day the Benson stage, in which robbery the suspected head of the outlaw faction, William "Curly Bill" Brocious, was identified by Wells Fargo detectives.

Wyatt read the article in disgust. "You seen this?" he asked, tossing the paper to Doc, who knew now that their respite had ended.

"I have," he said. He knew there was nothing further to say to Wyatt that could dissuade him.

Wyatt was already walking out the door as he said, "We leave six men here to take care of Virgil and Morgan and the women. . . . I've sent wires off to Jack Johnson, Jack Vermillion, and Sherm McMasters to join us, and I've got enough Federal warrants to bring in every one of Curly Bill's men. 'Cause I've had enough of laying low."

CHAPTER TWENTY-EIGHT

Within a week, Wyatt, Doc, McMasters, Johnson, and Vermillion led their posse of several dozen men down through the streets of Contention, a mining town not unlike Tombstone. The men carried shotguns, Henry rifles, and Winchesters as they dismounted and walked down the length and breadth of the street like an occupying army. Each of them had a set of "Wanted" posters, and the town shortly began to reverberate with the sound of posters being nailed into clapboard sides of buildings. Wyatt and his posse went looking everywhere. They had a tip that Curly Bill was holed up in Contention, and they turned over the town looking for him.

Wyatt entered a restaurant with Doc, Vermillion, and Johnson at his side, their rifles cradled in their arms. They spoke to no one, simply walked through the restaurant checking out every face. Seeing that neither Ike nor Curly Bill was there, Wyatt took out a sheaf of "Wanted" posters and put them in the proprietor's hands.

"Post these in a prominent place," he ordered.

There was one poster each for Curly Bill, Ike Clanton, Johnny Ringo, Frank Stillwell, Pony Deal, and the other members of the reconstituted Clanton gang.

"This ain't Tombstone," said the restaurant owner. "You got a war with the Clantons, that's none of *our* business. You can't tell us what to do."

When Wyatt spoke it was barely above a whisper. "I'm a deputy Federal marshal and those are Federal warrants. You help the Clantons and I'll make it my business."

At just about that time, a wagon loaded down with coops of chickens pulled along down Allen Street into Tombstone. The chickens were loud and filthy, flapping their wings, screeching, sending feathers and chicken droppings every which way. The wagon was drawn by a mean-looking old woman named Lina. She pulled her wagon up in front of the office of the sheriff of Cochise County. She went around to the back of the wagon and took off two coops, revealing the chicken-dropping-covered head of Ike Clanton.

"We here, Aunt Lina?" asked Ike.

"We're here," she said.

"You don't see any of 'em, do you, Aunt Lina?"

She looked around. "Nope," she said.

Inside his office, Johnny Behan sat playing cards with Harry Woods when in walked Ike Clanton, Phinn Clanton, and Pony Deal. All of them were besplattered with chicken droppings and feathers.

"Johnny, you got to help us," said Ike.

"What happened to you?" replied Behan. "You look like you've been tarred and feathered and you smell like . . ."

"Chicken crap," said Ike.

"What?" asked Behan.

"Chicken crap and feathers," said Ike. "We came in here in a spring wagon under a load a chicken coops. Hate them birds."

"Why?" asked the sheriff.

"Why?!" Ike fairly shouted. "You try ridin' twenty miles under a load of chicken coops and tell me if you don't hate them diarrhetic featherballs!"

Behan shook his head. "I meant," he said wearily, "*why* did you ride in a wagon *underneath* the chickens."

"Oh," said Ike, who paused and then realized he was meant to go on with an explanation. "Uh . . . Earp's out there with a hundred men. Maybe two hundred. From what .

I hear, could be as much as a thousand. What kinda chance do you think we'd have if he found us?''

"We want you to lock us up, Johnny," said Phinn Clanton.

"Shut up," Ike said to his brother, keeping up with the family tradition. Then, turning back to Behan, he said, "We want you to lock us up, Johnny. Stick us in your calaboose. It's the only place he can't get us."

Wyatt, Doc, Vermillion, Johnson, and McMasters led their posse back into the streets of Tombstone's Chinese section. All of the men were covered from head to toe in the fine white powdery dust that was so prevalent in the surrounding countryside. The white alkaline covering gave them all a ghostly appearance. As they rode through Hoptown the Chinese ceased what they were doing, fell silent, and looked upon these specters who came riding in like the Horsemen of the Apocalypse, their horses snorting and their eyes dead cold.

China Mary stood on the sidewalk in front of the Celestial Laundry watching Wyatt and his men. Her face was impassive, and then she took a step forward and called out to Wyatt, "I tell you . . . you go kill 'em. You remember? I say go kill 'em all. But you no do it. Because they just hurt Chinese man. So who give a care, huh? Now they trying to kill *you* . . . your brothers, your family. What you think about law and order now? Land of home . . . land of free. Ha ha ha ha . . . big joke, huh? You better off listen China Mary. Kill 'em all."

He looked over at Mary, the white alkali caking under his eyes. China Mary leaned out into the street, craned her neck, and when she spoke again, her gravelly voice had become seductive. "You better off kill 'em *all*."

When they had entered the business district John Clum saw them and hurried over to Wyatt, calling out his name.

Wyatt reined his horse and turned to him. "We couldn't find 'em," he said. "Any of 'em. They're all holed up someplace."

"Ike Clanton and his brother Phinn and Pony Deal are holed up in Johnny Behan's jail," said Clum.

"What?"

"He figured he was safer in there than with you out looking for him."

"I'm taking him," Wyatt said, striding toward the jail.

Clum caught up and restrained him. "You can't, Wyatt. He surrendered to Behan."

"Oh well, there's a piece of law enforcement," Wyatt said derisively.

"He's wanted for a crime committed in Behan's jursidiction and he's Behan's prisoner. It's the law," said the mayor.

"He's *using* the law, John!"

"And he has every right to, Wyatt," Clum said. "Just like any other citizen. It's what makes us civilized. It's what separates us from the red Indians. We're a *country* of laws."

"We're a country of lawyers," Wyatt said in disgust. He shook his head, turned around, and walked off in the other direction, looking up at Sherm McMasters. "Sherm," he said, "post six men around Johnny Behan's jail. People have a habit of checking out prematurely. If Ike tries it, kill him."

Sherm smiled. "You bet."

"I need a bath," Wyatt said.

Wyatt and Doc went into the Cosmopolitan Hotel, past their two guards at the door. Doc went off to the bar and Wyatt headed up the stairs. In his room, Mattie was out cold, snoring on the bed, her now ever-present bottle of laudanum clutched in her hand. Wyatt crossed to her, took the bottle away, and held it up to the light to see how much was missing. The door to his room was open, and Allie poked her head in.

"How's Virgil?" Wyatt asked.

"Ask him yourself," Allie said, cold and hateful.

Wyatt sighed. "The door was closed," he said, "I didn't want to disturb him."

"Who cares," said Allie, preparing to leave.

"Allie," Wyatt said.

"What?"

Wyatt held up the bottle of laudanum. "How much of this stuff does she take now?"

"What do you care?"

Wyatt looked first at her and then down at Mattie. He spoke without malice or sarcasm, just sadness. "I don't anymore."

The pitcher of hot water poured over his head, streaking the alkali on his face. Josie had set the bathtub up in the center of her room, and Wyatt, luxuriating in the hot bath, leaned back physically and mentally exhausted. "I'm so tired, Josie."

She rubbed his shoulders. "I know," she said softly, "I know." She hated to see this man who was once so in control, now just plain worn out.

"We're broke," he said. "You know? All the properties are mortgaged up to the hilt. . . . I've sold off my interest in the Oriental and that money's already gone for doctor bills. With Morg and Virg down, I'm the only one who's bringing in a paycheck, and it gets sliced pretty thin when you gotta cut it eight ways."

Josie rubbed soap into his hair and began to shampoo it.

"I swear, Josie . . . we *made* money here. Not a lot, but we made money. Doctors and lawyers and bankers . . . that's who it turns out I've been working for. We were gonna make our fortunes here, and nothin's left," he said. "Nothin's left."

She leaned in toward him and said, "Then there's nothing left to hold us here, either."

"There's my . . ." He stopped in midsentence. "I was gonna say there's my family . . ." Wyatt was silent.

"I'll be your family," said Josie.

But Wyatt either didn't hear or didn't care to. He continued in a monotone. ". . . But I don't know how much of that is left now either. Maybe we should all just go." Then he looked up at Josie. "What did you say?"

"I said *I'll* be your family. I'll give you children by the litter if that's what you want, and we'll make our own family. But don't paint rosy pictures that can't ever be."

"What do you mean?"

"I would *never* tell you," she said, "to choose between me and your brothers, but you shouldn't kid either one of us. Your brothers' wives will never accept me . . . never."

Wyatt looked up at her, smiling now for the first time she could remember. "Well, Josie, I wouldn't worry about it. They don't exactly care much for me either."

Just then the door crashed open, exploding off its hinges from the deafening blows of rifle butts. Wyatt whirled instinctively and picked up his six-gun, which lay by the side of the tub, only to find himself staring into one Winchester and one Henry rifle, each held by a grizzled cavalry trooper, one of whom was a sergeant.

"Drop it, please, Marshal Earp," said the sergeant. "I don't want to have to shoot."

"What's the meaning of this?" Josie demanded.

Wyatt still had not dropped his gun. He had it pointed at the sergeant's head.

"Marshal," said the sergeant, "I know you're a good shot and I heard what you did to those McLaury boys, but we start throwin' lead and this here lady's bound to catch some."

Just then a smart-ass cavalry lieutenant, no more than a boy really, and one who was clearly out of his depth, stepped into the doorway and audibly gasped as Wyatt's gun swung around toward him. "Marshal Earp," he said, trying to cover his fear with officialdom.

"If you're in charge, Lieutenant, start talking."

"Marshal Earp . . . I'll have to ask you to put your weapon down. I have a warrant for your arrest, sir."

"On what charge?" Wyatt asked, still not putting the gun down.

"It is a warrant charging you with the murder of Frank and Tom McLaury and William Clanton," said the lieutenant, unable to take his eyes off the gun barrel.

Josie stood up, wedging herself between Wyatt's gun and the lieutenant. "That was decided in a court of law," she said, her chin jutting forward, her hands on her hips. "Those charges were dismissed."

The lieutenant, who was actually mighty grateful for the shield she now provided him, spoke apologetically. "They were dismissed in Tombstone, ma'am," he said, still looking over her shoulder at Wyatt's gun. "They were refiled this afternoon in Contention."

Wyatt finally uncocked the revolver but still didn't put it down. "Refiled by who?"

The lieutenant read from the warrant. "By one Isaac Clanton, Marshal Earp."

"Ike Clanton's in jail!" Wyatt shouted, and damn near jumped out of the bathtub until he remembered he was butt naked; while he couldn't care less of what the lieutenant thought of him, he thought such an action would reflect poorly upon Josie. That was when he heard Johnny Behan's voice.

"Ike *was* in jail, Wyatt," Behan said smugly as he stepped into the room and looked over at Josie. "Miss Marcus . . ." he said, tipping his hat and smiling at what he hoped would be her discomfort.

"Go to hell," Josie said.

"What do you mean *was* in jail?" said Wyatt.

Like a wicked landlord in the classic melodrama, Behan did everything but twirl his mustache as he airily proclaimed, "He was ordered released for insufficient evidence. And the first thing he did was to ask me to file charges for him in Contention."

The lieutenant looked down at his boots and then up at Wyatt. "Sheriff Behan made a formal request of our assistance in serving this warrant. He said he feared for his life if he had to serve it alone."

"He was right," Wyatt said, looking at Behan and then back at the lieutenant. "And will you be escorting me to Contention as well, Lieutenant?"

"No, sir," said the young officer. "Our orders were simply to assist the sheriff in serving the warrant. He and his deputies have said they will see to it that you are taken to Contention."

"I bet they did," said Wyatt. And he was under arrest.

Wyatt and Doc and the still-wounded but ambulatory Morgan were shackled and chained one to the other and loaded into the back of a wagon. Behan sat facing them with a shotgun across his lap as Harry Woods drove the team.

"Hey, Doc," said Morgan. "What do you want to bet we don't make it to Contention alive?"

"Nothin'," said Doc, and Harry whipped up the team and started off. It was nighttime, and as the wagon rolled along out of Tombstone in the open countryside, the three prisoners saw the silhouettes of armed men riding out of the moonlight toward them.

"Here it comes," said Morgan.

" 'Evening, Sheriff Behan," said John Clum from one of the horses.

Behan looked and could now make out, next to Clum, Sherm McMasters, Jack Vermillion, Jack Johnson, and the other members of the Earp posse.

"What are you doing here, Clum?" he said. "This is no affair of yours. Or theirs."

"Miss Marcus said you might be taking a little ride to Contention," said the mayor. "It was such a lovely night, we thought we'd join you just to make sure your prisoners got there in one piece."

Behan and Woods exchanged looks. There was nothing they could do. The sheriff of Cochise County turned to his deputy in disgust and said, "Say giddap to the horses, Harry."

It took but little time to get the charges against them dismissed in Contention, for the point of the exercise had not been to try them in that town but murder them on the way to it. Once the case had been disposed of, Wyatt and Doc and Morgan prepared to return to Tombstone with Clum, McMasters, Vermillion, Johnson, et al. John Clum looked positively radiant at yet another triumph of justice.

"What are you looking so happy about, John?" said Wyatt.

"Well, because . . ." Clum said, "because the judge dismissed the case."

"The *case*!" said Wyatt. "The case that was filed against me by the man who tried to murder my brother who just got set free because of lack of evidence when everybody *knows* he did it. This is nuts, John. The whole thing. It's just nuts."

"Well," said Morgan, "what the hell. When we get back to Tombstone let's go have a beer . . . shoot some pool."

Doc put his arm around Morgan. "Play some cards, get drunk . . . and thank the Lord we're free."

At Hatch's Saloon in Tombstone that night, Wyatt sat as Doc and Morgan shot. Morgan bent over the table, took a shot, and his cue ball wound up in the worst possible place it could be. It seemed, Morgan thought ironically, that when your luck was down, it was down all the way around.

"Behind the eight ball," he said, shaking his head and smiling ruefully. "Wouldn't you know it."

Just then three shots rang out in rapid succession, crashing through the windows behind Wyatt and blowing open Morgan's back.

Instantly Doc and Wyatt had their guns drawn, but the assassins had already vanished.

Lou came running up the street within minutes and pushed her way into the saloon, which was ringed by curiosity seekers. After her followed Allie, helping the still-recovering Virgil down the street and into the saloon, followed by James and Bessie.

Morgan was laid out on the pool table. The doctor had already come, but there was nothing he could do. Morgan looked up at Wyatt and motioned for him to bend down. He was too weak to speak loudly, or perhaps he did not want these words to be heard. Wyatt bent down and put his ear next to Morgan's lips. Morgan whispered words that no one but Wyatt ever heard. Wyatt took Morgan's hand and held it to his chest, then nodded his head back and forth almost imperceptibly.

Lou looked down at her dying husband. Next to her, Allie looked at her favorite brother-in-law. Virgil stood next to her, and James brushed tears from his eyes as he leaned against Bessie, who stood like a statue. And behind them, cut off from the brothers by the wives, stood Doc Holliday, who wept uncontrollably. Tears welled up in Virgil's and Wyatt's eyes but did not fall.

Morgan, lying on his back on the pool table, had his mouth open, and now with every breath came a rattle back in his throat. The doctor leaned over with a clean cloth and wiped fluid and blood out of Morgan's mouth, but the horrible death rattle of his breathing labored on again. And again. And again . . . then stopped.

All was silent as his brothers and wife, sisters-in-law and Doc Holliday literally held their breaths waiting to see if Morgan would take another of his. He did not. The doctor took a pocket mirror and held it up to Morgan's open mouth. No fog formed on the mirror. The doctor then looked at his pocket watch.

"The time of death," he said, "will be fixed at eleven fifty-two P.M."

Later that night, after Mattie had given Lou some of her laudanum, after Virgil had been helped back to his room, and after Doc had finally drunk himself into unconsciousness, Wyatt stood at the window on the third floor, looking out, his face lit by moonlight. Josie appeared behind Wyatt and put her hand on his shoulder. He did not acknowledge her presence.

"What are you going to do?" she asked softly, already knowing the answer.

"Kill 'em all," Wyatt said.

CHAPTER
TWENTY-NINE

CHAPTER
TWENTY-NINE

There was little traffic in the streets of Tombstone early on that particular slate-gray morning, so the sound of a woman screaming was all the more noticeable. She stumbled as she ran, getting up crying, and running all the way to what had become known as the Earp fortress.

The Cosmopolitan Hotel once again had the appearance of a garrison under siege, with one unhappy addition. A hearse was parked out front bearing on its door the name Watt & Tarbell Undertakers. Standing next to the hack was the undertaker who had thought well enough to thank Wyatt for the business he had given them and pledged to stand ready to accommodate the Earp family's future needs as well. He directed two workmen who were similarly dressed in black as they carried a coffin into the hotel. The undertaker watched impassively as the frightened woman ran screaming up to the entrance. She was stopped by Sherm and Vermillion, who guarded the doorway with shotguns in hands and double bandoliers of shells crisscrossing their chests. The woman, Marietta Spence, showed the marks of another brutal beating. Her face was bloody, her clothing was ripped.

"Just hold it right there, lady," said Sherm.

"Madre de dios . . . let me in," she implored.

"No one's goin' in there," he said again.

"Josie," she said. "Miss Marcus . . . you tell her I'm here. You tell her Marietta Spence knows all about who killed Wyatt's brother."

Wyatt stood in Morgan's room looking on as the undertaker and two workmen hefted Morgan's body and placed it into the coffin on the floor from the bed. Lou stood next to the window, eyes wide open, looking like a terrified child as her husband's body was lowered down into the box. Johnson ducked his head into the room and whispered, "Josie needs to see ya outside, Wyatt."

Wyatt cut him off. "Not now."

"I think you better see her," said Johnson. "Marietta Spence was just talkin' to her."

Sherm and Vermillion stood at the entrance to the alleyway as Wyatt came down through the door of the Cosmopolitan. Several men gathered around him acting as bodyguards and indicated that Wyatt should head for the alley. Wyatt strode over past Sherm and Vermillion to Josie, who had an arm around Marietta Spence. Wyatt looked from one woman to the other.

"Tell him," Josie said to Marietta.

"If I tell you," Marietta said to Wyatt, "you get him?"

"Who?"

"Mi esposo."

"Pete Spence?" Wyatt asked.

Marietta nodded her head. "The men who kill your brother . . . ? Pete. Frank Stillwell. The one they call Indian Charlie . . ."

"Cruz?" said Wyatt. "Florentino Cruz?"

Marietta nodded her head and continued. "And Curly Bill . . . and Johnny Ringo. They're the ones behind it. The others actually did it. He threatened to kill me. He threatened to kill me and my mother. He'll do it, too."

"No," said Wyatt, "he will not." It was not a threat or a promise, it was a fact. Pete Spence would die, Wyatt would see to that.

"I don't have no place to stay," said the Mexican woman. Wyatt called out to Sherm, "Sherm! Take this lady upstairs. Find out where her mother is and bring her too. Make sure they're protected.''

"You kill him?'' Marietta said, grabbing Wyatt's arm. "I want him dead. . . . He put a knife to my throat. I want him dead!''

Wyatt took her hand off of him. "You go with Mr. McMasters,'' he said.

Sherm led Marietta off down the alleyway. Wyatt turned to Josie. Just then a cat jumped out of the garbage and Wyatt whirled, drew his gun, cocked and leveled it, slammed Josie back out of harm's way, and then saw that it was just a cat. He let out a long sigh and turned back to Josie.

"We're taking Morgan's body to my parents' ranch in California.''

"I want to go with you.''

"No.''

"Please,'' she said.

"I want you to go to Colorado. I want you to go find Bat Masterson. I'll send him a wire.''

"Wyatt . . .'' she said, trying to figure out a way to make him see.

"I can't be thinking about protecting you, Josie. You understand? I have things to do.''

They were both quiet, and then Josie said, "I'll do whatever you want me to.''

"I'll come to you as soon as I can,'' said Wyatt. "As soon as it's over . . . as soon as it's safe.'' He held her to him and then added, "I don't know when that will be, but I'll come to you.''

She put her head on his chest and he held her close. "Colorado's not like here,'' he said barely above a whisper. "It's green . . . it's so green. They have wildflowers there, and it's so green. . . .''

Morgan's coffin was loaded into the hearse by Watt & Tarbell's finest as Wyatt entered the hotel only to be stopped by Doc, who carried a telegram. "Wyatt,'' he said, handing him the wire. "It just came from Bob Paul in Tucson. He says he knows we're traveling to California for the funeral and he wanted to warn you that he's seen Ike Clanton, Frank Stillwell, and someone else he didn't know around the train yards. His guess is they're there to assassinate you.''

Wyatt read the telegram aloud: ". . . Therefore, my advice is to stay on the train and on your guard. My deepest sympathies to you and your family. Your friend, Bob Paul."

Lou came down the stairway dressed in black, her eyes red-rimmed. She passed Wyatt on the stairs and said nothing. Wyatt watched her pass for a moment, breathed out a sigh, and then continued up the stairs.

In his room Virgil finished reading the telegram Wyatt had given him. He was still bandaged across his chest and needed Wyatt's help as he slipped on his shirt.

"How're we gonna do it?" he asked his brother.

Then Wyatt began the most painful conversation of his life. The emotion drained from his face and voice, and what was left was strictly business. It was deadly serious business with no room for mistakes.

"We're not," Wyatt said, helping Virgil on with his remaining shirtsleeve.

Virgil looked up at him. "What are you talking about?"

"You're no good to me now, Virgil."

"Wyatt . . ."

"You're busted up and you're a liability."

Virgil looked down at his shoes as Wyatt buttoned Virgil's shirt. Virgil looked back up, tears in his eyes. "Damn, Wyatt," he said, "I could—"

"It's over, Virg," said Wyatt. "I'll handle it."

Wyatt buttoned the last button on Virgil's shirt. "You're the best of us, Virgil," Wyatt said. "You always were."

Mattie, dressed in black, sat on the edge of the bed staring at the opposite wall. Wyatt appeared in the doorway.

"It's time to go now, Mattie," he said.

Mattie looked up at him through the narcotic gauze of her addiction. "Sure, sugar," she said, and smiled a little smile, adding as if it was an afterthought, "Hmmm . . . You're the only brother who hasn't been shot. That's not fair."

So saying, she pulled out a gun and pointed it right at Wyatt's head. He ducked as she fired.

Out front of the hotel, Sherm and Vermillion heard the gunshot and raced back inside to be met by Doc, who already had his gun drawn. The three of them ran up the stairs to

Wyatt's open room. They stood in the doorway and saw
Mattie crumpled on the bed, sobbing. Wyatt held a small gun
in his hand. He turned to them and handed Sherm the weapon.

"There was an accident," he said. "Hold on to this. It
went off by accident."

Allie and Virg came down the stairs, Allie supporting Virgil, saying, "Maybe it'll work out for us. We can get a little
farm in California. Just us. Just the two of us."

Sherm and Vermillion came down the stairs with Mattie in
between them. Each of them held one of her arms. Her face
was twisted with dementia.

"Who'll take care of me?" she howled.

Next came James and Bessie. James was pickled and indignant.

"He doesn't ask me for help!" he slurred. "I could do
things. He never asks me!"

"Thank God you're a drunk, James," Bessie said, "or he
would."

Wyatt looked all around his room like a traveling salesman
who was trying to make sure he had left nothing behind in
his hotel. He reached over to the dresser and picked up a Colt
.45 and stuck it in his waistband.

Then he put on his gun belt with the heavy, long-barreled
Buntline Special, checking first to make sure it was loaded.
He picked up his old Wells Fargo days twelve-gauge double-
barreled shotgun, slipped in two rounds, snapped it shut, and
caught sight of himself in the dresser mirror. On his shirtfront
was a badge. He looked at his reflection long and hard. Then
he took off the badge and held it in his hand. He ran his
thumb slowly across the scratched face of it, across the words
"U.S. Deputy Marshal," then placed it in an open drawer
and slowly pushed the drawer shut.

The door of the baggage car was open with Morgan's coffin
sitting in the center of the car and Lou sitting in a chair next
to the coffin, motionless. The trainman grabbed the door, slid
it shut.

In a passenger car, Virgil and Allie sat side by side opposite
Mattie. James and Bessie sat on the next bench, James taking
a swig from his bottle and leaning across to pass it to Doc,
who sat across the aisle with Sherm McMasters, Vermillion,

and Johnson. Standing at the other end of the car was Wyatt, who was staring out the window at the undertaker hack. The undertaker looked up at Wyatt as the train pulled out, leaving behind it the station and the sign receding in the distance that said, "Tombstone."

In Tucson at sunset a little boy ate popcorn from a bag and held his father's hand as they pushed through the desert metropolis's streets on what to all appearances was a very festive occasion.

There was bunting everywhere of the Stars and Stripes, crowds of men, women and children converging on the town square, hawkers selling wares, families with picnic baskets. For tonight Tucson would inaugurate its new gaslight system. The whole town was there to celebrate. In the center of town there was a platform from which the mayor of the city addressed the citizenry and, to his mind, posterity.

"It won't be long now, my friends," he said. "As soon as yonder sun sets in the horizon, we will celebrate the dawning of a new age."

Ike Clanton and Frank Stillwell stood in the crowd of celebrants listening to the mayor's words. Ike pulled out his pocket watch, looked at it, and looked at the train schedule he held in his other hand as he heard the mayor say, "No, it won't be long now . . ."

The long, slow train was silhouetted black against the crimson and purple Arizona sunset. It chugged along through the desert, belching black smoke as it neared its destination.

"Ever since Adam and Eve were banished from the Garden of Eden," intoned the mayor, "man has feared the darkness of the night and been powerless against it.

"Certainly we who live on the frontier have known the blackest nights, where not even the glowing embers of the pioneer's lonely campfire were there to illuminate the barren mesas of the Southwest that it has been our manifest destiny to inherit."

In the crowd Ike turned to Frank Stillwell and smiled, checking the schedule and his watch once again. "Like Curly Bill used to say, it's killin' time."

He and Stillwell began pushing their way through the crowd

toward the train yard as the mayor continued his vision: "But tonight, we leave the past and the time of savages and cavemen behind as we enter a golden age of progress."

In the baggage compartment Wyatt, Doc, Sherm, Vermillion, and Johnson stood near the coffin, all of them with shotguns as Wyatt looked out the half-opened baggage compartment door for the men who would kill them. He knew they were out there waiting in the dark.

"Indeed," said the mayor, "as we leave the past behind and enter the bright golden dawn of a more civilized age, our fair city has become an island of light."

On the horizon, the last sliver of sun sank.

The mayor walked to the edge of the platform, where a noble young lad in short pants and gymnastics shirt stood holding a torch. Stretching down on the road in front of him were the gaslights spaced out at intervals, and by each gaslight a fresh-faced boy or girl dressed like Uncle Sam with a lamplighter pole waiting for the flame to come their way.

". . . And so," said the mayor, "my fellow Americans, my fellow Arizonians, fellow citizens of Tucson . . . I take great pride and pleasure in igniting this flame symbolic of the hopes and dreams which burn in our hearts as we stand poised at the edge of the new millennium. Welcome," he said, "to the future!"

He lit the torch and the bearer set off, torch held high in his hand, in a slow jog down the street as the brass band played and people cheered.

The train pulled slowly into the yard as Stillwell and Ike crossed the first set of tracks and pulled out their guns. Ike, who was evidently acting as field commander, motioned Stillwell to go in one direction while he went in the other.

The train had not yet come to a stop when the door to the baggage compartment slid open and Wyatt jumped down, then Doc, then Vermillion, then Sherm, and then Johnson, all of them with firearms at the ready.

A new cheer went up from the crowd as the first Uncle Sam lamplighter took fire from the torch that had reached him and lit the gas lamp with a whoosh and a puff like a stove catching fire, as Stillwell prowled through the darkened freight yard.

Wyatt climbed up onto a parked set of freight cars and

walked down the line on their roofs. Peering into the darkness, crouched low on top of a car, he saw something. Then, like a cat, he slipped down along the line.

Stillwell, down below, was unaware that Wyatt was stalking him from behind and above.

The torch runner was working up a slight sweat but smiling still, as he passed the flame to yet another lamplighter. Children waved the Old Glory back and forth in front of him, their faces lit yellow from torchlight.

A worried look crossed Stillwell's face as he felt the presence of danger close over his heart in an icy grip.

At the other end of the yard, Ike prowled through the darkness, and through the darkness, Doc was hunting too.

There were only three lamps left unlit on the street, at the end of which was a beautiful young woman, blond hair flowing back behind her, costumed as an idealized representation of Lady Liberty. She held her own torch up, smiling, waiting for the runner to light it.

Wyatt jumped down from the roof of the freight car inches behind Stillwell. Stillwell turned at the sound, stumbling back as he looked up into the dark face of Wyatt Earp.

Whoosh. Puff. Only one lamp remained as Lady Liberty smiled, stretching forth her lamp.

"Murder my brother, you son of a bitch?" Wyatt hissed as he raised the shotgun and trained it on Stillwell, who recoiled at the sight of his executioner, feebly raising up his own gun in faint hope of defense. As the runner reached the lady she held her torch high to meet his. With them both then bursting into flame, the street exploded in fireworks that lit up the skies, and Wyatt pulled the first trigger of the double-barreled gun that ripped its charge through Frank Stillwell.

Stillwell's innards and Wyatt's face shone in the skyrockets' white glare. A second rocket exploded phosphorus yellow as Wyatt loosed the contents of the other barrel, lifting Stillwell back off his heels and into the air.

In the city's square, happy townsfolk pulled out their side arms, shot into the air, and cheered. Men embraced the ladies and the band played loudly, muffling the sounds of gunfire.

Wyatt stood over the body of Frank Stillwell, watching the death throes. He pulled the pistol out of his waistband, and not hearing the patriotic airs wafting from the square through the train yard nor seeing the fireworks that lit the sky, he pumped all six shells into the dead body with his left hand. Simultaneously his right pulled out the Buntline Special. Then he emptied that gun into his brother's murderer as well.

Mixed into the sounds of the faraway fireworks Doc heard Wyatt's guns and took off at a run, and Ike, hearing the guns as well, ran and dove underneath a freight car, cowering like a dog.

"Jesus, Wyatt," Doc said when he got to his friend, who was firing his last two shots into the corpse, and saw Wyatt's face in the fading afterglow of Chinese gunpowder in the sky. Wyatt looked insane. Doc looked down at the body, full of bullet holes and blood. "Jesus," he said again, and Doc, looking at Wyatt, was for the first time in his life afraid of a gunman.

"Give me your gun," Wyatt said in a voice hoarse as brimstone.

"Why?" Doc replied.

"Give me your gun!"

Doc complied. Wyatt took it and started shooting rounds into the corpse. "Jesus, Wyatt, he's dead," Doc said in horror.

Wyatt fired yet another round.

"Come on, Wyatt! *I'm* supposed to be the crazy one."

Wyatt turned to look at him, and it was not Doc who looked crazy. Wyatt turned back to the corpse and fired the next three rounds, till the gun clicked and clicked again.

"Wyatt," Doc said, pulling at his friend's arm, "let's go."

For a moment Wyatt looked disoriented, dazed. Then he started back a step, turned on the corpse, coughed up, and spit on it.

"Great," said Doc, shaking his head ruefully. "You satisfied now? Can we go now?"

He pulled again at Wyatt's arm to turn him away. Wyatt at first went along passively, but then shrugged him off, turning back to Stillwell's corpse and kicking it as hard as he could with his boot, again and again as the last of the fireworks glimmered out in the sky.

CHAPTER THIRTY

Sunrise on the mesa. The flat land blended into purple sky streaked red, then orange that rose up over the horizon in a fiery ball. Five horsemen appeared: Wyatt, Doc, Vermillion, McMasters, and Johnson. Wyatt headed off in one direction and the other four in another.

When he reached Tombstone the next day, Wyatt rode down the street through the Hoptown section. China Mary sat out front of the Celestial Laundry in a rocking chair smoking a cigar. She looked up at Wyatt and saw the look on his face, and smiled a wicked, knowing smile.

Wyatt rode past the Wells Fargo office, and there in the window as if on watch for Wyatt's arrival was Wilbur, who got up and scrambled outside.

"Marshal Earp," he called. "Marshal Earp."

Wyatt reined in his horse.

"There's a wire just come in, Marshal Earp," said Wilbur. "For me?"

"No, sir," Wilbur said. "For Sheriff Behan."

"Then why you tellin' me, Wilbur?"

"Well, sir, it's a wire advising Sheriff Behan that there is a warrant out for your arrest, sir . . . for murder."

"Whose murder?"

"Fella by the name of Stillwell," said Wilbur. "Said they was close to twenty holes in him and that somebody seen you and Doc leavin' the train yard in Tucson."

"Has Behan seen that wire yet?" Wyatt asked, looking around.

"No, sir. I was kinda hopin' I'd see you first. I showed it to Mister Clum, though," Wilbur said, hoping he had done right by the marshal.

"I would appreciate it if Behan didn't see it for another half hour," Wyatt said.

"You bet," said the little man.

"Thank you, Wilbur."

Wilbur looked at him, and then said in a kind of awe, "You gonna kill 'em all, ain't ya."

Wyatt did not answer but rode on.

Clum was there with his copy boy, Wayne, when Wyatt came into the *Epitaph*. Clum turned to the lad. "You go out and get some lunch now, Wayne," he said.

"But it's not ten o'clock yet, Mister Clum," said the boy.

"Then go out and get some breakfast."

"But I already had—"

"Leave!" said Clum.

"Yes, sir."

Once Wayne was outside, Wyatt pulled an envelope from his inside coat pocket.

"Hello, John," he said.

"Johnny Behan's gonna be looking for you once he—"

"I already talked to Wilbur," said Wyatt. "I have a little time."

"Wyatt, what . . ." John Clum wore a pained expression. "You couldn't have been trying to arrest him . . . not with close to twenty bullet holes in his body."

"No," said Wyatt, "I wasn't trying to arrest him."

"I . . . I don't know what to say to that."

Wyatt handed him the envelope. "This is my will, John," he said. "I've named you as executor. Not that there's much left. The bank'll have the houses . . . but there are a few mining claims."

"It's vengeance, then," exclaimed the mayor. "Plain vengeance!"

"It's survival, John."

"This is not the jungle. We have laws!"

"Yes, we do," said Wyatt. "And if they think that they can exterminate my family and then hide behind alibis—and the technicalities of those laws—then they have missed their guess."

Clum considered all the ramifications, not just for Wyatt but for himself as well.

"I won't be able to help you," he said. "You've crossed the line, Wyatt."

"There isn't any line. Not anymore."

Wyatt rode his horse slowly down Fremont Street, past the O.K. Corral, past what folks called "Earp Corners," the four houses that belonged to the Earp brothers. The doors to the houses were open. On one house, the door hung on one hinge and a mattress was propped up against a window. It appeared that the houses had been vandalized and looted. Painted across the wall of Virgil's house was the word *Murderers*.

Just then Johnny Behan came up First Street. Behind him trailed Wilbur, and Behan held the telegram in his hand.

"Hold on there, Wyatt," Behan said.

Wyatt turned to look at him. The look was ice and brooked no misinterpretation.

"Uh . . ." said the sheriff, seeing the look. "I . . . uhh . . : I want to see you about this."

Then Wyatt said, "You might just see me once too often, Johnny."

And he rode slowly out of town.

A lone outlaw sentry stood on a rock watching the approach to the system of desert caves. In the distance he saw a rider kicking up dust as he came full tilt toward the hideout. The sentry took his rifle and just for the fun of it sighted on the rider.

"It's me, ya damn fool!" Johnny Behan called out to the sentry.

In Curly Bill's desert hideout, Behan addressed Curly Bill, Johnny Ringo, Ike Clanton, and sundry other outlaws. "Now we got him," he said. "We can shoot him on sight and the territorial government'll pay us to do it."

Ike perked up. "Uhh . . . how much?" he asked.

"Shut up," Ringo said.

"Well," said Ike, explaining himself. "Of course, I'd do it for nothing."

"Here. Put these on," said Sheriff Behan.

So saying, he pulled out a dozen silver stars with the words "Deputy Sheriff, Cochise County" emblazoned on each. The outlaws got a great giggle out of this.

"Well, I'll be," Johnny Ringo said.

"Deputies!" said Curly Bill.

"I'll be damned," chimed in Ike Clanton.

Like little children playing with a trunk of clothes, the outlaws pinned the badges on, pointing to one another and themselves, laughing at the law.

"You are all now a legally constituted posse of deputy sheriffs," said Johnny Behan, who remembered as an afterthought, "Oh . . . Raise your right hands and repeat after me."

Curly Bill, however, was in no mood to cooperate. "Shut up and let's ride," he said.

Behan backed down very quickly. "You bet," he said. "Whatever you say, Bill."

The outlaws all mounted up, and a disappointed Ike, who had missed his moment of glory, crossed to Behan.

"*I'll* raise *my* right hand, Johnny."

"Shut up," said the sheriff.

At about the same time, Wyatt, Doc and Sherm, Vermillion, and Johnson sat atop their horses on the rise overlooking a small ramshackle ranch.

"That's Pete Spence's ranch down there," Doc said.

"And Cruz was staying there too?" asked Wyatt.

"Yeah," said Doc.

"Let's go," Wyatt said, and the men rode down toward the ranch.

Out near the tumbledown cabin, Florentino Cruz, alias Indian Charlie, was chopping wood. He looked up as he heard horses approach, and though he wore no gun, a Henry rifle was propped up near the chopping block. He grabbed it and looked up at the approaching horsemen.

"Cruz? Florentino Cruz?" Wyatt called out, seeing him go for his weapon.

By way of response, Cruz drew a bead and fired. It was the only shot he got off. Wyatt and his men all pulled their weapons, spurred their horses, and charged cavalry-style at Cruz, firing their guns as they galloped toward him.

At the sight of Wyatt and his men bearing down on him, Cruz turned to run. Wyatt and his men continued firing even though his back was turned. Cruz was hit in the buttocks several times and fell to the ground.

"Oh, my butt," he called in agony. "Oh, my butt."

Sadly for him, those were his last words. More bullets ripped open his chest now and splattered on the earth and outbuildings behind him.

The sign on the Tucson sheriff's office said "Sheriff's Office—Robert Paul, Sheriff." Pete Spence walked in. Sheriff Bob Paul sat at his desk doing paperwork as Spence entered.

"Are you Sheriff Paul?"

"I am," said the sheriff.

Spence pulled out his gun and Paul went for his, misunderstanding the move.

"Whoa . . . Whoa!" said Spence hurriedly. "I ain't drawin' down, mister. I'm givin' up."

He dropped his gun.

"Who are you?" asked Sheriff Paul.

"I'm Pete Spence . . . and I shot Morgan Earp and I'm givin' up and I want you to put me in your jail before his maniac brother finds me."

"You're ready to sign a confession?"

"Mister," said Spence, "I'm ready to write a book if that's what it takes. Earp's already killed Stillwell and Cruz, and the way I figure, prison ain't near as confining as a grave."

For the next two weeks, Behan and his band of outlaws who were now supposedly lawmen combed the desert floor looking for Wyatt and his bunch of lawmen who were now outlaws. They crisscrossed each other's trails half a dozen times without another major run-in as they searched the canyons and arroyos in vain for each other.

The days began to lengthen and the sun took a long time to set in Mescal Canyon, the day refusing to give way to darkness without a fight. The yellows and reds stayed up there in the dark sky a long time after the sun was already gone. Curly Bill and his men were tired. They were also awfully hot. The dust caked on the sweat that poured from each of them. Johnny turned to Curly Bill.

"Bill, it's almost dark," he said. "It's been a long, hot day. Beans and bed would sure go good about now. We ain't gonna find anybody at night."

"Okay," said Curly Bill. "But no fires."

"I hate cold beans," Ike whined.

They dismounted and hobbled their horses.

Wyatt and his party were strung out with about twenty yards between each rider as they straggled through the canyon. They were likewise exhausted. Wyatt for the first time was showing signs of wear and tear, and he loosened his gun belt to its last notch and let out a sigh.

The land in this part of the countryside of Mescal Canyon was thick with mesquite and palo christi bushes so thick and so high that a man could travel ten paces from his group and no longer see them. And so it was now that Wyatt was out a little ways in front of his men so that they could not see him, and he quite literally rode right into the middle of Curly Bill's camp. Curly Bill and his men were all lying on blankets, eating beans, when Wyatt simply rode into their midst by mistake.

Curly Bill looked up. "What the . . ." he said, dropping his plate of beans and scrambling for his six-gun, which he had taken off.

Wyatt, for his part, was taken by surprise and horrified at finding himself all alone in the enemy's camp. Guns started coming out from every direction. There was no question that if he tried to wheel hs horse and run he would be shot down. He leaped off his horse, holding the reins to use it for cover. Unfortunately, because the gun belt with the Buntline Special had been loosened as he hit the ground, it slipped from his waist and fell down around his ankles, causing him to trip over it.

"Damn!" he cursed, reaching his hand up as shots rang out, one hitting his horse in the flank. Wyatt grabbed the shotgun from its scabbard and as his horse bellowed in pain and fell, Wyatt found himself face-to-face with Curly Bill, who was just as shocked to be staring into Wyatt's double barrels, which now promptly exploded and blasted him to perdition. The twelve-gauge at this range had cut him in half.

Doc and the others heard the gunfire. Doc drew his weapon and spurred his horse, riding straight into the camp, which was now full of men scurrying for their mounts. One outlaw was drawing down on Wyatt, who was bending over to pick up his gun. Just then Doc fired and that outlaw went down, dead.

"They got us surrounded!" Behan cried.

He and Ike and Johnny and the others leaped aboard their animals and spurred them off in all directions as Doc jumped off his horse. Wyatt appeared to him to have been hit.

"Wyatt, you hit?"

"I tripped," Wyatt said.

"What?"

"I got caught with my knickers down around my ankles, Doc, and I tripped."

An embarrassed Wyatt stood and pulled his gun belt back up around his waist as if pulling on his drawers, and cinched the belt.

"Jeez, that was close," Wyatt said, shaken. "I just rode into their camp, Doc. I mean, I just looked up and there they all were . . ."

"We could probably catch up to a few of them. . . . You wanna go after 'em?" Doc asked.

"No."

"Good," said Doc. "Neither do I."

"Scary," Wyatt said, shuddering. "Just plain scary."

At Fort Huachuca, Arizona, a tired and dirty Johnny Behan rode up to the gates.

A Captain Clark was the commanding officer of this frontier outpost. Johnny Behan stood in front of him, having fled the ambush and headed directly to the fort.

"The Earp gang," he said, "was responsible for the deaths of Frank and Tom McLaury and Billy Clanton. They got off on a legal loophole but now they've shown their true colors and they've gone and killed Frank Stillwell in cold blood. And they've gone and killed Florentino Cruz, also known as Indian Charlie, in cold blood. . . . And while I and my duly deputized posse were pursuing them, in a cowardly ambush they have murdered my deputy, William Brocious . . . and Johnny Barnes. They have become a scourge upon the land and are bent on continuing their reign of murderous terror. Now I am demanding Federal help in apprehending these killers who have overwhelmed the abilities of the office of the sheriff of Cochise County.''

Shortly thereafter, a mounted troop of cavalry rode through Tombstone ready for war. China Mary watched impassively as a young cavalry trooper pulled out a wanted poster and hammered it into place over a wanted poster that said, ''Wanted Dead or Alive for Murder—Curly Bill Brocious.''

The new one read: ''Wanted Dead or Alive for Murder— Wyatt Earp.''

CHAPTER
THIRTY-ONE

Johnny Behan left the office of the sheriff of Cochise County and walked down the street toward his house, dog tired and ready for a bath and a drink. Johnny pushed open the door of his house and walked in.

There sitting in a chair by the window was the silhouette of a man with a gun. Behan started backing up, his hands raised. "Wyatt, please, listen . . ." he pleaded.

Suddenly the silhouette spoke with a tone of panic in his voice as well.

"Wyatt?! Where?" said Johnny Ringo from the shadows.

"Who's there?" called Behan.

"Wyatt?" Johnny asked, frightened.

"Johnny?" Behan asked, confused.

"Yeah," Johnny Ringo said.

"You alone?" Behan asked.

"Yeah . . . You too?"

"Yeah," said Behan, relieved.

"Thank God," Johnny said.

Behan gingerly crossed over to a lamp and lit it, revealing the terrified-looking Johnny Ringo.

"You gotta help me," Johnny said. "I'm the only one left. The Earps are ridin' all through the territory to every water hole in the Whetstones shootin' everybody in sight who even knows me."

"Where's Ike and Phinn?" Behan asked.

"Who knows? I hear they went down to Mexico. I shoulda gone with 'em, but it's too late now. . . . I can't be out there. They're killin' everybody."

"The Federals are out lookin' for 'em now," Behan said.

"Oh, them blue boys couldn't find shit in an outhouse. Did you see how he blew Curly Bill apart? Cut him in half with that shotgun of his."

Behan shuddered as he remembered. "You want a drink?" he asked.

"I want a lot of drinks," Johnny said.

Behan took a bottle, took a swig, and passed the bottle to Johnny, who took a long, long swig.

"Twenty bullet holes in poor old Frank Stillwell," he said, "not countin' the shotgun. . . . What kinda animal is he, anyway? Damn maniac. How dead you gotta be before he stops shootin' at you?"

He took another swig off the bottle. "I'm movin' in with ya, if it's all the same to you," said Ringo.

"Well, now wait a second," said Behan. "Maybe it isn't all the same—"

"I'll pay ya," said Johnny. "I got money. Fat lot a good it's gonna do me with Wyatt out there waitin' to shoot me twenty times with those Colts of his."

Johnny took another long swig. "I been sittin' here countin' stiffs . . . countin' ghosts, you know?" he said. "I know more dead people than I know live ones—all on account a Earp. What's it take to kill that guy, anyway?"

He took another long drink that killed the bottle.

The front of the Cochise County sheriff's office now bore a mighty resemblance to the way the front of the Cosmopolitan Hotel had looked. Sandbags were piled up at the windows, revealing gun portals. Armed men with bandoliers stood at the rooftops of buildings and blue-uniformed cavalrymen patrolled the streets.

*　*　*

Out in the desert there was a mighty dust storm blowing and the cavalrymen, heads down, bent against the wind, pushed on through the harsh countryside.

From behind boulders Wyatt watched them through his telescope. Next to him were Doc, Sherm, Vermillion, and Johnson. The wind kicked up the sand, biting into their faces.

Wyatt passed the telescope to Doc, who looked down at the horse soldiers. "Shoot," he said, "you'd think we were the entire Apache nation on the warpath from the number of blue coats they got out lookin' for us."

Sherm was reading a well-worn week-old newspaper. "Says here Johnny Behan sent a wire to the President demanding Federal troops be sent in to stop the wholesale slaughter," he said.

"Why'd the President listen to him?" said Doc. "We're Republicans . . . why doesn't he listen to us?"

"I don't see how we're gonna be able to get past all of 'em," Sherm said.

"There's gotta be some way," said Wyatt.

Doc turned to him. "Wyatt," he said.

"What?"

"You remember back in Tombstone after Virgil got shot when I told you it was time to lay low?"

"Yeah," said Wyatt.

"It's that time again."

Wyatt looked at him, questioning with his look if Doc was giving up.

"Don't look at me like that," said Doc. "I want to see Johnny Ringo just as dead as you do. But when the rabbit goes into the hole, it's time to . . . it's time to . . ."

It was clear that Doc had gotten lost in this metaphor.

"It's time to *what*, Doc?" said Wyatt.

"Oh, how should I know," Doc said. "I'm a dentist and a gambler and a gentleman. It's time to grow carrots, okay? It's time to get out of these godforsaken dust storms. It's time for a drink and a bath and a hard mattress and a soft woman and the hell with rabbits. God, how I hate the desert!"

It was ten days' hard ride out of Arizona into New Mexico and then shooting straight up to Colorado. Wyatt came up out of red rock and purple sky and pink stone mountains like statues where the Indians sat on top and talked to God. The sand turned fine to dust and covered every part of man and horse alike. He lived it, breathed it, tasted it there on his teeth and in his nostrils, and the wind blasted the sand and grit hard against his skin. And then, like a miracle, there came Colorado.

A ranch sat in a tiny valley wedged in between two mountain ranges. A full creek ran down the middle of the valley, bisecting it into two lush meadows gone crazy with the colors of wildflowers sprinkled throughout. The mouth of the canyon was the only way in, and from the vantage point of the small homesteaders' cabin tucked way in a corner of the valley you could see anyone approaching. If you needed to run you could follow the creek back up into the mountains to any one of several dozen trails. It was, in short, an idyllic place for laying low.

Into that valley rode Wyatt. His horse and clothes and face were caked with trail dust that made him look foreign in this lush green setting: a visitor from a far-off harsh, dry land. The look on his face was one of relief and release, a sinner on a twenty-four-hour pass in paradise, and up ahead of him he saw Josie. She had planted a small garden next to the homesteaders' cabin. Her hair was down and long, and patches of light played on it through the trees. The setting was so beautiful and so different from all he had just been through that when he swallowed now, it was not gulping trail dust as much as choking back the emotion of coming home to a place he'd never seen before.

Josie looked up startled, not from any sound but from a feeling of awareness at the back of her neck or perhaps a tickle in her throat, something that not even forest animals could see or hear or smell, something that let her know her love was near. She turned to him, spoke his name, Wyatt, without any sound, rushed to him, said it again in a rush in a whisper in a prayer in Thanksgiving, Wyatt, in rejoicing. . . .

"Wyatt!" she cried.

And into each other's arms, she kissing him, he luxuriating in the touch of her lips on his skin, breaking through the caked-on dust, breaking through with kisses and tears, she kissed him again.

She said his name over and over again, as if with each utterance she could make him be more real, planted there in front of her in this valley and not just in her imagination or dreams.

"Wyatt . . . Wyatt . . . Wyatt . . ."

As if overcome with both their emotions and the beauty of the place, they sank down into the grass holding on to each other, little whimper sounds rising from both their throats. He kissed her now, full on the mouth and hard, to make her forget, to give them a way to hide and be hidden. But there was something in that kiss that Josie sensed. It wasn't passion for her, nor longing for her. She put her fingers up to his lips to stop him, to give a moment for the rush of blood to leave her head so she could think and understand, and then she did and there was a look on her face, neither of terror nor even disappointment—just heartrending sadness.

"It's not over yet . . . is it?" she said.

And Wyatt shook his head, no, and she sighed and pulled his head down onto her breast.

"Hide here," she said in a voice soft as her breasts felt to him against his cheek. "Let me hide you. . . . You hide here for a while."

She pulled him in tighter, rocking him slowly, rocking slowly.

A bathtub of soapy water sat in the center of the room, a fluffy white towel was on the floor, and a freshly bathed, hair-still-wet Wyatt was in bed with the woman he loved. He reached across and pulled her to him, buried himself in the touch and the feel and the smell of her, traced along her mouth with his fingers and then let them play down across her neck as his lips found hers. The fireplace crackled and an orange light from the fire played out across their bodies.

The next day there was the hard *thwack* of a log being split as Wyatt chopped fuel for the fireplace. Josie smiled up at him from where she knelt, weeding the garden.

There were days when Wyatt and Josie walked next to each other, a picnic basket between them, each of them holding one of the handles, till a checked tablecloth was spread out along with good things to eat, corn on the cob and rosy apples, home-baked bread and yellow and orange cheeses that neither of them touched as they lay in the tall grass and Wyatt play-fully laced wildflowers into her hair.

One day there was a deer in the woods. It stood there frozen with fear as Wyatt sighted it through his favorite old Henry rifle. His finger started to squeeze the trigger, and then he lowered the rifle.

The deer looked at him quizzically.

"Shut up," Wyatt said quietly to the animal, and the deer just continued to look at him.

"Well, go on, shoo . . . ya dumb deer," he said, and went home to Josie.

Josie was bent over a cooking fire in the cabin. She looked up as Wyatt entered with the rifle in his hand and no meat for dinner.

"No luck?" she asked.

Wyatt put something on the table. She could not see what it was.

"Carrots," Wyatt said. "It's what you grow when the rabbit goes into the hole."

The next day, Wyatt was working in the garden. There was no gun belt at his hip. Nearby, Josie was gathering eggs from the chicken coops.

Four horsemen dressed in black rode up from far away across the meadow with the sun behind them so he could not make out who they were. Only the way they rode and the rifles sticking up in their scabbards told him these men were not homesteaders.

Josie looked up, frightened. "Wyatt . . . ?" she said.

Wyatt saw them, squinted his eyes against the sun, dropped the hoe, and picked up the rifle leaning against the cabin.

"Get in the cabin, Josie," he said.

She moved to the cabin as Wyatt cocked the rifle. He shaded his eyes against the sun, trying to make out who the riders were. Behind him the cabin door opened and Josie came out carrying the shotgun, into which she rammed two shells and snapped the action shut.

"Wyatt!" the rider called.

Wyatt squinted his eyes even more and then recognized Bat Masterson.

"Oh . . ." he said, trying to act nonchalant. "Hi."

With Bat was Marsh Williams, a fellow by the name of Fred Dodge, and Sherm McMasters.

"Hello, Marsh," Wyatt said. "Long time no see. . . . Sherm, I thought you were in Denver with Doc."

"Marsh here wanted to see you, Wyatt," said Bat. "And for some reason he thought I might know where you were."

"Wyatt," Marsh said, "this is Fred Dodge. He is an undercover detective for Wells Fargo."

The table was set outside under a tree, where Wyatt sat with Marsh, Bat, Sherm, and Fred. The men drank coffee and ate corn bread with big slabs of fresh churned butter.

"You boys did quite a job, Wyatt," Fred Dodge said. "We haven't had a stage hit or a bank robbed or any cattle rustled for the last three months. Seems like everybody who ever rode with the Clantons is either dead or departed for parts unknown. If you ask me, they ought to elect you governor instead of havin' your face on 'Wanted' posters."

"And that's the way Wells Fargo feels as well," said Marsh. "Whatever influence we have is going to be used with the governor of Colorado to fight your extradition."

Wyatt looked at him long and hard.

"Well, I appreciate that, Marsh," he said. "But I don't believe that's what you came all this way to tell me."

"It is part of the reason, Wyatt," Marsh replied. "We like things as quiet as they are. We'd like to see to it that they stay that way.

"Sooner or later word's going to get out that you're laying low and Johnny Ringo may get the idea that he can start back up again right where he left off. He's the only one left who could do that."

"And . . . ?" said Wyatt.

"He *was* one of the men who killed Morgan," Marsh said.

"I'm aware of that," Wyatt said evenly.

"We could help you get him if you're still of a mind to do that," said Marsh. "Fred here has any number of informants who would keep tabs on Johnny, and the minute he comes up for air you would know about it. We could help provide horses and way stations to allow you to get back into Arizona and out again without anyone being the wiser. . . . And I

have been authorized to tell you that the home office would
be willing to express its appreciation with a reward for you
or your men upon presentation of suitable proof that Ringo
has been eliminated."

Wyatt just looked at him.

"Now, I cannot provide documentation for that offer," he
continued, "and I would call you a liar if you ever quote me
. . . but the offer is there nonetheless. You want Ringo dead
for family reasons. For the home office it's just good business."

Wyatt looked up at Josie, who watched him from the cabin
and then went sadly inside, knowing that the time of killing
and waiting and dread was about to begin all over again.

The windows of the office of the sheriff of Cochise County
were sandbagged, and as before there were armed guards out
in front of the sheriff's office. From inside was heard a whoop
and a holler from Johnny Behan.

"He's dead!" Behan shouted. "That son of a bitch is
dead."

Out came Behan, followed by an ebullient Harry Woods.
Behan clutched a newspaper as though it were the Holy Grail.
With more whoops and hollers he raced down the street
toward his house.

The windows of Johnny Behan's house were also sandbagged, and there was an armed guard perched behind a
sandbagged emplacement to the right of the building. Behan
and Harry Woods came up laughing and holding the newspaper.

Johnny Ringo, pale and drunk, sat at a table cheating at
solitaire when Behan and Woods entered. Johnny almost
jumped at the sound and reached for his gun.

"Put down the cannon, Johnny m'lad," Behan said cheer-
ily. "You're free and so am I."

"What are you talkin' about?" Johnny said.

"Read and rejoice, old son," Behan said, tossing the newspaper onto the table.

"That paper just come in from New Mexico," said Woods.
"I'm gonna reprint that story word for word in the *Nugget*."

"He's dead, Johnny," Behan said.

"Who?" asked Johnny.

"Who would ya most like to *see* dead?" asked the sheriff.

"Earp? He's dead?"

"Killed in a barroom brawl," Woods said.

"Shot twice through the heart," Behan added. "Or at least where they think it might have been. But no matter that . . . he's dead, Johnny."

The crowd of cowboys all looked up as a jubilant Johnny Ringo crashed through the swinging doors holding the newspaper in his hands.

"Drinks all around on me!" he called to one and all. "Wyatt Earp is dead!"

Through the window of the saloon Wilbur watched the celebration, then walked down to the Wells Fargo office.

A telegraph message was received presently at the Wells Fargo office in Gunnison, Colorado. A few moments thereafter, a twelve-year-old boy with a Wells Fargo cap on his head and a message in his hand ran across the street and into a saloon. The boy went into the saloon, up to a man with his back to the bar.

"Are you Mr. Smith, sir?" the boy asked.

"I am today," Wyatt said.

He tipped the boy and took the message and read it. Then he turned to Doc Holliday, who stood next to him.

"They fell for it," Wyatt said.

Doc smiled and raised his glass in a toast. "Confusion to our enemies."

The train sped along through the backcountry. Wyatt and Doc sat with their hats pulled low, staring out at the countryside. Opposite them sat a traveling salesman.

"We're slowing down," said the salesman. "I certainly hope nothing's the matter."

He looked out the window, craning his neck to see what could be holding up the progress of the train. Then he turned back to Wyatt and Doc, his traveling companions. "I certainly hope . . ." the salesman began, but they were already gone.

The train slowed to a crawl, allowing Wyatt and Doc time to jump down at the place where Fred Dodge waited with two fresh horses.

Doc and Wyatt and Fred Dodge rode full tilt through the countryside to the Hooker Ranch, not far from Tombstone.

Marsh Williams was there, waiting for them. Cowhands were readying fresh mounts for all of them. In addition, there were several other gunmen who were preparing to leave with Wyatt.

"Frank Leslie spotted Ringo leaving Tombstone," Marsh reported. "He trailed him up toward Turkey Creek Canyon. He just sent back word with Billy."

"Any idea where he's headed?" Wyatt asked.

"Probably the Smith place or the Sanders. Mrs. Smith and Mrs. Sanders both think of him as one of their favorites. They keep a pot of beans on for him night and day."

"Let's go," said Wyatt.

The party mounted up, Wyatt, Doc, and Fred Dodge and the others. Marsh Williams looked up at them.

"I won't be here when you get back," he said.

"I didn't figure you would," said Wyatt.

Wyatt and his party rode up through the canyon at dusk. Up ahead of them was Frank Leslie, a very tough-looking customer. He motioned them to be quiet. Wyatt halted his horse, handed the reins to Doc, and walked over to Frank.

"He's up there, Wyatt. Maybe a quarter of a mile. He's pretty drunk; he's been celebrating ever since he heard you were dead."

Johnny rode along very drunk up Turkey Creek in a wonderful mood, singing softly to himself.

Wyatt, Doc, and their party circled up on foot, spreading out as if on a deer hunt. It was dark by now.

Johnny, still mounted, took a swig out of his flask and replaced it. Then he heard something. He reined in his horse and listened for footfalls in the dark. The horse snorted, and he smacked its head with an open palm. "Shhhh."

Wyatt, some fifty yards away, circled up in front of Johnny, who peered out into the night.

Johnny seemed to make something out and then heard the worst sound imaginable for him.

"Hello, Johnny," Wyatt said.

"Earp . . . ?"

Wyatt raised his rifle. "Let's end it, Johnny," he said.

Johnny wheeled his horse around as Wyatt fired, the shot missing, and Johnny raced up into the canyon, spurring his horse as fast as it would go. Other shots rang out behind him.

"Damn it!" said Wyatt, disgusted with missing his target.

He and the others ran down to their horses, which were hobbled below.

Johnny spurred his horse on, then reined it in and got an idea. He took his Winchester rifle out of its scabbard and dismounted. He pulled his boots off and looped them around the saddle, then smacked the horse hard and it took off.

"Yeah . . . we'll let you follow him for a while," Johnny said.

He took a step and oooched and eeeched and ouched. He sat down and tore his undershirt out from underneath his shirt, ripped it into strips, and tied them around his feet.

Then he took his rifle and got around to the back of a tree and set up an ambush position. He pulled out his flask and took a long, long drink to calm his nerves.

Wyatt, Doc, Fred, and the other members of their party combed the canyon quietly, looking for their prey.

A very drunk Johnny finished the last swallow from his flask. He was angry that it was empty and he tossed it, then regretted having made the noise. He put his index finger up to his lips. "Shhhh!" he admonished himself. He curled up on his left side, holding his pistol in his hand, the rifle off to the side, and went to sleep.

The sun was just coming up as Wyatt and Doc found Johnny's horse with the boots slung over the saddle. They fanned out.

Johnny was asleep at the foot of the large tree where he had planned his ambush. He stirred softly in his sleep as the sound of footfalls approached and then a boot gently kicked Johnny's leg. Johnny's eyes opened. He heard the hammer on a weapon cocking back.

Standing over him, his gun pointed down at Johnny's head, was Wyatt Earp.

"It's over, Johnny," he said, and shot him.

Wyatt then went to get the horses and when he got back, he saw Fred Dodge standing a little ways off from the three other members of their party. The men had now propped Johnny's body up in the bole of the tree. Doc came over to him.

"I got the horses," Wyatt said. "Let's . . ." Then he looked closer and a slow look of disbelief came over his face. "What are they . . ."

By way of explanation, Fred said, "They're scalping him, Wyatt."

Wyatt's eyes opened in amazement, and he took a step forward as if to stop them.

"It's the only way they're gonna collect the bounty," said Doc, "is if they have proof."

There was a moment of horror for Wyatt. His head shook back and forth, almost like an old man with the tremors. His voice came out in broken whispers. "I . . . won't allow . . ."

Doc stepped in front of him, setting him straight on the facts of life.

"It's business with these boys, Wyatt," he said. "It's not their hobby."

Wyatt looked at Doc as if not knowing him.

"Business?" he said. He looked at Doc a long time, at what his best friend had become, at what had become of all of them. "Good-bye, Doc," Wyatt said, and he turned and mounted his horse.

"Good-bye, Doc?!" said Doc.

Wyatt did not respond or turn back to look as he rode away.

"Good-bye Doc? We're supposed to be friends," Doc called, but there was no answer. His only friend was gone.

POSTSCRIPT

Wyatt Earp married Josephine Sarah Marcus. They were wed on board a ship off the coast of San Francisco. Sometime later, Mattie Blaylock Earp died of an overdose of laudanum. Her death was ruled a suicide. In November 1887, John H. "Doc" Holliday, at thirty-six years of age, died alone of tuberculosis. That same year, Judge Wells Spicer, who presided over the O.K. Corral inquest, was found in the desert with a single bullet hole in the brain. Ike Clanton was also killed that year. He was forty years old.

The next thirteen years were uneventful ones for the Earps. Then, in 1900, Warren, Wyatt's youngest brother, was murdered in Arizona. It is rumored that Wyatt and Virgil returned to Arizona and killed his assailants. Five years later, Virgil Earp died peacefully of pneumonia in Nevada at the age of sixty-two. Johnny Behan died in Tucson, Arizona, in 1912. He was sixty-seven years old and had had an active life in Arizona politics.

Bat Masterson, after a lifetime of adventure, became a reporter for the New York *Morning Telegraph*. He published numerous short stories and a book of memoirs. When he died in 1921, it was not with his boots on in a blazing gun battle;

it was sitting at his desk trying to meet a deadline. He was sixty-seven years old. James Earp, on the other hand, defying all predictions of an early death due to an overworked liver, proved the value of a dissolute but contented lifestyle. He died in Los Angeles, California, in 1926 at the age of eighty-five.

Wyatt Earp died in 1929. He was eighty years old. Among the pallbearers at his funeral were John Clum and William S. Hart. He was buried in Hills of Eternity Cemetery in Colma, California. Josie died in 1944 at the age of eighty-three. She was buried next to Wyatt. They had been together forty-five years, in which time Josie had suffered numerous miscarriages. They had no children. They had only each other.